ARS LITURGIAE

Worship, Aesthetics and Praxis

◆

Essays in Honor
of
Nathan D. Mitchell

ARS LITURGIAE

Worship, Aesthetics and Praxis

◆

Essays in Honor
of
Nathan D. Mitchell

EDITED BY CLARE V. JOHNSON

LITURGY
TRAINING
PUBLICATIONS

ARS LITURGIAE: WORSHIP, AESTHETICS AND
PRAXIS copyright © 2003 Archdiocese of
Chicago: Liturgy Training Publications, 1800
North Hermitage Avenue, Chicago IL 60622-
1101; 1-800-933-1800, fax 1-800-933-7094,
e-mail orders@ltp.org. All rights reserved.
See our website at www.ltp.org.

This book was edited by Victoria M. Tufano.
Audrey Novak Riley was the production editor.
The design is by Lucy Smith, and the typesetting
was done by Anne Fritzinger in Bembo and
Optima. The art on the cover and interior is by
Steve Erspamer, SM. The photograph of Nathan
Mitchell on page vi courtesy of the Notre Dame
Center for Pastoral Liturgy, University of Notre
Dame, Notre Dame, Indiana.

Library of Congress Control Number:
2002117764

Printed in the United States of America.

1-56854-488-X
ARTLIT

Contents

THE 1998 BERAKAH AWARD
TO
Nathan D. Mitchell

Gifted teacher, nurtured on Hoosier soil
in the spirit of St. Benedict,
brilliant writer,
sustained by poets, artists and theologians,
lover of the liturgy,
whose quarrel with untruth
cries out from the Amen Corner,
You have plumbed the depths of anaphora
and psyche,
of cult and controversy, eucharist, ministry
and our very posture before God.
For your sense and sensibility,
sharpened by knowing
omnia exeunt in mysterium;
for your *ora et labora*
we give thanks.

◆

Proceedings of the North American Academy of Liturgy
(Evanston: North American Academy of Liturgy, 1998), 16.

Introduction

In the Supplement to the *Hadrianum,* an eighth-century sacramentary attributed to Pope Gregory I, Saint Benedict of Aniane (d. 821) gathered together a variety of liturgical resources such as votive Masses, reconciliation services, funerals, exorcisms, morning and evening prayer and other miscellaneous blessings. In his introduction to the Supplement, Benedict writes:

> *Since there are other liturgical materials which Holy Church finds itself obliged to use, but which [Pope Gregory] omitted because he knew they had already been produced by other people, we have thought it worth our while to gather them like spring flowers, arrange them in a beautiful bouquet and—after carefully correcting and amending them and giving them appropriate titles—present them in this separate work so that diligent readers may find everything they need for the present.*[1]

Taking our lead from Benedict of Aniane, we present in this volume a small "mixed bouquet" of essays in honor of Nathan D. Mitchell on the occasion of his sixtieth birthday.

Historian, theologian, liturgiologist, teacher, musician, poet, artist of the liturgy—these are some of the titles that can be used to describe Nathan. Born in Richmond, Indiana, on March 9, 1943, Nathan has been a lover of the liturgy his whole life. Classical languages and literature, history, theology and liturgical studies were all elements of the education he gained at St. Meinrad College in Indiana (BA, 1966, MDiv, 1970), Indiana University, Bloomington, Indiana (MA, 1971), and the University of Notre Dame, where he completed his PhD in liturgical studies in 1978.

Nathan is a gifted teacher who began his career as an associate professor in the school of theology at St. Meinrad (1974–82) where he was a member of the Benedictine community from 1964 to 1982. Nathan has had a long and close association with the University of Notre Dame, which started when he was a doctoral student and continued when he was invited back as a visiting professor (1982–83). Later Nathan became associate director for research at the University of Notre Dame Center for Pastoral Liturgy (1990 to present), and is also presently a concurrent professor of liturgical studies in the department of theology at Notre Dame.

Nathan's remarkable contribution to the field of liturgical studies has come predominantly through his writing, though he is also a frequent presenter, lecturer and teacher throughout North America. The book for which Nathan is probably best known is *Cult and Controversy: The Worship of the Eucharist Outside Mass.*[2] In addition to this masterly work, Nathan has written eight other books, including *Mission and Ministry: History and Theology in the Sacrament of Order,*[3] *Eucharist as Sacrament of Initiation,*[4] *Real Presence: The Work of the Eucharist,*[5] *Liturgy and the Social Sciences,*[6] and *Table, Bread and Cup: Meditations on Eucharist—Selections from Assembly.*[7] A prolific writer, Nathan has published over 200 articles, and in addition to his own extensive writing, has acted as editor for *Assembly* and *Liturgy Digest,* both of which are publications of the Notre Dame Center for Pastoral Liturgy.[8]

Nathan's is the persistent voice that has sounded forth from the pages of "The Amen Corner" bimonthly since 1991 in the liturgical journal *Worship.* In his tenure as author of "The Amen Corner" Nathan has provided informed and insightful commentary on myriad topics. Always abreast of the latest liturgical developments, Nathan effortlessly weaves together everything from politics, papacy and pop stars[9] to arts, aesthetics and architecture,[10] offering his readers a measured and critical view of the most recent happenings and topical issues of both a secular and sacred nature.

Among Nathan's many gifts, arguably his greatest is his aptitude for synthesis. The ability to interlace artistically the historical, theological, ritual, aesthetic and pastoral dimensions of liturgical studies is something that seems to come naturally to Nathan. Spread throughout this volume are various quotes from Nathan's writing in "The Amen Corner," exemplifying well some of his synthetic abilities.

A self-described "card-carrying Vatican II progressive,"[11] Nathan has made no apology for his unceasing promotion of the ideals and vision of the Second Vatican Council in his writings and work. He never hesitates to take the opportunity to affirm the liturgical principles outlined by the Council, frequently advocating a vision of liturgy that recognizes the active agency of the assembly in the liturgical event[12] as both subject and recipient of the sacramental action.[13] Nathan has also been an advocate for the use of inclusive language,[14] the inculturation of the liturgy[15] and the need for an active ethical response to flow from the liturgy out into the world.[16]

Nathan was a charter member of the North American Academy of Liturgy at its formation in Scottsdale, Arizona, in 1973, and was honored by the Academy in 1998 with the Berakah Award for his outstanding contribution to the field of liturgical studies. In his response to receiving the Berakah Award, Nathan characteristically attempted to deflect the recognition offered by this honor away from his individual accomplishment and toward the broader scholarly discipline of liturgiology, stating "together, we concelebrate this award."[17]

In this collection of essays we honor Nathan for his outstanding individual accomplishments in liturgical studies and for his contribution to the broader church as scholar, teacher and author. It was our intention in compiling this volume to try to reflect in its contents at least some of Nathan's numerous scholarly interests, from eucharistic reservation practices to aesthetics and poetics, and from liturgically-based spirituality to architecture and preaching. And so we have gathered together a varied array of essays written by eleven of Nathan's colleagues and friends, in which "the art of liturgy" is explored in terms of three broad categories: Worship, Aesthetics and Praxis.

Robert F. Taft, SJ, opens the Worship section with an essay tracing the practice of eucharistic reservation and self-communion at home in the late antique East. Taft offers a detailed study of eucharistic practices among the laity, monastics, solitary ascetics and hermits, uncovering a fascinating but little known aspect of the history of the eucharist beyond actual eucharistic celebration, from the perspective of Eastern Christianity.

Continuing on with the theme of eucharistic practices outside of liturgy, Maxwell E. Johnson presents a study of eucharistic reservation in Lutheranism in the United States. Johnson's essay touches on the questions "What is the underlying theology of real presence operative in Lutheran eucharistic practices?" and "What is the relationship between eucharistic reservation and real presence?" He provides a critique of contemporary Lutheran liturgical-pastoral practice in light of historical perspectives on reservation and communion in the Lutheran tradition.

In his essay John F. Baldovin, SJ, explores and breaks open the theories of one of the most abstract thinkers to enter liturgical scholarship in recent years, Cambridge academic Catherine Pickstock. Baldovin analyzes critically Pickstock's treatment of the medieval Roman Mass and the conclusions she draws not only for modern liturgical practices since Vatican II, but also for the relationship between liturgy, art, politics and society in general.

In the final essay in the Worship section, Michael S. Driscoll examines marriage rites in eighteenth-century Vienna, the time of Mozart. Driscoll considers the differences in marriage practices according to social class and the effects on the marriage rite itself as a result of the power struggle between emperor and pope for jurisdictional control over marriage practices.

Edward Foley, CAPUCHIN, introduces the section on Aesthetics with an essay on the aesthetics of liturgical performance. Foley notes the tendency of recent official liturgical reforms to over-emphasize the intellectual aspect of liturgical texts as part of the attempt to assure universal accuracy of textual translations. Foley reminds us of the need to recognize and reaffirm the embodied and performative nature of the liturgy as the praxis of a living body of worshipers rather than simply as a text on a page.

In his essay entitled "Let the Poet Speak," Gilbert Ostdiek, OFM, provides an insightful reflection on the relationship between liturgy and poetics. Ostdiek notes that exploring the artistry of the poet can offer to the liturgist new ways of perceiving reality, unveiling deeper meanings of the words we employ in liturgy and allowing for new understandings to arise. Ostdiek explains that poetics is not restricted solely to words, but extends to gestures in worship and also to the use of liturgical space.

Patrick W. Collins rounds out the Aesthetics section with his essay on spirituality, imagination and the arts. In this essay Collins discusses the power of the arts to ignite the imagination, which in turn feeds the development of spirituality. It is through the power of the imagination that we gain access to the world of the spiritual and the mystical, in order to encounter what is most real and most true in the world. Collins suggests that the arts serve to engage the imagination on an intuitive level, enabling deeper insights into faith and spirituality.

John Allyn Melloh, SM, begins the section on liturgical Praxis with a consideration of the vocation of the preacher. Drawing insights from four disciplines—systematic theology, liturgical theology, biblical theology and ritual studies—Melloh explores what it means to have a vocation to preaching. He suggests that preaching is a task that involves not only speaking words of truth and offering praise and glory to God, but also voicing the laments of a community, naming sin and grace in light of gospel truth and negotiating the shared vision of the communal reality borne out in ritual engagement.

Andrew D. Ciferni, OPraem, continues the theme of preaching with an essay on preaching at the eucharist on high holy days. Ciferni highlights the importance of locating preaching within the liturgical context of the feast or holy day being celebrated, and of allowing the homily to provide a strong link between the liturgy of the word and the liturgy of the eucharist. He offers suggestions as to how this can be accomplished, emphasizing the need to locate the homily in the here-and-now, and the need to bring the particular feast being celebrated into dialogue with the lives of the gathered community.

In his essay on reading as a transformative spiritual practice, Raymond Studzinski, OSB, offers a glimpse into the art of religious reading *(lectio divina)*. Studzinski suggests that reading done slowly and meditatively actually transforms the reader, as the words penetrate the consciousness of the reader, enabling him or her to see beyond the written text of Christian scriptures to the text of the world created by God. Studzinski describes the ways in which reading can become a transformative spiritual exercise, and what the resultant outcomes of such a practice in the life of the Christian person might be.

R. Kevin Seasoltz, OSB, concludes the Praxis section of this volume with an essay on Irish church architecture. In his essay Seasoltz considers how the changes in worship practices after the Second Vatican Council have influenced the styles of architecture employed in church building in Ireland. He describes the historical development of architectural styles and outlines four main design categories which have predominated in Irish churches in the twentieth century. Seasoltz also discusses the importance of using the artwork and furnishings of distinguished local artists, in the final appointment of new church buildings.

As editor of this collection, I would like to express my sincere thanks to Victoria Tufano and Liturgy Training Publications for their support and willingness to publish this volume. Special thanks are due to Professor Maxwell E. Johnson for his generous guidance and encouragement throughout the production process. Thanks also to Joseph Weiss, SJ, acting director of the Center for Pastoral Liturgy at the University of Notre Dame, for his assistance in discreetly providing a copy of Nathan's curriculum vitae and photograph without alerting Nathan to the project in progress.

As the first dissertationist to work under Nathan's direction, I join with many of his current and former students who are indebted to him for his guidance, patience and kindness. This volume is a token of the gratitude of many to Nathan, not only for his scholarship, generosity and mentoring, but also for his remarkable contribution to the field of liturgical studies, his unstinting promotion of the liturgical vision of Vatican II and his eminent skill as poet, prophet and pedagogue. May Nathan—a true artist of the liturgy—continue to ponder, promote and practice *ars liturgiae* for many years to come.

Clare V. Johnson

1. "English Translation of the Preface to the Supplement: *Hucusque.*" Quoted in Cyrille Vogel, *Medieval Liturgy: An Introduction to the Sources,* trans. and rev. by William Storey and Neils Rasmussen (Washington: The Pastoral Press, 1986), 87.

2. *Cult and Controversy: The Worship of Eucharist Outside Mass* (New York: Pueblo / Collegeville: The Liturgical Press, 1982).

3. *Mission and Ministry: History and Theology in the Sacrament of Order* (Wilmington: Michael Glazier / Collegeville: The Liturgical Press, 1983).

4. *Eucharist as Sacrament of Initiation,* Forum Essays 2 (Chicago: Liturgy Training Publications, 1994).

5. *Real Presence: The Work of the Eucharist* (Chicago: Liturgy Training Publications, 1998); new and rev. ed., 2001.

6. *Liturgy and the Social Sciences,* American Essays Series, ed. Edward B. Foley (Collegeville: The Liturgical Press, 1999).

7. *Table, Bread and Cup: Meditations on Eucharist—Selections from Assembly* (Notre Dame: Notre Dame Center for Pastoral Liturgy, 2000).

8. A bibliography of Nathan's works is included at the end of this volume.

9. See "The Amen Corner: Rocking toward the Third Millennium," *Worship* 72:1 (January 1998): 81.

10. See, for example, "The Amen Corner: Being Good and Being Beautiful," *Worship* 74:6 (November 2000): 550–8, and "The Amen Corner: Believe in the Wind," *Worship* 73:4 (July 1999): 363–4.

11. "The Amen Corner: Rocking toward the Third Millennium," 80.

12. "The Amen Corner: How We Belong," *Worship* 76:4 (July 2002): 367.

13. Ibid.

14. See "The Amen Corner: Reform the Reform," *Worship* 71:6 (November 1997): 555–63.

15. See "The Amen Corner: Liturgy as *Lingua Franca,*" *Worship* 75:2 (March 2001): 181–2.

16. See "The Amen Corner: Being Good and Being Beautiful," 557.

17. Nathan D. Mitchell, "Notes toward a Supreme Fiction," *Proceedings of the North American Academy of Liturgy* (Evanston: North American Academy of Liturgy, 1998), 18.

The eucharist, after all, is not a precious object, but a sacred outcome—a verb, not a noun, a deed, not a devotion.

Nathan Mitchell, "The Amen Corner: Eucharist without Walls," *Worship* 73:2 (March 1999): 186.

Home-Communion in the Late Antique East

Robert F. Taft, SJ

In this volume of essays honoring Nathan Mitchell, I would like to return to a theme Nathan himself wrote on some twenty years ago, the eucharist apart from the actual eucharistic celebration.[1] Nathan's study dealt more with the Western material, and with issues concerning the cult of the eucharist outside Mass. Here I shall try to complement that study with the relatively sparse Eastern evidence, especially regarding eucharistic reservation and communion at home, which in my view have not yet received adequate treatment for the late antique East. This is especially true of the hagiographical evidence,[2] a source of liturgical research that has interested me especially in recent years, as I come to see more and more that liturgy from the top down—that is, liturgy as reflected in the official liturgical, magisterial, and canonical sources—is but part of the picture.[3]

Home-Communion of the Laity

That home-communion was frequent in early Christianity is accepted as established.[4] For instance ca. 150 CE, Justin, *Apology* I, 65.5, says: " . . . those we call 'deacons' give communion to each of those present from the eucharistized bread and wine with water, and bring it to those who are not present."[5] Justin repeats the same in 67.5: " . . . communion from the eucharistized things is given to each one, and sent via the deacons to those not present."[6] The so-called *Apostolic Tradition* of Pseudo-Hippolytus (third/fourth century?)[7] and numerous other sources from the third through the seventh centuries[8] confirm that it was customary for the faithful to take home from the Sunday synaxis enough of the consecrated species—doubtless only the consecrated bread—for communion on weekdays, when there was normally no eucharistic liturgy except in special circumstances.[9] They also brought communion to members of the local community unable to attend the eucharistic service.[10] These absent members were not just the infirm: during the persecutions communion also had to be brought, doubtless clandestinely, to Christians languishing in prison.[11]

Furthermore, in late antiquity churches were mostly urban, travel difficult, transportation slow or non-existent, and many Christians in the countryside (which in most areas did not begin to have a resident clergy until the fourth century) lived too far away from a church to be present at the Sunday synaxis except sporadically if at all. Though 1 Clement 42:4, at the end of the first century, already speaks of bishops being instituted for the faithful "in the countryside and towns,"[12] it is generally accepted that throughout the third century the church was well ensconced only in urban areas. The organization of a resident clergy in the countryside had to await the so-called "Peace of Constantine" in 312. This occurred more rapidly in some places, more slowly in others. For instance, already by the end of the fourth century the bishop of Caesarea in Cappadocia was assisted by fifty "chorbishops" serving the surrounding countryside.[13]

But even as late as the end of the sixth century, some remote regions were ill-served by clergy, and the people went without the eucharist and other sacraments. Monophysite author John of

Ephesus (ca. 507–586), born in Ingila (modern Egil in Turkey) on the Tigris in Mesopotamia, in the Roman province of Armenia IV, recounts in his *Life of Symeon the Mountaineer* how the saint encountered Christian peasants living isolated in the mountainous district of Mesopotamia east of the Euphrates, near Melitene, who were totally ignorant of the eucharist. They would bring their children to the nearest church to be baptized, but knew no other church services whatever—a deplorable situation Saint Symeon hastened to remedy. He found and repaired an abandoned church in a nearby hamlet, instructed the people, gave them penance, then celebrated the divine mysteries for them and even tonsured some of the children as "children of the covenant"—that is, monastics.[14]

It should not surprise us, then, that lay home-communion lasted much longer in the East than in the West, where, by the end of the Golden Age of the Fathers, home-communion seems to have died out. Nußbaum claims Saint Augustine (d. 430), *Contra Julianum* III, 162, is our last Western witness to the practice.[15] In the East the evidence shows it lasted at least through the seventh century.[16] This is especially true for Palestine. John Moschos (d. 619), *Pratum spirituale 79*, a major source for Palestinian monasticism ca. 600, relates how the laity took the Holy Thursday eucharist home and kept it for over a year.[17] The consecrated bread was even carried on trips as a sacred object, as one might carry an icon or relic today.[18] As late as Saint Anastasius (fl. 640–700), monk of the Monastery of St. Catherine on Sinai, *Question 113,* we still find reference to carrying the eucharist on trips.[19]

The practice of lay home-communion seems to have been especially common during the Monophysite crisis, when the non-Chalcedonians could not be sure of finding a eucharist at which to communicate that was acceptable to their conscience. *Plerophoriai* 10 of John Rufus (John of Antioch), an Arab from southern Palestine who became Monophysite bishop of Maiuma near Gaza (491–?), and wrote his *Plerophoriai* or *Convictions: Testimonies and*

Revelations Against the Council of Chalcedon during the patriarchate of Severus of Antioch (512–518),[20] confirms that Monophysite faithful took home the eucharistic species they had received from their own clergy and gave themselves communion so as not to have to receive the sacrament from the Chalcedonians.[21] Later Sophronius, briefly patriarch of Jerusalem in 634–638, in his *Miracles of Saints Cyrus and John*[22] tells of a Monophysite, forced by illness to stay at the shrine of Menouthis, then in the hands of the Chalcedonians. He refused to receive there the Chalcedonian eucharist, saying that one of his relatives was going to bring him the eucharist of his own confession that same day.[23] According to *Plerophoriai* 78, however, this Monophysite practice did not pass unchallenged. Some Alexandrian Monophysite faithful resident in Beirut were in the habit of keeping at home the eucharistic species they had received from their own clergy and giving themselves communion on Sundays. But a stylite reprimanded them, saying seculars could not do this; they should receive communion in church from the hands of the clergy.[24]

Monastic Indifference toward the Liturgy

Surprisingly, in the light of these monastic witnesses to lay home-communion in late antique Palestine, the evidence for the same practice among solitaries in this cradle of Eastern monasticism is sparse. This may be due to the somewhat ambiguous, even indifferent attitude toward liturgy one finds in some early monastic sources.

Eusebius of Caesarea in Palestine (ca. 265–ca. 340), in *Demonstratio Evangelica* I, 8, written probably between 312 and 320, has this to say about the worship of ascetics:

> *Following on the Master's instructions, the disciples adapted*
> *his teaching to the various capacities of the multitude. . . .*
> *Henceforth, two manners of life are seen in Christ's Church.*
> *The first surpasses nature and the common way of living, for*

*it allows neither marriage nor procreation, commerce nor
possessions. Filled with divine love it runs from everyday life,
vowing itself exclusively to God's service. . . . Those who follow
this path are consecrated, they come before the God of heaven
and earth as representatives of all humanity—not with bloody
and smoking sacrifices, not with libation and incense offering,
but, as the nature of a life truly devoted demands, with words
and deeds expressive of inner virtue. By this means they appease
God, rendering Him service for themselves and their neighbors.
So much for the perfect. Others go by a less exalted way. Living
chastely in marriage, they give themselves to the procreation of
the race, to military, family and commercial affairs. . . . For
them, one special hour is set aside for devout exercises, and
certain days are consecrated to religious instruction and reading
God's law.*[25]

From that last sentence one might infer that the church's liturgical assemblies were meant for the laity. And indeed, some early
monastics took just that stance, perceiving a conflict between the
demands of solitude and participation in the public, ecclesial action
of the liturgy. Although the evidence shows considerable variety in
eremitical usage, and one finds widely varying attitudes toward
monastic indifference to the sacraments, the problem, especially
acute among the Messalians, an oriental sect of pseudo-mystics,[26]
was a real one also in orthodox monastic circles.

Some Syriac texts attributed to Saint Ephrem (ca. 306–373)
go so far as to imply that monastic asceticism replaces even the
eucharistic liturgy:

> . . . and instead of the buildings of the church they [the
> monastics] became the temples for the Holy Ghost, instead of the
> altars (are) their spirits; as sacrifices their prayers are being offered
> to the Godhead.
>
> They serve as priests for themselves, and they celebrate
> (offer) their sufferings . . . their fasts are their Eucharist and their
> vigils their libations . . . their faith is a sanctuary, their minds
> are the altars, their virginity the perfect sacrifices, their chastity
> a veil (of the altar) and their humility a censer of incense.[27]

The same approach is reported even more trenchantly by
Anastasius of Sinai (fl. 640–700), *Question 2,* in the response given
to one who had manifested perplexity at a certain solitary's sedu-
lous avoidance of the church and its synaxes. The anchorite is said
to have replied:

> All such synaxes and liturgies and feasts are done above all . . .
> so that man may be free from his sins and God may dwell in
> him, as it is written. . . . But once man has been made into
> a living temple of God, the God-led soul is removed from all
> desire for sensible churches and synaxes and human festivities.
> For he has in himself the Father and the High-priest Son, and
> the Spirit, the true fire; within is the sacrifice to God in truth,
> the contrite spirit; within is the altar . . . within is the kingdom
> and Jerusalem on high.[28]

This attitude becomes even more problematic in the case of
solitaries who not only avoided the church's public synaxes but in
some instances even disdained them. Palladius (ca. 363–ca. 431),
bishop of Helenopolis in Bithynia (ca. 400–406), exiled because of
his support for John Chrysostom, and later bishop of Aspuna in
Galatia from ca. 412, had spent the years 388–400 in Egypt and
Palestine, and his account of Egyptian monasticism in the *Lausiac
History,* written ca. 419, is especially rich in such tales, probably

because Palladius felt the need to address the problem head-on. The most explicit case is the visionary ascetic Valens, who stated baldly: "I have no need of communion; for today I saw Christ."[29] Another solitary, Ptolemy, lived in such total isolation that "he became a stranger to the teaching of holy men . . . and the constant communion of the mysteries, and diverged so greatly from the straight way that he declared these things were nothing"; and the monk Heron alternately refused to attend the eucharist or subsisted on the mysteries alone without other nourishment.[30]

Even the strict cenobotism of the Pachomian Tabennesiots was not immune to a somewhat laissez-faire approach to the sacraments. The *Vita bohairica* of Pachomius, §§86–94, tells of a monk-catechumen allowed to die without baptism, which the angels ministered to him after death.[31] A similar indifference—even disrespect—toward church and sacraments can be seen in the behavior of "holy fools" who sought humility and contempt by aberrant behavior. Leontius of Neapolis, *Life of St. Symeon the Fool,* written in Cyprus in 642–649 but set in the Syrian city of Emesa during the sixth century,[32] is a case in point. Chapter 12 describes the fool's violently disruptive behavior during Sunday services.[33]

No wonder Benedictine Eligius Dekkers' ironically entitled article, "Were the Early Monks Liturgical?"[34] poured cold water on the romanticism of the nineteenth-century Benedictine revival à la Guéranger and its resumption of the Cluniac *monachus propter chorum* ideology, which considered the monk a *homo liturgicus par excellence.*

Home-Communion among Male Solitaries

Counterbalancing such monastic rejection of the liturgy, however, are other miracle stories showing that the requirements of eucharistic participation by all Christians, laity and hermits included, were not so easily dismissed. In this category are the miraculous stratagems that enabled solitaries to participate in the eucharistic liturgy or communion, thereby reconciling the need to preserve their seclusion while at the same time satisfying the demands of sacramental participation. In another anecdote from Palestinian monasticism,[35] Anastasius of Sinai (fl. 640–700) recounts how three solitaries, miraculously rendered invisible so they could take communion unseen, came frequently to communicate themselves from the eucharist reserved in a pyx *(skeuophorion)* in the monastery. Eventually the monk in charge of the reserve noticed that particles of the consecrated bread were disappearing, so the ascetics appeared to him and admitted their responsibility.[36] In the same period and area, ca. 600, John Moschos (d. 619), *Pratum spirituale* 122, tells how two nude anchorites—their fierce asceticism included going about naked—received communion invisibly at the Holy Thursday monastery eucharist, while in chapter 127 another miraculously communicated at the Holy Saturday eucharist in the Jerusalem basilica of the Anastasis.[37] And while Saint Symeon Salos (the Fool) would not go to church services without acting disruptively lest he renounce his chosen role of "fool for Christ's sake," he denounced others for not communicating frequently.[38]

The Communion of Women Solitaries

Circa 419, Palladius, *Historia Lausiaca* 59.2, tells—with no hint of disapproval—how the virgin Taor, for thirty years a nun in one of the twelve Pachomian women's monasteries in Antinoe, Egypt, refused to go out with the other nuns to the church on Sunday for communion not because she disdained the sacrament, but because she valued her solitude and chastity more.[39] So even among recluses who did not reject sacramental life *per se,* many refused to abandon their solitude even to attend the Sunday eucharist.[40] This was especially true of women, for obvious reasons in the culture of those times.

As for women ascetics who lived deep in the wilderness far from any *lavra* or church, living without the eucharist for years seems not to have been unusual. The legendary seventh-century *Life of St. Mary of Egypt,* 32–38, has the anchorite spend forty-eight years in the desert without ever participating in the eucharistic liturgy until a Sabaitic priest-monk, who had retired to the desert for Lent, brought her holy communion on the last Holy Thursday before she died.[41] This tale is a topos recounted about other recluses,[42] especially women, such as the one in the *Life of St. Cyriacus* (449–556) 18, by Cyril of Scythopolis (ca. 512–d. ca. 558), who went for eighteen years in the wilderness without seeing a priest.[43] And in the first half of the ninth century, the *Vita* (ca. 913/19) 18–20 of Saint Theoktiste of Lesbos says she had not participated in the eucharist at all while in solitude for thirty-five years on the small, otherwise uninhabited island of Pharos. Eventually she ran into a hunter from neighboring Eubeae and asked him to bring her the sacrament in a vessel when he sailed over to hunt the following year, which he did, whereupon she communicated and died.[44]

Rituals of Eremetical Communion

Back in Palestine, the incipit (f. 72r-v) of one of the "night chants" of the midnight office in the ninth-century Horologion manuscript *Sinai Gr. 864,* written for use by a solitary, reads: "We have received your flesh, O Christ, and we have been deemed worthy of your blood, we have run the course of the day, grant us the repose of the night. . . . "[45] As Maxime Leila Ajjoub, the editor of this private Horologion, notes, this seems to imply that the recluse for which it was written communicated regularly, even daily.[46] And unless the recluse was a priest, this had to be from the eucharistic reserve.

Another Palestinian Horologion manuscript of that period shows us how the solitary's private communion took place while at the same time resolving for us an anomaly in today's Byzantine Liturgy of the Hours. The latter has before the Table Service (that is, the blessing of the main meal) and None[47]—the Slavonic books place it before Vespers[48]—an office known as the Typika (Slavonic *Izobrazitel'nyja* or *Obednica*),[49] which is used only on aliturgical days, that is, on days of fast and penance when the full eucharistic liturgy is not celebrated.[50] Its non-lenten form in the Greek Horologion now comprises the following elements:[51]

Psalm 102
Psalm 145 + *"Ho Monogenes* (O Only-begotten Son)"[52]
The Beatitudes (Matthew 5:3–12) with versicles[53]
Troparia (refrains)
Creed
Prayer of Absolution
Our Father
Kontakion (variable refrain)
Kyrie eleison 40 times
"Blessed be the name of the Lord for ever" (= Psalm 112:2)
   3 times
"Glory be to the Father . . . both now and ever . . ."
Psalm 33
Apolysis (dismissal)

Today this service is seemingly without purpose. But its earliest extant witness, entitled "Horologion According to the Rule of the Lavra Our Holy Father Sabas" in the ninth-century manuscript *Sinai Gr. 863,* bears the title "At Communion *(eis ten metalipsin),"* showing that the Typika was originally a Palestinian monastic communion service to provide the monks an opportunity to communicate even on aliturgical days when the eucharistic sacrifice was not celebrated.[54] This is clear from the conclusion of the pristine service, obviously modeled on the communion rite of hagiopolite cathedral Liturgy of the Presanctified Gifts,[55] with elements like the Lord's Prayer, the communion call "Holy things for the holy!" and its response, the hagiopolite koinonikon or communion responsory (LXX Psalm 33 + alleluia), plus a postcommunion thanksgiving.[56]

Here is the full outline of the original service as found in *Sinai Gr. 863* († = parallels in hagiopolite Liturgy of the Presanctified Gifts as indicated in the notes):

The Beatitudes
†Antiphon: troparion "The angelic choirs," LXX Psalm 33:6, troparion again
Doxology[57]
Creed[58]
†Our Father[59]
Kyrie eleison 3 times
†"One is holy" (incipit of the *Sancta sanctis* response)[60]
†Hagiopolite koinonikon: LXX Psalm 33:9, alleluia, Psalm 33:1–2, doxology[61]
Postcommunion Prayer
†Prayer of Thanksgiving after Communion[62]

The only other manuscript I have seen thus far that still indicates the Typika as a communion service is the Horologion appended to the Psalter of *Harvard University Houghton Library Ms. Greek 3* (1105), which presents on folios 247^{v}–8^{v} a structurally more developed Typika service with this rubric after Psalm 33:9 (f. 248^{v}): "Before the Communion of the Divine and Holy Mysteries *(Pro tes ton theion kai hagion mysterion metalepsios).*"[63]

The *Vita* of Saint Luke the Younger (d. 953), thaumaturge and founder of the Monastery of Hosios Loukas in Phokis, Greece,[64] confirms the use of the Typika rite as a presanctified communion service for monks living in isolation. Chapter 42 of this *Vita,* which dates from after the Byzantine conquest of Crete in 961,[65] reports the following dialogue between Saint Luke and the Archbishop of Corinth, who had stopped by the monastery on his way to Constantinople[66] soon after 927:[67]

> 1. *Then he [Luke] asked the archbishop, . . . saying, "Tell me, O master, how those of us who settle in the mountains and the deserts on account of the great number of our sins—how may we*

participate in the divine and awesome mysteries? For you see that we lack not only a congregation but even a priest?" 2. He [the archbishop] commended him for his inquiry and said, "Father, you do well to inquire about this good and important matter, 'for the good is not good unless the outcome is good.' 3. Now to begin with, a priest should be present, but if he is unavoidably absent, place the vessel with the presanctified [gifts] on the holy table if it is a chapel, but if it is a cell, [put it] on a very clean bench. 4. Then, spreading out a small veil, place the holy particles on it, and, lighting the incense, sing the psalms of the typika *or the* Trisagion *along with the Creed. 5. After three genuflexions, fold your hands and take with your mouth the venerable Body of Christ our God, saying the Amen. 6. In place of the eucharistic wine you may drink a cup of ordinary wine, but this cup should not be shared afterwards for the use of another. 7. Next, put the remaining particles with the veil in the vessel, taking all care lest a pearl*[68] *fall out and be trampled.*[69]

The scenario is perfectly clear. The only perplexity arises from §4. Since the Typika service already includes the Creed and Trisagion, as in the outline above, then the intended sense of §4 could be: "say the Typika service, comprising the psalms, the Trisagion, the Creed, and so on."

At any rate, we clearly have here a presanctified communion service designed to permit solitaries to partake of the eucharist outside the liturgy and in the absence of a priest—a possibility still envisaged by Slavonic Orthodox sources right through the nineteenth century, some of which, indeed, cite this chapter of the Lukan *Vita* in justification of the practice.[70] But that was long after the Typika had ceased to be used for communion: I know of no witness to that practice after the medieval Byzantine monastic rules.[71]

When the monks of Constantinople, who already had such a communion service in their Byzantine cathedral Liturgy of the Presanctified Gifts, adopted the Sabaitic Horologion in the course of the Studite reform,[72] this Palestinian monastic communion rite was apparently used as a surrogate communion service for aliturgical days during the minor Lents preceding Christmas and Holy Apostles (Saints Peter and Paul, June 29).[73] During Great Lent preceding Easter, when the Liturgy of the Presanctified Gifts served as the communion rite for aliturgical days, the Typika service was downgraded to a rite for the distribution of the *antidoron,* or blessed bread, left over from the *prosphora* offered for the eucharist but not consecrated.[74] In a still further development, we see the beginning and end of the Typika rite added to the Divine Liturgy in the twelfth-century Typikon of the Monastery of the Theotokos Evergetis, founded in 1049.[75] The beginning of the rite, comprising Psalm 102, Psalm 145 plus the *Ho Monogenes,*[76] and the Beatitudes, replaced the three traditional antiphons at the opening of the liturgy,[77] where they remain to this day in some liturgical usages.[78] Its end, Psalm 112:2, Psalm 33 accompanying the distribution of the blessed bread, or *antidoron,* and the concluding *apolysis,* or dismissal prayer, were appended to the end of the Divine Liturgy, after the original dismissal, Opisthambonos, and Skeuophylakion prayers with which the liturgy had traditionally concluded.[79]

Conclusion

Though this evidence is sporadic and largely anecdotal, it is widespread enough to prove that home and eremitical eucharistic reservation and communion were still practiced widely in the Christian East, especially in Palestine and later Byzantine Orthodoxy, long after it had disappeared in the West. If we add to this the abundant later evidence from Byzantine Orthodoxy of communion administered in special circumstances by non-priests and even laity— Emperor Justinian I (527–565), *Novella* 123.36, authorizes nuns to choose either a priest or deacon approved by the bishop to bring them communion; they could also choose a layman, but then, if the bishop judged him worthy, he would have to receive ordination at least to the diaconate;[80] canon 58 of the Qunisext Council "in Trullo" in 691 or 692 decrees that the laity may not give themselves communion if a bishop, presbyter or deacon is at hand to do so, which must mean the laity were allowed to give themselves communion if no clergy were available;[81] patriarch Photius (877–886), writing to Archbishop Leo of Calabria in 885 or 886, permits even deaconesses to bring communion to Christians in captivity;[82] and as late as Symeon of Thessalonika (d. 1429), *Responsiones* 40, a deacon, in the absence of a priest, is allowed to give the presanctified eucharist to one in danger of death[83]—then perhaps post–Vatican II Catholic innovations such as "extraordinary ministers" of the eucharist, which some self-appointed guardians of the tradition find reprehensible, are not such novelties after all. There is nothing like a knowledge of the sources to put things in perspective. Indeed, there is nothing else that can do it—and that, among other things, is what the history of liturgy is for.

◆───

Abbreviations used in notes

BBTT= *Belfast Byzantine Texts and Translations* (Belfast Byzantine Enterprises, Institute of Byzantine Studies, the Queen's University of Belfast).

BHG= François Halkin, *Bibliotheca Hagiographica Graeca*. Subsidia Hagiographica 8a, 3rd ed. Bruxelles: Société des Bollandistes, 1957.

BSLT= *Byzantine Saints' Lives in Translation*, series editor Alice-Mary Talbot (Washington: Dumbarton Oaks Research Library and Collection).

CCL= *Corpus Christianorum*, series Latina.

CPG= *Clavis Patrum Graecorum*, 5 vols., ed. M. Geerard, F. Glorie; & *Supplementum*, ed. M. Geerard, J. Noret (Turnhout: Corpus Christianorum, 1974–1998).

CSCO= *Corpus Scriptorum Christianorum Orientalium*.

DACL= *Dictionnaire d'archéologie chrétienne et de liturgie* (Paris: Letouzey et Ané, 1924–1953).

Dmitrievskij I–III = A.A. Dmitrievskij, *Opisanie liturgicheskix rukopisej xran-jashchixsja v bibliotekax pravoslavnogo vostoka,* I–II (Kiev: Tipografia G.T. Korchak-Novitskago, 1895, 1901); III (Petrograd:V. F. Kirshbauma, 1917).

OC= *Oriens Christianus.*

OCA= *Orientalia Christiana Analecta.*

OCP= *Orientalia Christiana Periodica.*

ODB= *The Oxford Dictionary of Byzantium,* ed. A. Kazhdan et al., 3 vols. (New York/Oxford: Oxford University Press, 1991).

PE= A. Hänggi, I. Pahl, *Prex eucharistica,* vol. 1: *Textus e variis liturgiis antiquioribus selecti.* Spicilegium Friburgense 12, 3rd ed. by A. Gerhards and H. Brakmann (Freiburg: Éditions universitaires, 1998).

PG= *Patrologia Graeca.*

PO= *Patrologia Orientalis.*

PRES= The Liturgy of the Presanctified Gifts.

SC= *Sources chrétiennes.*

1. Nathan Mitchell, *Cult and Controversy:The Worship of the Eucharist Outside Mass* (New York: Pueblo, 1982).

2. On this see Evelyne Patlagean, "Ancient Byzantine Hagiography and Social History," in *Saints and Their Cults: Studies in Religious Sociology, Folkore and History,* ed. S.Wilson (Cambridge: Cambridge University Press, 1983), 101–21, esp. 110ff.

3. See R. F.Taft, *Beyond East and West. Problems in Liturgical Understanding,* 2nd ed. (Rome: Edizioni Orientalia Christiana, Pontifical Oriental Institute, 1997), 292–3. This interest has, of course, been fueled by the ever-increasing availability of sources and translations of sources, as reflected in the wonderful work of the Jesuit Société des Bollandistes in Brussels with their publications *Acta Sanctorum,* the periodical *Analecta Bollandiana,* and the monograph series *Subsidia Hagiographica.* To this longstanding scholarly effort one must now add the "Dumbarton Oaks Hagiography Project," a *Hagiography Database for the Byzantine World* created under the direction of Alice-Mary Talbot and the late Alexander Kazhdan of the Dumbarton Oaks Center for Byzantine Studies in Washington, D.C., as well as the saints' lives appearing in the BSLT series translation under the direction of Prof.Talbot: *Holy Women of Byzantium. Ten Saints' Lives in English Translation,* BSLT 1, ed. A.-M.Talbot (Washington: Dumbarton Oaks Research Library and Collection, 1996); ed. idem, *Byzantine Defenders of Images. Eight Saints' Lives in English Translation,* BSLT 2 (Washington: Dumbarton Oaks Research Library and Collection, 1998); *The Life of Lazaros of Mt. Galesion:An Eleventh-Century Pillar Saint,* BSLT 3, intro., trans., and notes by R. P. H. Greenfield (Washington: Dumbarton Oaks Research Library and

Collection, 2000). On this and other recent signs of growing interest in hagiography, see U. Zanetti, "The 'Dumbarton Oaks Hagiography Project.' Reflections of a User," *Analecta Bollandiana* 115 (1997): 166–93; also "Congresses and "Periodicals" on the Bollandist website (http://www.kbr.be/~soc.boll).

4. H. Leclercq, "Communion eucharistique (fréquente)," DACL III.1:515–52; id., "Communion fréquente" and "Communion quotidienne," *Dictionnaire de théologie catholique* (Paris: Letouzey et Ané, 1923–50), III.2:2454–5, 2457–62; J. Duhr, "Communion fréquente," *Dictionnaire de spiritualité* (Paris: G. Beauchesne et ses fils, 1932–95), 2:1234–92; E. Herman, "Die häufige und tägliche Kommunion in den byzantinischen Klöstern," in: *Mémorial Louis Petit. Mélanges d'histoire et d'archéologie byzantines,* Archives de l'Orient chrétien 1 (Bucharest: Institut français d'études byzantines, 1948), 203–17, here 203–4; Taft, *Beyond East and West,* 88–9.

5. PE 70 = PG 6:428B.

6. PE 70 = PG 6:429C.

7. B. Botte, *La Tradition apostolique de S. Hippolyte. Essai de reconstitution,* Liturgiewissenschaftliche Quellen und Forschungen 39 (Münster: Aschendorff, 1963), 82–5; *Hippolytus: A Text for Students,* Grove Liturgical Studies 8, intro., trans., commentary and notes by G. J. Cuming, (Bramcote, Notts.: Grove Books, 1976), 27. Regarding the so-called *Apostolic Tradition* once attributed to Hippolytus of Rome but generally judged not to be authentic by recent scholarship despite some clearly Hippolytan vocabulary in the document, the dust has not yet settled on its dating, provenance, and so forth. Christoph Markschies of Heidelberg asserts: "Hardly a sentence here [that is, of the *Apostolic Tradition*] can be taken unchecked as witness of a church order of the third century": "Neue Forschungen," 597–8 (article cited in full below in this note). Challenges to the authenticity of this "prétendue Tradition apostolique" began to surface in articles by M. Metzger, "Nouvelles perspectives pour la prétendue Tradition apostolique," *Ecclesia Orans* 5 (1988): 241–59; id., "Enquêtes autour de la prétendue Tradition apostolique," ibid., 9 (1992): 7–36; id., "A propos des règlements ecclésiastiques de prétendue Tradition apostolique," *Revue des sciences religieuses* 66 (1992): 249–61. See most recently: A. Brent, *Hippolytus & the Roman Church in the Third Century: Communities in Tension Before the Emergence of a Monarch-Bishop.* Supplements to *Vigiliae Christianae,* 31 (Leiden: E. J. Brill, 1995), 184–203, 458–540 passim; P. F. Bradshaw, "Redating the Apostolic Tradition: Some Preliminary Steps," in *Rule of Prayer, Rule of Faith: Essays in Honor of Aidan Kavanagh, OSB,* eds. N. Mitchell and J. Baldovin (Collegeville: Pueblo/The Liturgical Press, 1996), 3–17; id., "The Problems of a New Edition of the Apostolic Tradition," in *Acts of the International Congress Comparative Liturgy Fifty Years after Anton Baumstark (1872–1948), Rome, 25–29 September 1998,* OCA 265, eds. R. F. Taft and Gabriele Winkler (Rome: Pontifical Oriental Institute, 2001), 613–22; Ch. Markschies, "Neue Forschungen zur sogennaten *Traditio apostolica,*" ibid., 583–98;

M. Metzger, "Tradition orale et tradition écrite dans la pratique liturgique antique. Les recueils de traditions apostoliques," ibid., 599–612. These issues need not detain us, however, for the evidence in this document serves our purposes equally well regardless of whether its date is third/fourth century or even later.

8. For example, third century Tertullian (d. *post* 220), *De oratione* 19.4, CCL 1:268; *Ad uxorem* 2, 5:2–3, CCL 1:389–90; *De exhort. cast.* 7.3–6, CCL 2:1024–6; Cyprian (d. ca. 258), *De lapsis* 26, CCL 3:235; fourth/fifth century Jerome (ca. 347–419), *Ep. 49,* 15 (= *Apologeticum ad Pammachium,* 393), *Corpus Scriptorum Ecclesiasticorum Latinorum* (Vindobonae: F. Tempsky, 1910–8), 54:377. For the dating of Jerome's life and works see Ferdinand Cavallera, *Saint Jérôme. Sa vie et son œuvre* (Louvain: Spicilegium Sacrum Lovaniense, Bureaux, 1922), II, 153–65; Augustine, (d. 430), *Contra Julianum* III, 162, PL 45:1315; sixth century *Ep. 93,* attributed to Saint Basil the Great (d. 379): S. Basile, *Lettres,* 2 vols., ed. Yves Courtonne (Paris: Les Belles Lettres, 1957, 1961), 1:203–4 = PG 32:484–85, but certainly not authentic according to S. J. Voicu, "Cesaria, Basilio *(Ep. 93/94)* e Severo," *Augustinianum* 35 (1995): 697–703, who argues convincingly for the authorship of Severus (d. 538), Monophysite patriarch of Antioch 512–8; John Moschus (d. 619), *Pratum spirituale* (ca. 600), 30, PG 87:2877 = *The Spiritual Meadow (Pratum Spirituale)* by John Moschos (also known as John Eviratus), Cistercian Studies Series 139, intro., trans., and notes, John Wortley (Kalamazoo: Cistercian Publications, 1992), 21–2; further references in O. Nußbaum, *Die Aufbewahrung der Eucharistie,* Theophaneia 29 (Bonn: Königstein/Ts.: Hanstein, 1979), 266ff; Mitchell, *Cult and Controversy,* 10–19; and, especially for the later period, the sources cited below.

9. On the frequency of eucharistic celebration in the early and late antique church, see Taft, *Beyond East and West,* 88–9.

10. See, for example, Justin (ca. 150), *Apology* I, 65.5, 67.5, PE 70 = PG 6:428–32, cited above at notes 5–6; Pope Damasus I (305–84), *Elogium S. Tarsicii* no. 15, in *Epigrammata Damasiana,* Sussidi allo studio delle antichità cristiane 2, ed. A. Ferrua (Vatican: Pontificio istituto di archeologia cristiana, 1942), 117. Cf. F. J. Dölger, *ICHTHYS: Das Fischsymbol in frühchristlicher Zeit,* 2 vols., I, 2nd ed. (Münster: Aschendorff, 1928); II (Münster: Aschendorff, 1922) II, 534–5; Taft, *Beyond East and West,* 89; Nußbaum, *Die Aufbewahrung,* 177–8; further references, especially Western, in D. Callam, "The Frequency of Mass in the Latin Church ca. 400," *Theological Studies* 45 (1984): 613–50, here 615ff.

11. Severus of Antioch (d. 538) *Ep. 93,* S. Basile, *Lettres,* ed. Courtonne 1:203–4 = PG 32:484–5, refers explicitly to the persecutions as a reason for this practice. See also Callam, "Frequency," 616; W. H. Freestone, *The Sacrament Reserved: A Survey of the Practice of Reserving the Eucharist, with Special Reference to the Communion of the Sick, during the First Twelve Centuries,* Alcuin Club Collections 21 (London/Milwaukee: Alcuin Club, 1917), 44–5.

12. K. Bihlmeyer, *Die apostolischen Väter,* Neubearbeitung der Funkischen Ausgabe. Sammlung ausgewählter kirchen- und dogmengeschichtlicher Quellen schriften, 2. Reihe, 1. Heft, 1. Teil (Tübingen: J.C.B. Mohr, 1924), 58.

13. P. Joannou, "Chorbishop," *New Catholic Encyclopedia,* 15 vols. (New York: McGraw-Hill, 1967), 3:625–6. On the whole question, see C. Rupe, "Parish," ibid., 10:1017; H. Dressler, "Asia Minor, Early Church in," ibid., 1:955–57; A. von Harnack, *The Mission and Expansion of Christianity in the First Three Centuries,* 2 vols., (London: Williams and Norgate, 1908), I: 445–82, II: 89ff, 324–37; G. W. O. Addleshaw, *The Beginnings of the Parochial System* (London: St. Anthony's Hall Publications, 1953), 7ff; and especially *The Church in Town and Countryside,* Studies in Church History 16, ed. D. Baker (Oxford: Basil Blackwell, 1979). On the institution of chorbishops or "country bishops," see F. Gillmann, *Das Institut der Chorbischöffe im Orient* (Munich: 1903); T. Gottlob, *Der abendländische Chorepiskopat,* Kanonistische Studien und Texte 1 (Bonn/Cologne: K. Schroeder, 1928, repr. Amsterdam: P. Schippers, 1963); H. Hess, *The Canons of the Council of Sardica, A.D. 343, A Landmark in the Early Development of Canon Law* (Oxford: Oxford University Press, 1958), esp. 100–3; E. Kirsten, "Chorbischof," *Reallexikon für Antike und Christentum* 2 (1954): 1105–14; H. Leclercq, "Chorévêques," DACL 3.1:1423–52; id., "Périodeute," DACL 14.1:369–79; J. Parisot, "Les chorévêques," *Revue de l'Orient chrétien* 6 (1901): 157–71, 419–43.

14. John of Ephesus, *Lives of the Eastern Saints,* 16, ed. E. W. Brooks, PO 17:233–47. On the "children of the convenant," see A. Vööbus, *Celibacy, a Requirement for Admission to Baptism in the Early Syrian Church* (Stockholm: Esthonian Theological Society in Exile, 1951); G. Nedungatt, "The Covenanters of the Early Syriac-Speaking Church," OCP 39 (1973): 191–215, 419–44.

15. PL 45:1315; cf. Nußbaum, *Die Aufbewahrung,* 270.

16. Nußbaum, *Die Aufbewahrung,* 269, 274; Herman, "Kommunion," 206.

17. PG 87.3:2396–97 = Wortley 64.

18. F. J. Dölger, "Die Eucharistie als Reiseschutz. Die Eucharistie in den Händen der Laien," *Antike und Christentum* 5 (1936): 232–47; Freestone, *The Sacrament Reserved,* 55–6; Callam, "Frequency," 616–17, esp. note 11; R. F. Taft, *A History of the Liturgy of St. John Chrysostom,* vol. V: *The Precommunion Rites,* OCA 261 (Rome: Pontifical Oriental Institute, 2000), 404–12; id., "One Bread, One Body: Ritual Symbols of Ecclesial Communion in the Patristic Period," in *Nova Doctrina Vetusque: Essays on Early Christianity in Honor of Frederic W. Schlatter, SJ,* eds. Douglas Kries and Catherine Brown Tkacz (New York: P. Lang, 1999), 23–50, here 28–32.

19. PG 89:765AB; regarding authenticity see CPG §7746.

20. PO 8:6–7; G. Fedalto, *Hierarchia Ecclesiastica Orientalis,* 2 vols. I: *Patriarchatus Constantinopolitanus;* II: *Patriarchatus Alexandrinus, Antiochenus, Hierosolymitanus* (Padua: Edizioni Messaggero, 1988), II: 1027 §99.22.15.

21. PO 8:24.

22. BHG 477–479, XXXVI, 15.

23. *Los «Thaumata» de Sofronio: contribución al estudio de la «incubatio» cristiana.*
Consejo superior de investigaciones científicas, Instituto «Antonio de Nebrija»,
Manuales y anejos de «Emerita» 31, ed. N. F. Marcos (Madrid: Bolaños y Aguilar,
1975), 325 = PG 87.3:3553B.

24. PO 8:134–35.

25. *Eusebius Werke 6,* Die griechischen christlichen Schriftsteller 23., ed. I. A.
Heikel (Leipzig: J. C. Hinrichs, 1913) 39 = PG 22: 76C–77A; English trans.
from E. Dekkers, "Were the Early Monks Liturgical?" *Collectanea Cisterciensia*
22 (1960): 120–37, here 134–35 (emphasis added).

26. Dekkers, "Were the Early Monks Liturgical?" 126. On Messalianism, see
I. Hausherr, "L'erreur fondamentale et la logique du Messalianisme," OCP 1
(1935): 328–60 = id., *Études de spiritualité orientale,* OCA 183 (Rome:
Pontifical Oriental Institute, 1969), 64–96.

27. Cited in Syriac with English translation by A. Vööbus, *History of Asceticism in the
Syrian Orient,* vol. 2, CSCO 197, Subsidia 17 (Louvain: Secrétariat du CSCO,
1960), 311. Authors note a similar indifference toward the external sacramental
life of the church elsewhere in the Syriac literature, for example, in the late
fourth century *Liber Graduum,* Memra 12, *Patrologia Syriaca* 3:284–303; cf. A.
Kowalski, *Perfezione e giustizia di Adamo nel Liber Graduum,* OCA 232 (Rome:
Pontifical Oriental Institute, 1989), 216–17; also in the writings of John the
Solitary (second half of fourth century): Jean le solitaire (Pseudo-Jean de
Lycopolis), *Dialogue sur l'âme et les passions des hommes,* traduit du syriaque sur
l'édition de Sven Dedering par I. Hausherr, OCA 120 (Rome: Pontifical
Oriental Institute, 1939), 101–2; and in John of Apamea (late fifth/early sixth
century): W. Strothmann, *Johannes von Apamea,* Patristische Texte und Studien
11 (Berlin: De Gruyter, 1972), 79–80. See R. Murray, *Symbols of Church and
Kingdom. A Study in Early Syriac Tradition* (Cambridge: Cambridge University
Press, 1975), 129, 262–76 passim.

28. PG 89:344–52.

29. Chapter 25.2–5, Palladio, *La Storia lausiaca,* testo critico e commento a cura di
G. J. M. Bartelink, traduzione di Marino Barchiesi. Vita dei santi 2 (Milan:
Fondazione Lorenzo Valla: A. Mondadori, 1990), 134–7; cf. V. Déroche,
"Représentations de l'Eucharistie dans la haute époque byzantine," (in press).
I am indebted to Prof. Déroche of the Collège de France and CNRS for
sending me a pre-publication copy of his important paper, to which I owe
some of the references I exploit in this study.

30. Chapter 26.2, 27.2: Bartelink 138–39, 142–43. Note, however, that the same
chapters of the *Lausiac History* roundly condemn these attitudes they recount,

and chapter 17.9 tells of a laywoman who was turned into a mare because she had stayed away from communion for five weeks: Bartelink, 74–5.

31. *S. Pachomii vita bohairica scripta,* ed. L.-Th. Lefort. Text found in: CSCO 89, Scriptores Coptici series 3, vol. 7 (Louvain: Secrétariat du CSCO, 1925), 86–94; translation found in CSCO 107, Scriptores Coptici series 3, vol. 7 (Louvain: Secrétariat du CSCO, 1936), 57–62.

32. D. Krueger, *Symeon the Holy Fool. Leontius's "Life" and the Late Antique City,* The Transformation of the Classical Heritage 25 (Berkeley: University of California Press, 1996), 4ff.

33. Léontios de Néapolis, *Vie de Syméon le fou et vie de Jean de Chypre,* Édition commentée par A. J. Festugière en collaboration avec Lennart Rydén. Institut français d'archéologie de Beyrouth, Bibliothèque archéologique et historique, tome 95 (Paris: P. Geuthner, 1974—appeared in 1977), 79–80, 133; cf. V. Déroche, *Études sur Léontios de Néapolis,* Acta Universitatis Upsaliensis, Studia Byzantina Upsaliensia 3 (Uppsala: Uppsala Universitet, 1995), 194–5. See also the *Vita* 190 of St. Andrew the Fool, PG 111:836CD.

34. In *Collectanea Cisterciensia* 22 (1960): 120–37; trans. from id., "Les anciens moines cultivaient-ils la liturgie?" *La Maison-Dieu* 51 (1957): 31–54, an earlier redaction of which first appeared in *Vom christlichen Mysterium. Gesammelte Arbeiten zum Gedächtnis Odo Casel OSB,* ed. A. Mayer, J. Quasten, B. Neunheuser (Düsseldorf: Patmos-Verlag, 1951), 97–114, and a German translation of the more recent French redaction in *Liturgie und Mönchtum* 22 (1958). See also Friedrich Wulf, "Priestertum und Rätestand," *Geist und Leben* 33 (1960): 109–18, 246–61; and the discussion in Taft, *The Liturgy of the Hours in East and West,* 2nd rev. ed. (Collegeville: The Liturgical Press, 1993), 362–3.

35. See *Narrationes utiles animae* 30, a collection of edifying tales judged as authentic.

36. F. Nau, "Le texte grec des récits du moine Anastase sur les saints pères du Sinaï," Oriens Christianus 2 (1902): 77–8. On the question of authenticity, see CPG §7758 B9[9].

37. PG 87.3:2983–6, 2998–9 = Wortley 99–100, 103. In Palladius, *Historia Lausiaca* 18.25, the Egyptian monk Mark receives communion from an angel, not from the priest, even during the eucharistic liturgy: Bartelink 92.

38. L. Rydén, *Das Leben des heiligen Narren Symeon von Leontios von Neapolis,* Acta Universitatis Upsaliensis: Studia Graeca Upsaliensia 4 (Uppsala: Uppsala Universitet, 1963), 145–6, 162; English trans. Krueger, *Symeon the Holy Fool* 150–1, 165; cf. Déroche, Léontios 194–5.

39. Bartelink 260–1.

40. On this issue, see L. von Hertling, *Antonius der Einsiedler,* Forschungen zur Geschichte des innerkirchlichen Lebens 1 (Innsbruck: Felizian, 1929), 80–6.

41. Trans. M. Kouli, in Talbot, *Holy Women* 88–90, cf. 67 (= BHG 1042).

42. Nau, "Le texte grec des récits du moine Anastase," 67: §XII.

43. *Kyrillos von Skythopolis,* Texte und Untersuchungen 49:2, ed. E. Schwartz (Leipzig: J. C. Hinrichs, 1939), 233 = Cyril of Scythopolis, *The Lives of the Monks of Palestine,* Cistercian Studies Series 114, trans. R. M. Price, annotated by J. Binns (Kalamazoo: Cistercian Publications, 1991), 257. On the question of Byzantine female eremitism, see A. M. Talbot, "A Comparison of the Monastic Experience of Byzantine Men and Women," *The Greek Orthodox Theological Review* 30 (1985): 1–20, here 16–8.

44. Trans. A. C. Hero, BSLT 1:111–13 (= BHG 1723–4).

45. Sr. Maxime Leila Ajjoub, *Le codex Sinaiticus 864 (IXe siècle). Horologion,* 2 vols. (PHD diss., Pontifical Oriental Institute, Rome, 1986), §38, Greek text II, 40; French translation I, 30–1; commentary I, lv–lxi. For the location of these chants within the mesonyktikon, see the schema of the office (I, xxxiii–iv). The publication of this study in the SC series has been announced. I am indebted to S. Parenti for this reference. The text of the chant has also been edited from codex *Erlangen 96* (1025CE), f. 53, and 15th-century *Barberini Gr. 307,* f. 301, by P. Maas, *Frühbyzantinische Kirchenpoesie.* Kleine Texte für Vorlesungen und Übungen 52/53, hrsg. H. Lietzmann (Berlin: Weidmann, 1931), 6–7 §4; cf. 1–2. On the chant in question, see also A. Baumstark, "Ein frühchristliches Theotokion in mehrsprachiger Überlieferung und verwandte Texte des ambrosianischen Ritus," OC new series 9 (1920): 54; id., "*Te Deum* und eine Gruppe griechischer Abendhymnen," OC 34 = series 3, 12 (1937): 25.

46. "Le scribe de *l'horologion* ne pourrait être qu'un moine solitaire qui a le souci de former un manuel pour sa prière individuelle": Ajjoub I, xxxviii, 40 note 1.

47. *Horologion* (Rome: Pontifical Oriental Institute, 1937), 181–94.

48. *Ierejskij molitvoslov* (Rome: Pontifical Oriental Institute, 1950), 222–37.

49. For the corresponding Armenian office see note 54 below.

50. See J.-M. Hanssens, *Institutiones liturgicae de ritibus orientalibus* II–III (Rome: Apud aedes Pontificium Universitatis Gregorianae, 1930, 1932): II, §§186–95, though §§192, 194 must be now corrected on the basis of the discoveries of Mateos and Anderson, cited below at notes 52, 63. See also R. Stichel, "Homiletik, Hymnographie und Hagiographie im frübyzantinischen Palästina," in: eds. W. Hörander, J. Koder, O. Kresten, *ANDRIAS. Herbert Hunger zum 80 Geburtstag* = *Jahrbuch der österreichischen Byzantinistik* 44 (1994): 389–406, here 395–7.

51. *Horologion,* 181–94. For the Typika in earlier manuscript sources see John E. Klentos, *Byzantine Liturgy in Twelfth-Century Constantinople: An Analysis of the Synaxarion of the Monastery of the Theotokos Evergetis* (codex *Athens Ethnike Bibliotheke 788*), (PHD diss., University of Notre Dame, 1995), 186–9.

52. The *Ho Monogenes* chant is the *perisse* or final refrain that now concludes the second antiphon of the Byzantine Divine Liturgy. See J. Mateos, *La célébration*

de la parole dans la liturgie byzantine. Étude historique, OCA 191 (Rome: Pontifical Oriental Institute, 1971), 50–2; R. F. Taft, "Monogenes, Ho," ODB 2:1397.

53. The Slavonic redaction of the Typika service inserts an Epistle and Gospel here, after the Beatitudes.

54. J. Mateos, "Un horologion inédit de S. Sabas. Le codex sinaïtique grec 863 (IXe siècle)," in *Mélanges E. Tisserant,* III.1, Studi e testi 233 (Vatican: Biblioteca apostolica Vaticana, 1964), 47–76, esp. 54–5; cf. Mateos, *Célébration,* 68–71. For further sources of what A. Baumstark calls "the Old Palestinian Melkite Rite," see his *Comparative Liturgy* (Westminster, Md.: Newman Press, 1958), 223–4; R. F. Taft, *The Byzantine Rite. A Short History,* American Essays in Liturgy (Collegeville: The Liturgical Press, 1992), 56–7 and the literature cited there, 64–5 notes 26–31. For the corresponding Armenian office, the Armenian Third or Noon Hour *(Chashu Zham),* see M. Findikyan, "Bishop Step'anos Siwnec'i: A Source for the Study of Medieval Armenian Liturgy," *Ostkirchliche Studien* 44 (1995): 171–96; and most recently, G. Winkler, "Über die Bedeutung einiger liturgischer Begriffe im georgischen Lektionar und Iadgari sowie im armenischen Ritus," *Studi sull'Oriente cristiano* 4:1 (2000): 133–54, here 142–7, 149–54. On the possible relation of the Armenian *Chashu Zham* to the Byzantine Typika communion service, see R. F. Taft, review of *Commentary on the Divine Liturgy by Xosrov Anjewac'I,* Armenian Church Classics, intro., and trans. S. Peter Cowe (New York: Department of Religious Education, Diocese of the Armenian Church, 1991), OCP 59 (1993): 274–6; id., review of the same in *Journal of the Society for Armenian Studies* 7 (1994): 174–7; id., "The Armenian Liturgy: Its Origins and Characteristics," in Treasures in Heaven: Armenian Art, Religion, and Society (New York: Pierpont Morgan Library, 1998), 13–30, here 19–20; and esp. id., "The Armenian 'Holy Sacrifice *(Surb Patarag)*' as a Mirror of Armenian Liturgical History," in *The Armenian Christian Tradition,* OCA 254, ed. R. F. Taft (Rome: Pontifical Oriental Institute, 1997), 175–97, here 185–8. An analogous monastic service for communion outside the liturgy existed also in the West, according to Aurelian, bishop of Arles (546–551), *Rule for Monks* 57:11–12, composed between 534 and 542. Mass was a exception even on Sundays and feasts, when the monks normally received communion from the reserved species at the end of terce: "Every Sunday . . . after terce, however, say the *Our Father* and, chanting psalmody, let all communicate. Do the same on feast-days. But when it seems suitable to the holy abbot, then let there be masses": PL 68:396B = *Règles monastiques d'occident, IVe–VIe siècle, d'Augustin à Ferréol,* introd. et notes par V. Deprez, préface par A. de Vogüé, Vie monastique 9, Bégrolle-en-Mauges, (Maine-et-Loire: Abbaye de Bellefontaine, 1980), 248–9.

55. This provenance was first suggested by S. Parenti, private communication; cf. A.-A. Thiermeyer, "Das Typikon-Ktetorikon und sein literarhistorischer Kontext," OCP 58 (1992): 475–513, here 482; and most recently developed by

A. Pentkovskij and M. Jovcheva, "Prazdnichnye i voskresnye blazhenny v vizantijskom I slavjanskom bogosluzhenii VIII–XIII vv.," *Palaeobulgarica* 25:3 (2001): 31–60, here 33ff. The largely unstudied hagiopolite PRES can be seen in a few extant sources, in chronological order: the so-called Typikon of the Anastasis in the Greek codex *Jerusalem Stavrou 43* (1122 CE), ed. A. Papadopoulos-Kerameus, *Analekta Hierosolymitike Stachyologia,* 5 vols., (St. Petersburg: V. Kirsvaoum, 1894–98), II: 49–51, 65–6, 78–83; two variant Georgian redactions of hagiopolite PRES from codices *Graz Georgian 4* (tenth century) and *Vatican Borgia Georgian 7* (thirteenth/fourteenth century): *Liturgiae Ibericae antiquiores,* ed. M. Tarchnishvili, CSCO 122–3, Scriptores Iberici 1–2, series I, vol. 1, (Louvain: Secrétariat du CSCO, 1950), 71–3 and 78–80 respectively; Greek hagiopolite PRES in codex *Sinai Gr. 1040* (1156–69 CE): F. E. Brightman, *Liturgies Eastern and Western* (Oxford: Clarendon Press, 1896), 494–500; Dmitrievskij II, 134–5.

56. On the elements of the precommunion ritual, see the relevant chapters in Taft, *Precommunion.*

57. Tarchnishvili, *Liturgiae,* I.1, 71.

58. In PRES of *Graz Georgian 4* (tenth century), however, the Creed is explicitly excluded by the rubric: *"Non dicitur Credo,"* ibid., 74.

59. Ibid., 74.

60. Ibid., 75.

61. Ibid., 79, but cf. 75, where the PRES fragment in *Vatican Borgia Georgian 7* (thirteenth/fourteenth century), has Psalm 148 + alleluia.

62. Cf. ibid., 75.

63. For this transcription and all information on this source, I am indebted to Prof. Jeffrey C. Anderson of George Washington University, Washington, D.C., who discovered this Horologion text, brought it to my attention, and is editing it for publication in the OCA series.

64. *The Life and Miracles of Saint Luke of Steiris,* eds. Carolyn L. Connor and W. Robert Connor (Brookline: The Archbishop Iakovos Library of Ecclesiastical and Historical Sources 18, 1994) = BHG 994. This reference to the Typika at communion was brought to my attention by Basil Lourié of St. Petersburg in his paper "Svataja Chasha v rannexristianskix chinoposledovanijax domashnogo prichashchenija (s zamechaniem koptskom chine Ispolnenija Chashi)," in *Srednovekovoe pravoslavie. Ot prixoda do patriarxata,* Vypusk 2., ed. N. D. Barabanov (Volgograd: 1998), 4–29.

65. Connor & Connor, ix.

66. As recounted in chapter 41 of this *Vita.*

67. Date from A. Kazhdan, "Hagiographical Notes," *Byzantinische Zeitschrift* 78 (1985): 49–55, here 54. In §12: "The Hermits of around 900 and the Problem

of the Liturgy," ibid., 53–5, Kazhdan discusses the problem of providing the eucharist for non-ordained anchorites, but does not recognize the parallel between the *Vita* and the Typika service.

68. That is, *margarites,* common Greek term for the consecrated bread.

69. Connor & Connor, 62–5 (translation slightly amended, with numbers added to facilitate reference); cf. commentary, ibid., 161.

70. A. Almazov, *Tajnaja ispoved' v Pravoslavnoj vostochnoj cerkvi. Opyt vneshnej istorii. Issledovanie preimushchestvenno po rukopisjam,* 3 vols. (Odessa: 1894, reprint Moscow: 1995) II: 116–38, III: 26–8; cf. Lourié, "Svataja Chasha," note 18.

71. On which, see Thiermeyer, "Das Typikon-Ktetorikon"; A.-M. Talbot, "Typikon, Monastic," ODB 3:3132; the new series of translations in *Byzantine Monastic Foundation Documents,* 5 vols., Dumbarton Oaks Studies 35, eds. J. Thomas and A. Constantinides Hero (Washington, D.C.: Dumbarton Oaks Research Library and Collection, 2000); and the new Belfast translation of the Evergetis Synaxarion cited in note 75 below.

72. On the Studite reform, see R. F. Taft, *The Byzantine Rite. A Short History,* chapters 5–6; and, most recently, Th. Pott, *La réforme liturgique byzantine. Étude du phénomène de l'évolution non-spontanée de la liturgie byzantine,* Bibliotheca Ephemerides Liturgicae, Subsidia 104 (Rome: CLV-Edizioni liturgiche, 2000), chapter 4.

73. Klentos, *Evergetis,* 186–9, 233.

74. Cf. Hanssens, *Institutiones* II, §§189–95, citing several sources from Dmitrievskij I, 233, 248, 603, etc.; Symeon of Thessalonika (d. 1429), *Dialogus* 330, PG 155:596AD. On the antidoron see Taft, *Precommunion* 217–20, 405–13; id., "One Bread, One Body," 28–32.

75. Mateos, *Célébration,* 70. On the important and highly influential Constantinopolitan Monastery of the Theotokos Evergetis, see the growing body of literature produced by the Theotokos Evergetis Project of Queen's University: *The Theotokos Evergetis and Eleventh-Century Monasticism. Papers of the Third Belfast Byzantine International Colloquium, 1–4 May 1992,* BBTT 6.1, eds. Margaret Mullet and Anthony Kirby (Belfast: Queen's University, 1994); see also *Work and Worship at the Theotokos Evergetis 1050–1200. Papers of the Fourth Belfast Byzantine International Colloquium, Portaferry, Co. Down, 14–17 September 1995,* BBTT 6.2, eds. idem (Belfast: Queen's University, 1997), 166–77. For the influence of Evergetis on Byzantine monasticism, see esp. Barbara Crostini, "Towards a Study of the Scriptorium of the Monastery of the Theotokos Evergetis: Preliminary Remarks," in Mullet-Kirby, *Theotokos Evergetis,* BBTT 6.1: 1176–97; Robert Jordan, "The Monastery of the Theotokos Evergetis, its Children and Grandchildren," ibid., 215–45; John Thomas, "Documentary Evidence from the Byzantine Monastic *Typika* for the History of the Evergetine Reform," ibid., 246–73; on the influence of Evergetine liturgical usages, see esp. Klentos, *Evergetis;* also Mullet-Kirby,

Theotokos Evergetis, BBTT 6.1, studies 16–7, 19; idem., *Work and Worship,* BBTT 6.2, studies 19–23. The only complete edition of the liturgical Typikon or Synaxarion remains Dmitrievskij I, 256–656, but the first volume of the excellent new Belfast critical edition with facing English translation is now available: *The Synaxarion of the Monastery of the Theotokos Evergetis. September–February,* BBTT 6.5, text and trans. Robert H. Jordan (Belfast: Queen's University, 2000). The administrative Typikon Ktetorikon has been critically edited by Paul Gautier, "Le Typikon de la Théotokos Évergétis," REB 40 (1982): 5–101.

76. See note 52 above.

77. We first see this in the early Georgian version of the Liturgy of St. John Chrysostom in the eleventh-century Palestinian manuscript *Sinai Georg. 89.* See A. Jacob, "Une version géorgienne inédite de la Liturgie de S. Jean Chrysostome," *Le Muséon* 77 (1964): 65–117, here 90–2. For Evergetis, see Dmitrievskij I, 256–656 passim; Mateos, *Célébration* 69–70; and especially Klentos, *Evergetis* 225–9, 233–4.

78. For the antiphons, see Mateos, *Célébration* 71; for the end of the liturgy, see the Slavonic *Sluzhebnik* (Rome: 1956), 291–2, 403–4, 468–9.

79. Dmitrievskij I, 603, cf. 515; Mateos, *Célébration* 70; and, most thoroughly, Klentos, *Evergetis,* 225–9, 233–4.

80. *Corpus iuris civilis,* III: *Novellae,* ed. R. Schoell, G. Kroll (Berlin: 1928), I: 620. In the West, this ministry could be exercised even by a subdeacon or a layperson: cf. P. Browe, "Die Sterbekommunion im Altertum und Mittelalter," *Zeitschrift für katholische Theologie* 60 (1936): 1–54, here 3.

81. *The Council in Trullo Revisited,* Kanonika 6 (Rome: Pontifical Oriental Institute, 1995), 138 = J. D. Mansi, *Sacrorum conciliorum nova et amplissima collectio,* 53 tomes in 58 vols., eds. G. Nedungatt and M. Featherstone (Paris: H. Welter, 1901–27), 11:969.

82. *Reg* 531: 4 = *Les Regestes du Patriarcat de Constantinople I: Les actes des patriarches,* fasc. 1–3, Le Patriarcat byzantin, série I, ed. V. Grumel (Kadiköy-Istanbul: Socii Assumptionistae Chalcedonenses, 1932, 1936); fasc. 1, 2nd ed. (Paris: Institut français d'études byzantines, 1972); fasc. 4, ed. V. Laurent (Paris: Institut français d'études byzantines, 1971); fasc. 5–7, ed. J. Darrouzès (Paris: Institut français d'études byzantines, 1977, 1979, 1991): references are to the documents, which are numbered consecutively throughout, in chronological order.

83. PG 155:889B. Almazov, *Tajnaja ispoved'* II, 116–26, cites evidence to show that such practices continued in some Byzantine Orthodox Churches up through the seventeenth century.

However legitimate acts of eucharistic adoration and devotion may be, they are not the primary reason for real presence in the eucharist. Even tradition-minded Catholics can agree that Christ did not institute the sacrament of the Supper primarily so the consecrated species could be "reserved, carried about, lifted up, or worshiped." The primary purpose was eating and drinking—the food and actions of a meal become the sign and cause of Christ's union with us and ours with him. That is why our eucharistic prayers ask that we who partake of the hallowed elements may become "one body, one spirit in Christ."

Nathan Mitchell, "The Amen Corner: Becoming Eucharist," *Worship* 72:3 (May 1998): 280.

Eucharistic Reservation and Lutheranism: An Extension of the Sunday Worship?

Maxwell E. Johnson

Ecumenical students and teachers of liturgy owe a great debt of gratitude to the careful scholarly work of Nathan Mitchell in general and, in particular, to his various works on the eucharist. It is indeed safe to say that all who have been educated in good graduate programs in liturgical studies in the United States since 1982, regardless of their denominational affiliation, know what they know about the eucharist, especially about extra-liturgical veneration and devotion to the eucharist in the West, because of Nathan's now classic work, *Cult and Controversy: The Worship of the Eucharist Outside Mass.*[1]

In ecumenical conversations Roman Catholics frequently ask Lutherans something like this: "If you Lutherans really believe in the real presence of Christ in the eucharist as you say you do, then why don't you normally reserve the eucharist in your churches?" This is, of course, a most legitimate question for Lutherans to be asked by Roman Catholics. But there is a rather interesting assumption behind this question, namely, that the practice of eucharistic reservation in one Christian tradition can be some kind of litmus test for determining whether another Christian tradition really holds to a theology of real presence. Is this necessarily the case? What *is* the precise relationship between eucharistic reservation and real presence? This particular essay in thanksgiving to and in honor of Nathan will deal with these questions from a Lutheran theological perspective in light of the early history of the practice of reservation and communion, related doctrinal and/or dogmatic issues, and current Lutheran liturgical-pastoral practice. In spite of their long history of not doing so, might there be ways today in which Lutheranism could embrace some form of eucharistic reservation without compromising its confessional position? I believe that such could, indeed, be possible.

A Variety of "Lutheran" Practices

Let us imagine four Evangelical Lutheran Church in America (ELCA) congregations existing in various places within the same large city, all of which celebrate the eucharist at every Sunday liturgy and on major festival days.[2] The first congregation, Transfiguration Lutheran Church, has three Sunday eucharists, one on Saturday evening and two on Sunday morning. Real bread is used for the celebrations. All of the bread and wine needed for all three celebrations is placed on the credence table before the Saturday evening liturgy and, hence, whatever remains of those elements after the first or second liturgies is simply used again (= reconsecrated) at the next liturgy. At the end of all three liturgies any remaining bread and wine is scattered and poured on the ground outside. The theological rationale for both practices (using what remains at the next liturgy and eventually disposing of them on the ground) is that Lutherans believe that after the liturgy the bread and wine, which *were* the body and blood of Christ, are no longer that body and blood but revert back to common food and drink.

A similar practice and theological rationale is present at the second imaginary congregation, Faith Lutheran Church. At Faith, however, any hosts remaining after its two Sunday celebrations are simply stored with unconsecrated ones and any wine remaining in the flagon is poured back into the bottle in preparation for the next Sunday's celebrations. At both Transfiguration and Faith, distribution of communion to the sick and homebound requires the presence of the pastor who will use an occasional service called "Celebration of Holy Communion with Those in Special Circumstances," a service which includes two short eucharistic prayers containing the words of institution.[3]

The third congregation, Saint Paul's Lutheran Church, practices a custom different from either that of Transfiguration or Faith. At Saint Paul's any of the elements remaining after each of its two Sunday eucharists are reverently consumed by the pastor and assisting ministers, a portion is sent with lay communion ministers to the sick and homebound, who will use a service called "Distribution of Communion to Those in Special Circumstances,"[4] and another portion is reserved for the future communion of the sick in what is essentially a tabernacle on the former altar in the very center of the back wall of the church. Until only recently this "tabernacle" was kept in the sacristy. At Saint Paul's the obvious theological rationale is that there is a permanence to the real presence of Christ "in, with and under" the bread and wine, a presence that does not somehow cease after the celebration of the eucharistic liturgy itself.

The practice of the fourth imaginary congregation, Christus Rex, is similar to that of Saint Paul's but actually goes one or two steps further. That is, Christus Rex regularly sends lay communion ministers out to the sick and homebound from its single Sunday celebration and reserves both elements in an "aumbry" within a side wall of the sanctuary. But, in obvious imitation of Roman Catholic practice, Christus Rex celebrates a "Mass of the Presanctified" on Good Friday, wherein elements consecrated at the

Maundy Thursday eucharist are distributed to the congregation. And further, in equally obvious imitation of an unfortunately common Roman Catholic practice—a practice, in fact, that Roman Catholic liturgists consider to be liturgically scandalous![5]—Christus Rex *regularly* distributes holy communion at the time of distribution not only from what has just been consecrated at the Sunday liturgy but from the *reserved* sacrament as well! Indeed, there is no question but that approximately half of the relatively small congregation at Christus Rex receives holy communion from the *reserved* sacrament each week.

While it is certainly true that no liturgical or extra-liturgical cult of the blessed sacrament exists at Saint Paul's or at Christus Rex, the mere fact that the eucharist is reserved in these congregations under both elements indicates that within the ELCA—even within the same city—there is no consistency whatsoever in eucharistic practice, especially with regard to the question of what to do with elements remaining after the liturgy itself. Nevertheless, if I were to speculate on which of these four congregations best reflects the most common practice in the ELCA, I would have to say that probably that of both Transfiguration and Faith does, where what has been consecrated is either reused or used to feed the birds. The question, therefore, naturally arises: Which of these imaginary congregations is most Lutheran in its eucharistic practice and theological interpretation?

That is not an easy question to answer for the simple reason that, while strongly affirming the real presence of Christ in the eucharist, at times even in language that approximates the Roman Catholic doctrine of transubstantiation,[6] the Lutheran Confessions do not deal *in detail* with the *duration* of Christ's eucharistic presence. What they do say on this issue, however, if limited, is rather significant. In relationship to Corpus Christi processions, for example, Article XXII of the Augsburg Confession states, "Because the division of the sacrament [= the withdrawal of the cup] is contrary to the institution of Christ, the customary carrying about of the sacrament in processions is also omitted by us."[7] If this article might be interpreted as but critiquing a misuse or abuse of the sacrament, the Formula of Concord, Solid Declaration (1580) is much stronger in its approach. In its rejection of the specific doctrine of transubstantiation, Article VII states:

> [T]hey assert that under the species of the bread, which they allege has lost its natural substance and is no longer bread, the body of Christ is present even apart from the action of the sacrament (when, for instance, the bread is locked up in the tabernacle or is carried about as a spectacle and for adoration). For nothing can be a sacrament apart from God's command and the ordained use for which it is instituted in the Word of God.[8]

Such statements would seem to support the practice of either Transfiguration Church or Faith Church. Without the sacramental action, the "ordained use" of the eucharist, frequently interpreted as the reception or *sumptio* of the body and blood of Christ in communion (often times called "receptionism"), the eucharist is not the eucharist and the body and blood of Christ are not present.

But is it really that simple? Herman Sasse, in his now classic study of Luther's eucharistic theology, *This Is My Body,* wrote:

> Luther and the early Lutheran Church avoided forming any theory about the "moment" when the Real Presence begins and the "moment" when it ceases. Some later orthodox theologians advanced the theory that Christ's body and blood are present only at the "moment" when they are being received. This is frequently regarded, within and without the Lutheran Church, as the genuinely Lutheran doctrine. . . . [But] as far as Luther himself is concerned, there cannot be the slightest doubt that he never did limit the Real Presence to the instant of distribution and reception. He never abandoned the view that by the words

of consecration bread and wine "become" the body and blood of Christ. Otherwise neither the elevation, which was in use at Wittenberg up to 1542, nor the adoration of Christ, who is present in the elements, could have been justified. He always regarded it as Zwinglianism to neglect the difference between a consecrated and an unconsecrated host, and it has always been the custom of the Lutheran Church to consecrate the new supply of bread or wine or both if more is needed than originally was provided for. The rule that Luther, like Melanchthon and the Lutheran Confessions, followed was that that there is no sacrament, and consequently no presence of the body and blood of Christ, "apart from the use instituted by Christ" or "apart from the action divinely instituted." Since the word usus *is explained by* actio *it cannot mean the same as* sumptio. *If it has sometimes been understood in this way, it must be said that neither Luther nor the Formula of Concord . . . identified the* sumptio *(eating and drinking) with the use or action of the sacrament.*[9]

In a related footnote Sasse adds:

Luther demanded the dismissal of a pastor who had given to a communicant an unconsecrated host instead of a consecrated one, which had been dropped. This unfortunate man was imprisoned. Luther does not approve of such punishment, but he thinks him unfit for the Lutheran ministry: "He should go to his Zwinglians" (Letter of January 11, 1546; WA Br 11, No. 4186). In 1543 Luther and Bugenhagen gave their opinion in a controversy about the question whether consecrated hosts could be preserved together with unconsecrated ones for another consecration. Luther criticizes this. Nothing of the consecrated elements should be saved, but must be consumed. In this connection he gives a clear definition of the sacramental "time" or "action": "sic ergo definiemus tempus vel actionem sacramentalem, ut incipiat ab initio orationis dominicae et duret, donec omnes communicaverint, calicem ebiberunt, particulas*

comederint, populus dimissus et ab altari descessum sit."
(WA Br 10, No. 3894, lines 27ff.). In a Table Talk of 1540
Luther goes so far as to allow the blessed sacrament to be carried
to another altar (in the same church) or even, as was still custom-
ary in some churches, to be brought to the sick in their home
(WA TR 5, No. 5314), provided this could be regarded as part
of the "action." This was tolerated as an exception. However, a
reservation of the sacrament was not allowed. The remnants of
the elements should be either consumed or burned.[10]

On the basis of the above two quotations from Sasse, it would seem, then, that all four of our ELCA congregations are, in various ways, at odds with the Lutheran sacramental tradition. Both Transfiguration and Faith are at odds in their practice of mixing unconsecrated bread and wine with consecrated bread and wine, either from one service to the next or in preparation for the following week's liturgies. Certainly Transfiguration is at odds by scattering the remaining bread and pouring out the remaining wine on the ground rather than consuming both reverently. But Saint Paul's and Christus Rex are also at odds with that tradition in their own ways. Consistent with Luther's permitted exception of allowing the eucharist to be taken to the sick as an "extension of the action," both Saint Paul's and Christus Rex do send lay communion ministers out from the liturgy to the sick and homebound. It would seem, however, that they both depart from the Lutheran tradition in their practices of eucharistic reservation. Here, especially, it would appear that is the practice of Christus Rex which represents the most radical departure in regularly distributing communion from the reserved sacrament during Sunday liturgies and in adopting the "Mass of the Presanctified" for Good Friday.

If this is true, however, that all of these congregations seem to depart in some way from the Lutheran tradition, the reason for that must certainly be that the tradition itself is not all that clear. As we noted in Sasse above, "Luther and the early Lutheran Church avoided forming any theory about the 'moment' when the Real Presence begins and the 'moment' when it ceases." Consequently, even today the avoidance of forming any such theory is expressed in various ways. On the one hand, *The Use of the Means of Grace* can direct that "any food that remains is best consumed by the presiding and assisting minister and by others present following the service."[11] On the other hand, regarding the communion of the sick and homebound the same document says: "*Occasional Services* provides an order for the Distribution of Communion to Those in Special Circumstances. As an extension of the Sunday worship, the servers of Communion take the elements to those unable to attend."[12] But, when one reads the rubrics of this particular service it becomes clear that "extension of the Sunday worship" is interpreted as an *immediate* extension of the distribution of communion from the Sunday worship:

> *To underscore the significance of bringing the congregational Eucharist to those unable to participate in the assembly, the Communion should be carried to the absent without delay following the congregational celebration. Sufficient ministers should be appointed so that all the absent may receive Communion within a few hours of the congregation's service that day.*[13]

In other words, one does not get the impression that distribution on Tuesday or Wednesday of the following week, for example, is quite viewed as a similar "extension of the Sunday worship." And, consequently, one starts asking theologically, just how long *does* the presence of Christ remain in the bread and wine as this extension of the Sunday worship? A few hours? A few days? And if the body and blood of Christ do remain in the elements for the purposes of communing the sick and homebound on *Sundays*, does that presence disappear if the communion minister does not arrive at the place of the sick or homebound until Monday or Tuesday? Is the real presence of the body and blood of Christ in the bread and wine a permanent presence which remains as long as the bread and wine themselves remain as recognizable food and drink? To ask such questions, naturally, is to ask the question of the theological and liturgical propriety of eucharistic reservation itself. It is important here to look at this in the context of its early historical development rather than from the ideological and polemical stances of a later period.

Eucharistic Reservation and Communion in Historical Perspective

Lutherans (and, undoubtedly, many Roman Catholics), both at the time of the Formula of Concord and today, tend to forget that the reservation of the eucharist and communion from the reserved eucharist antedate the thirteenth-century doctrine of transubstantiation by centuries. Similarly, the practice of eucharistic reservation is no more intrinsically connected to the doctrine of transubstantiation than transubstantiation is itself intrinsically connected to the doctrine of the real presence! Even the Council of Trent said only that transubstantiation was the "most apt" and "most appropriate" way to refer to the change of the bread and wine into the body and blood of Christ![14] And, certainly the longstanding traditions of the Eastern Orthodox churches remind us that it is possible and traditional to acknowledge the real presence of Christ in the eucharist, to reserve the eucharist, to celebrate liturgies of the "presanctified" (at least in Lent) and to commune the sick from the reserved sacrament without any recourse to the Western medieval doctrine of transubstantiation and without any concomitant cult of the blessed sacrament (for example, Corpus Christi processions, benedictions and so on).

Thanks to the work of Nathan Mitchell and others,[15] the history of this topic is now easily narrated. Our earliest reference to the distribution and reception of communion *outside* of the liturgy appears already in the middle of the second century (ca. 150), in Justin Martyr's *First Apology* 65. Herein Justin indicates that, at the conclusion of the liturgy, "deacons" carried the eucharist to those who were absent from the community's celebration, a practice seemingly consistent with the distribution to the sick and homebound as the "extension of the Sunday worship" in the ELCA today. A short time later in North Africa, Tertullian witnesses to the fact that the faithful regularly took the eucharist home with them from the Sunday celebration for the reception of communion during the week (at least on the "station" or fasting days of Wednesdays and Fridays).[16] In the middle of the third century, Cyprian of Carthage also refers to this practice and informs us that the consecrated bread was kept in little boxes called *arcae* (or chrismals).[17] These *arcae* were either worn around the neck of believers or kept in their homes.

If Tertullian and Cyprian seem to refer only to the reservation and reception of the body of Christ in this context, rubrics preserved in the so-called *Apostolic Tradition,* ascribed to Hippolytus of Rome (ca. 215),[18] not only corroborate the practice of home reservation and communion, but make it clear that the ritual of communion included reception from the cup as well:

> *[H]aving blessed the cup in the name of God, you received as it were the antitype of the blood of Christ. Therefore do not pour any out, as though you despised it, lest an alien spirit lick it up. You will be guilty of the blood, as one who despises the price with which he has been bought.*[19]

It is quite possible, then, notes Mitchell, that early Christian domestic rituals of communion from the reserved eucharist included blessing the cup by means of dropping a small portion of the consecrated bread into it, a consecration by contact. Such a method of consecrating the wine, in fact, has continued to the present day in the Liturgy of the Presanctified and distribution of communion to the sick within various rites of the Christian East.[20]

That the practice of domestic eucharistic reservation and reception continued into the late fourth century is clearly attested by Basil of Caesarea (d. 379), who in reference to desert monastics and others writes:

> *All the solitaries in the deserts, where there is no priest, keep the communion by them and partake of it by themselves. At Alexandria, too, and in Egypt, each one of the laity, for the most part, keeps the communion at home, and whenever he wishes partakes of it himself. For after the priest has completed the sacrifice and distributed it, he who then received it in entirety . . . must believe that he duly takes and receives it from the hand that first gave it. For even in the church, when the priest distributes each portion, he who receives takes it into his complete control, and lifts it to his mouth with his own hand. It comes to the same thing, whether one or many portions at a time are received from the priest.[21]*

In light of the contemporary ELCA practice of carrying communion to the sick and homebound as an extension of the Sunday worship, it is interesting that Mitchell comments on the words of Basil, noting:

> *quite clearly, Basil regards communion at home as simply an extension of the public liturgy in church; postponing the consumption of some of the bread until a later time is quite inconsequential, since one still "takes and receives it from the hand that first gave it."*[22]

Nevertheless, if still in the fourth century eucharistic reservation at home and domestic rituals of communion reception on days when the eucharistic liturgy itself was not celebrated in church were rather common and approved, the custom of taking the eucharist home came to be discouraged for a variety of reasons. Jerome, for example, expressed his strong disapproval regarding those banned from receiving communion publicly in church, who yet received privately in their homes.[23] Similarly, the Council of Saragossa (ca. 379–381), perhaps out of fear of the eucharist falling into the hands of heretics (that is, the Priscillianists), decreed: "If anyone is found guilty of not consuming *in church* the eucharist he has received, let him be anathema."[24] At the same time, it *is* documented that the practice of home reservation and communion did continue in some places until the seventh and eighth centuries.

If home reservation and communion would cease for a variety of reasons, however, the reservation of the eucharist in churches, especially for the communion of the sick and for public distribution of communion on fasting days, certainly continued. Canon XIII of the Council of Nicea refers to the necessity of viaticum being given to the dying, but it is the late fourth-century *Apostolic Constitutions* (ca. 381) which contains our first clear reference to the reservation of the eucharist in the church (that is, in the sacristy).[25] For several centuries the reserved eucharist was frequently kept inside an *arca,* chrismal or pyx within a sacristy cupboard, and it is quite possible in some places, as a letter of Chrysostom indicates, that the wine was also reserved.[26] There is no reason to think that these practices were new developments in the fourth century but rather a continuation of what had already been evolving previously. A *Life of St. Basil* attributed to Amphilochius of Iconium indicates that Basil had commissioned a golden dove, into which he had placed a portion of the eucharist. This was then suspended over the altar "as a figure of the sacred dove that appeared at the Jordan over the Lord during his baptism."[27]

What is most interesting to note in this overall context, however, is the close relationship that seems to develop in some quarters between the practice of eucharistic reservation and christological orthodoxy. This becomes the case especially within the context of the fifth-century Nestorian controversy.[28] Whatever the eucharistic theology and practice of Nestorius himself might have been in Constantinople, the followers of Cyril of Alexandria apparently interpreted the strict christological diophysitism of Nestorius and his followers as leading to a eucharistic practice which held that there could be no complete or permanent union between the divine Logos and the bread and wine. Hence, the body and blood of Christ were present in holy communion but only *temporarily* and limited to the day of the eucharistic liturgy itself. What remained of the eucharistic elements until the next day was no longer considered to be Christ's body or blood. Already Cyril of Alexandria had attacked this approach:

> *I hear that some people say that the mystical blessing is no longer active to effect sanctification when the eucharist is left over to the next day. Those who reason this way are insane. For Christ does not become different, and his holy body does not undergo any change. On the contrary, the effectiveness of the blessing and the life-creating grace in It remains unchanged.[29]*

Further, for Cyril the very question of the life-giving nature of the eucharist was at stake in this controversy. That is, for him Nestorius had so separated the divine and human natures in Christ from each other that in the eucharist itself only the "human" body and blood of Christ could be received.[30] Cyril writes:

> *Not as common flesh do we receive it, not at all, nor as a man sanctified and associated with Word according to the unity of dignity, or as having had a divine indwelling, but as truly the life-giving and very flesh of the Word himself. For he is life*

according to his nature as God, and when he became united to his flesh, he made it life-giving.[31]

What Nestorius and his followers might have actually held and taught about the reservation of the eucharist theologically, however, is difficult to uncover and one must always be cautious of discerning a position based on the critique of opponents. The fact that the ancient Assyrian Church of the East did not historically—and still does not—reserve the eucharist nor celebrate the Liturgy of the Presanctified is what undoubtedly has led others to make certain assertions about eucharistic theology in that tradition. For example, according to N. Uspensky and other Orthodox theologians, eucharistic reservation and the Liturgy of the Presanctified in the Byzantine tradition signify the victory of Orthodox christology over "Nestorianism" in that both practices presumably safeguard the unity of the person of Christ in the eucharist as the God-man whose body and blood are life-giving.[32] The only problem is that they do not produce any hard evidence to support such a claim.

What is most likely the case is that the practice of the ancient Assyrian Church of the East regarding eucharistic reservation is nothing other than a continuation of early Christian liturgical diversity and the survival of one ancient practice. That is, some early Christian communities clearly reserved the eucharist and regularly communed the sick from the reserved sacrament. Others did not do so but simply carried the eucharist to the sick on the same day as the celebration. In fact, it may well be that Justin Martyr's own description of deacons carrying communion to the absent in his *First Apology* is quite consistent with the practice of the Assyrian Church of the East, and that Justin's own (Syrian?) community at Rome did not practice reservation. But only later within the developing homogeneity of liturgical practice across ecclesial boundaries and within the context of a developing christological orthodoxy, would certain practices come to be criticized and even condemned in light of those developments. Indeed, it would be preposterous to assume that prior to the Council of Ephesus (431) East Syrian Christians regularly reserved the eucharist and then stopped reserving in response to the christological position of the other churches that had now become recognized as the orthodox position. Does it not make more sense to see non-reservation as one ancient practice that was reinterpreted later on, reinterpreted not by those who followed the practice, but by those who sought to critique and condemn that practice in terms of their own christological position? Even today, according to Mar Bawai Soro, Western California Bishop of the Assyrian Church of the East:

> *The Church of the East holds that once the eucharistic elements are consecrated, they become really, truly and permanently, the body and blood of Christ. This theological statement can clearly be seen in Church of the East's liturgical-eucharistic texts, the writings of the Fathers, and in canonical legislation. Church of the East official texts do not dispute or contradict the common orthodox, catholic faith of the real and permanent presence of Christ in the Holy Qurbana. Now, concerning the practice of eucharistic preservation and the Presanctified: at present, we certainly do not preserve the eucharist, nor am I aware of any such practice in the past. Yet, as recently as the early 1990s, the Holy Synod (not the Patriarch) allowed priests to take the consecrated Holy Qurbana to the sick out in hospitals and homes. Sometimes, it may be through the overnight that the patient receives the eucharist. But there is still definitively no practice of preserving the Qurbana in our churches.*[33]

Hence, in spite of the approaches of Uspensky and others, there is no necessary correlation whatsoever between eucharistic reservation and the theology of Christ's real presence in the eucharist itself. Those who reserve and those who do not reserve might both assert Christ's real and permanent presence!

Further developments regarding eucharistic reservation and even the developing cult of the reserved eucharist in the medieval West and at the time of the Protestant Reformation are more widely known than are the practices from the patristic period. Hence, these developments need not be treated in detail here. At the risk of oversimplification, however, it is important to note that the very criticisms of the Lutheran Confessions against late medieval Roman practice (for example, reservation of the host and Corpus Christi processions) are those which arose because the cult of the blessed sacrament outside Mass—including an emphasis on the elevation of the host in Mass—had come to be in practice the practical surrogate for the reception of communion itself. That is, the desire to see and adore the host (spiritual and ocular communion) became, in the words of Joseph Jungmann, the "be all and end all" of eucharistic devotion and the host itself became the supreme relic among many lesser relics.[34] And yet, it was only after the Protestant Reformation, and in response to what was perceived to be a denial of the real presence on the part of the reformers, that, increasingly, the eucharist became reserved in tabernacles placed in the center of the main altar of Roman Catholic churches. Hence, for Roman Catholics the reservation or non-reservation of the eucharist became most closely associated with the affirmation or denial of Christ's real presence.[35]

Mitchell summarizes the development of the eucharist outside the eucharistic liturgy *per se* as the story of a significant shift from "eucharist as meal" to "eucharist as food," increasingly separated from the context of the meal itself.[36] If this is so, then the concern of the Lutheran Reformers for *usus* and *actio* and their suspicion of the external eucharistic cult associated with the reserved sacrament—"nothing can be a sacrament apart from God's command and the ordained use for which it is instituted in the Word of God"—might surely be viewed as nothing other than a concern for restoring the very meal character of the eucharist itself.

In other words, without questioning the meaning of the "eucharist as food," and while strongly affirming the real presence of Christ in, with and under the "food," the Lutheran reformers were adamant that such "food" was not an object to be adored *outside* of the overall liturgical *actio* but a gift to be received within that *actio* ("eucharist as meal") itself. If this seems so obvious to us now, it was surely not so obvious in a late medieval context where communion was received by the laity at most four times a year, and, at the least, by law, once during Easter, as decreed by Lateran IV (1215). What David Holeton has written with regard to the cessation of infant communion in the medieval West is certainly related to our topic here as well:

> *A Christian society that has degenerated to such a state that it becomes necessary to legislate that Christians need receive the eucharist once a year is fertile for most everything to take place in the context of baptism and the eucharist. The whole vision of what the eucharist was, and what its relationship was to the community, had . . . changed.*[37]

Eucharistic Reservation and Lutheranism Today

In light of the previous section, it would seem that the variety of Lutheran practices represented by our four contemporary ELCA congregations, with some exceptions, might all be considered somehow consistent not only with Lutheran sacramental theology and practice but with the variety of sacramental practices known throughout the history of the church. That is, the practice of non-reservation of the eucharist represented by Transfiguration and Faith Churches is surely consistent with the emphasis in both Luther and the Lutheran Confessions as well as with the continuing practice of the ancient Assyrian Church of the East. Indeed, with the concerns expressed both by Luther and the Formula of Concord against reservation and about the proper *usus* and *actio* of the sacrament within the context of the eucharistic liturgy itself, one wonders if the early Lutheran movement did not somehow accidentally restore that ancient eucharistic practice still characteristic of the Assyrian Church of the East. Here it is interesting to note that certain polemical Eastern Orthodox theologians, who have condemned "Nestorian" eucharistic practices, have seen in those practices the origins of Protestant "receptionism."[38]

What is very significant, however, is that the lack of reserving the eucharist in the Assyrian Church of the East has *not* been a factor in the very recent determination of pastoral guidelines for communion reception between the Assyrian Church of the East and the Chaldean Church, the latter of which is the closely related Eastern Catholic Church in communion with Rome. Beginning in 1994 with a *Common Christological Declaration between the Catholic Church and the Assyrian Church of the East,* continued ecumenical dialogue and convergence led in 2001 to a document entitled *Guidelines for Admission to the Eucharist between the Chaldean Church and the Assyrian Church of the East.* While these guidelines are ecumenically significant for a variety of reasons, it is clear that eucharistic reservation was and is not a related issue in this context. That is, even without the practice of eucharistic reservation, the *Guidelines* state clearly that "the Assyrian Church of the East has . . . preserved a full eucharistic faith in the presence of our Lord under the species of bread and wine."[39] In other words, as this development surely confirms, the reservation of the eucharist can *not* be a litmus test for determining the orthodoxy of a particular church's theology of the real presence of Christ in the eucharist. Consequently, in dialogue between Roman Catholics and Lutherans on the question of the real presence the issue of reservation might appear to be similarly moot.

At the same time, the apparent careless disregard for the elements remaining after the eucharistic liturgy at Transfiguration and

Faith must also be addressed. That is, reusing and mixing consecrated and unconsecrated elements, or using what remains to feed the birds and squirrels, belies an un-Lutheran notion of "receptionism," which cannot be supported theologically. The Lutheran reformers may well have considered various extra-liturgical practices associated with the eucharist (for example, processions and the like) to be abuses, but they did not teach a "receptionism." Hence, if the remaining eucharistic elements are to be reverently consumed or burned in the Lutheran tradition it is because they *are* consecrated and cannot be returned simply to common use, mixed for reuse or scattered on the ground. Indeed, to paraphrase an early Christian document, the *Didache,* "one does not give what is holy to dogs" (or to birds and squirrels).

What then of the practice of eucharistic reservation at both St. Paul's and Christus Rex? While there may be an accidental parallel in the practice of non-reservation and belief in the real presence within both the Assyrian Church of the East and the Lutheran churches, this parallel certainly fails when it is remembered that Lutherans chose deliberately in the sixteenth century to stop reserving the eucharist in their churches. With regard to specific Lutheran-Catholic dialogue and sacramental praxis today, then, the question of reservation is not really so moot at all since the cessation of reservation among Lutherans was a decision consciously directed against Roman Catholic praxis.

But must this still be the case in light of modern ecumenical convergence? That is, can there be a place in Lutheranism for a eucharistic reservation which does not compromise the Lutheran Confessional focus on sacramental *usus* or *actio?* One might surely think so and congregations like St. Paul's and Christus Rex have obviously concluded that eucharistic reservation is an appropriate Lutheran option today.

In an article on eucharistic reservation in contemporary Roman Catholicism Peter Fink has written:

> *The food of the eucharist is reserved after the eucharistic cele-*
> *bration primarily to extend the nourishment and the grace of*
> *Christ's table to those unable to participate in the liturgy itself,*
> *particularly the sick and the dying. This is clearly stated in the*
> *1967 instruction* Eucharisticum mysterium: *"the primary*
> *and original purpose of the reserving of the sacred species in*
> *church outside Mass is the administration of the Viaticum"*
> *(E.M. III, I, A.).*[40]

Of course, even the Council of Trent had made essentially the same
point:

> *The custom of reserving the Holy Eucharist in a sacred place is*
> *so ancient that even the period of the Nicene Council recognized*
> *that usage. Moreover, the practice of carrying the Sacred Eucharist*
> *to the sick and of carefully reserving it for this purpose in churches,*
> *besides being exceedingly reasonable and appropriate, is also found*
> *enjoined in numerous councils and is a very ancient observance*
> *of the Catholic Church. Wherefore, this holy council decrees that*
> *this salutary and necessary custom be by all means retained.*[41]

Similarly, the significant 1982 ecumenical convergence statement
of the Faith and Order Commission of the World Council of
Churches, *Baptism, Eucharist, Ministry,* suggests:

> *on the one hand, it be remembered, especially in sermons and*
> *instruction, that the primary intention of reserving the elements*
> *is their distribution among the sick and those who are absent,*
> *and on the other hand, it be recognized that the best way of*
> *showing respect for the elements served in the eucharistic*
> *celebration is by their consumption, without excluding their use*
> *for communion of the sick.*[42]

Closely related is the classic statement often attributed to early liturgical movement Belgian pioneer Lambert Beauduin that "the

eucharist is adored *because* it is reserved. It is not reserved in order to be adored." Clearly, the primary motive is for the communion of the sick and dying. Any other acts of devotion or adoration of the presence of Christ associated with reservation are secondary in nature.

Together with the service called "Distribution of Communion to Those in Special Circumstances," and in light of a renewed Roman Catholic emphasis on eucharistic reservation as an extension of "the nourishment and the grace of Christ's table to those unable to participate in the liturgy itself, particularly the sick and the dying," it should be possible for Lutheranism to re-evaluate and, in some contexts, at least, to embrace a limited practice of eucharistic reservation today. With the relatively rare exception of congregations like St. Paul's and Christus Rex, the fact that Lutherans have not traditionally reserved the eucharist has tended to put Lutheranism at odds with what early on became the practice of the *dominant* ecclesial traditions of Christianity in both East and West. Further, reservation of the eucharist and communion from the reserved eucharist, as we saw above in no less than Basil of Caesarea, can be viewed simply as the extension of the distribution of holy communion from the Sunday eucharist throughout the week. In this way Lutherans and Lutheran theology could embrace a practice of eucharistic reservation in ways that do not violate the Lutheran confessional stance about "action" and "use." That is, the reservation of the eucharist for the purposes of the reception of communion by the absent *is* nothing other than the extension of the eucharistic *actio* of the Sunday liturgy itself. Surely such an understanding of reservation for the purposes of communion reception on the part of the sick, homebound and dying can be seen today as part of "God's command and the ordained use for which it is instituted in the Word of God." At the time of the Lutheran Reformation this focus may well have been obscured by a non-reception piety and a reservation practice viewed primarily for purposes of adoration. But that is hardly a danger today when both

Lutherans and Roman Catholics place a similar emphasis on the reception of communion in the eucharistic liturgy and where both now send out communion ministers from the Sunday assembly to the sick and dying.

This does not mean, however, that either St. Paul's or Christus Rex is completely off the hook in their reservation and communion practices. The previous reservation practice of St. Paul's, with their tabernacle kept in the sacristy, was certainly much more consistent with the ancient Christian practice of reserving the eucharist for the sick, homebound and dying in sacristy aumbries. In fact, it is hard not to interpret the moving of this tabernacle from the sacristy to the former main altar in the church as anything other than an attempt at imitation of (post-Trent) Roman Catholic or Anglo-Catholic practice. Certainly Christus Rex needs to address its practice of communing the assembly from the reserved eucharist at the Sunday liturgy. What Robert Taft has said about Roman Catholic practice applies doubly to congregations standing in the Lutheran tradition of the *usus* and *actio* of the meal:

> [I]t is clear that there has to be a better way of narrowing the gap between theory and execution. When one can still now, already generations after Benedict XIV (Certiores effecti 3) and Pius XII (Mediator Dei 118), go to Sunday Mass in a Roman Catholic parish church almost anywhere—even one whose pastor has an advanced degree in liturgical studies, pastoral theology, or some allied area—and be subjected to communion from the tabernacle, that monstrous travesty of any true eucharistic symbolism whereby in a single moment common gifts are offered, blessed, distributed, shared—then there must indeed be a better way.[43]

One has to wonder, similarly, why it is that Christus Rex has also embraced the Roman Catholic "Mass of the Presanctified" for Good Friday. Indeed, the reception of communion from the reserved sacrament on Good Friday is itself a rather late development in the history of the Good Friday liturgy. The core of the ancient Good Friday liturgy, preserved in the current *Lutheran Book of Worship*—and in the Ambrosian Rite of the Roman Catholic Archdiocese of Milan, Italy—is the Passion of St. John 18–19, the solemn intercessions, and the meditation, veneration or adoration of the cross. In other words, a communion rite is not an essential part of the Good Friday liturgy and it is difficult to understand why Lutheran congregations would want to embrace something that is so foreign to their tradition. If Lutherans are to adopt the practice of eucharistic reservation, therefore, they need not directly imitate Roman Catholic reservation practices, and especially they do not need to imitate "that monstrous travesty of any true eucharistic symbolism" by distributing communion from the reserved eucharist at the Sunday liturgy.

Conclusion

In ecumenical dialogue and conversation, Roman Catholics are absolutely correct in pressing Lutherans on the question of belief in the real presence of Christ in the eucharist in relationship to the reservation of the eucharist. But, as I have attempted to demonstrate in this essay, there is no necessary correlation between a firm belief in the real presence of Christ in the eucharistic liturgy and meal and the practice of eucharistic reservation. That is, as the practice of the ancient Assyrian Church of the East indicates clearly, not all churches who hold a high doctrine of Christ's real presence have reserved the eucharist historically. Further, lack of reserving the eucharist in the Assyrian Church of the East has not been a factor in entering recently into a situation of shared eucharist with the Chaldean Church. Perhaps, the traditional Lutheran practice of non-reservation could be viewed in the same ecumenical light today.

At the same time, however, I have suggested that Lutherans *could* reserve the eucharist as but "an extension of the public liturgy in church" (Basil of Caesarea), an understanding toward which the occasional service called "Distribution of Communion to Those in Special Circumstances" already begins to point indirectly. Such a view of reservation, I have argued, does not conflict with the classic Lutheran emphasis of *usus* or *actio*. Indeed, if as the "extension of the Sunday worship" the eucharist can be carried to the sick, homebound and dying within "a few hours" on Sunday afternoons then certainly the distribution of the Sunday eucharist can be extended in this way for a "few days" during the week. For, whether "a few hours" or "a few days," the presence of Christ obviously remains somehow beyond the strict confines of the eucharistic celebration *in* church.

Finally, there may yet be another reason why modern Lutheranism might want to reconsider embracing the practice of eucharistic reservation. It is certainly true, as both traditional Lutheran and Assyrian Church of the East practice demonstrates, that belief in the real presence of Christ in the eucharist does not lead necessarily to eucharistic reservation and, hence, reservation itself cannot be considered a necessity for Lutherans. But it is equally true that in those churches which do reserve the eucharist there is little question about their belief in the real presence of Christ! It cannot be forgotten that in the medieval West, where communion reception was but an occasional act, it was precisely the practice of reservation along with associated devotional activity that not only preserved the eucharist as central in the life of the church, but also safeguarded belief in the real presence. If at the time of the Lutheran Reformation the issue was the restoration of the meal character of the eucharist, perhaps in our own day and age it is the theology of and belief in the real presence itself. Indeed, were Lutherans to begin reserving the eucharist as the "extension of the Sunday worship," consistent with the practices of some in early

Christianity, it might put to rest once and for all the erroneous notion that Lutheran theology of the real presence is some form of "receptionism." Ironically, Lutheran reservation of the eucharist today may be one of the best ways to preserve what Lutheranism actually believes, teaches and confesses about the eucharist, especially in light of recent ecumenical developments in the ELCA with the Episcopal Church, U.S.A., and various Reformed churches in the United States.

◆————————————————————————

1. New York/Collegeville: Pueblo, 1982.

2. Although the names of the congregations have been changed, these congregations and the practices described in them do exist and I have experienced them often. Also, while I have indicated that these are all ELCA congregations, I suspect that a similar variety of practices could be found also in congregations of the Lutheran Church–Missouri Synod.

3. Lutheran Church in America, *Occasional Services: A Companion to Lutheran Book of Worship* (Minneapolis: Augsburg Fortress, 1982), 82–8.

4. Ibid., 76–81.

5. See below, note 42.

6. Article X of the Augsburg Confession, for example, states that "the true body and blood of Christ are really present in the Supper of our Lord under the *form* of bread and wine. . . ." *The Book of Concord,* ed. T. Tappert (Philadelphia: Fortress Press, 1959), 34 (emphasis added).

7. Tappert, 51. Unfortunately, Melanchthon does not deal with this particular issue further in his *Apology.*

8. Ibid., 588.

9. Herman Sasse, *This Is My Body: Luther's Contention for the Real Presence of Christ in the Sacrament* (Minneapolis: Augsburg Publishing House, 1959), 173–4. In this context one might nuance Sasse's remarks to say that it is only recently among Lutherans that consecrating new elements was the custom. In the current ELCA statement on sacramental practices, *The Use of the Means of Grace* (Minneapolis: Augsburg Fortress, 1997), 50, for example, the following appears: "in the rare event that more of either element is needed during distribution, it is not necessary to repeat the words of institution." But no clear rationale is given for what amounts to a departure from Lutheran tradition in this context.

Sasse (and probably Luther himself) would have found this statement as undoubtedly indicative of a Zwinglian approach to the eucharist in modern American Lutheranism.

10. Ibid., 174. The Latin phrase quoted above can be translated as: "In this way, therefore, let us define sacramental 'time' or 'action': that it might begin at the prayer of the Lord *[orationis dominicae]* and remain until all will have communed, the chalice will have been drunk, the particles [of bread] will have been eaten, and the people dismissed and left the altar." It is difficult to know here if *"orationis dominicae"* means the Lord's Prayer (= Our Father) or is a reference to the institution narrative. Since this definition was given in 1543 it is possible that the reference is to the Our Father in the *Deutsche Messe* which actually precedes the institution narrative. But such an interpretation is not likely.

11. *The Use of the Means of Grace,* 50.

12. Ibid., 51.

13. *Occasional Services,* 79 (emphasis added).

14. H. J. Schroeder, *The Canons and Decrees of the Council of Trent* (St. Louis: B. Herder, 1941), Session XIII.4.

15. In addition to Mitchell, 10–19, the following historical survey is based on Robert Taft, "The Frequency of the Eucharist Throughout History," in idem. *Beyond East and West: Problems in Liturgical Understanding* (Rome: Edizioni Orientalia Christiana, Pontifical Oriental Institute, 1997), 87–110; Edward Foley, *From Age to Age* (Chicago: Liturgy Training Publications, 1991), and, of course, the classic study of O. Nußbaum, *Die Aufbewahrung der Eucharistie,* Theophaneia 29 (Bonn: Königstein, 1979).

16. See *Ad uxorem* 2:5, 2ff, and *De oratione* 19.4.

17. Cyprian, *De Lapsis* 26. See also Foley, p. 38.

18. *Apostolic Tradition,* chapters 36–8. *Hippolytus: A Text for Students,* ed. and trans. G. Cuming (Bramcote: Grove Books, 1976), 28.

19. *Apostolic Tradition,* ch. 38, ibid.

20. Mitchell, 12.

21. Basil, *Letter 23* as quoted in Mitchell, 17–18.

22. Mitchell, 18 (emphasis added).

23. See ibid., 17.

24. See ibid., 18–19.

25. *Apostolic Constitutions* 8.13.17. See also Foley, 60.

26. John Chrysostom, *Ep. Ad Innoc.,* 3.

27. Text as quoted by Foley, 60.

28. See N. D. Uspensky, *Evening Worship in the Orthodox Church* (Crestwood: St. Vladimir's Seminary Press, 1985), 154–6.

29. Cyril of Alexandria, *A Letter to Calosirius,* as translated in Uspensky, 154.

30. On this see the classic article by Henry Chadwick, "Eucharist and Christology in the Nestorian Controversy," *Journal of Theological Studies,* New Series 2 (1951): 145–64. Unfortunately, Chadwick does not deal with the question of reservation.

31. Cyril of Alexandria, *Letter* 17.3. English translation in D. Sheerin, *The Eucharist,* Message of the Fathers of the Church, vol. 7 (Wilmington/Collegeville: Michael Glazier, 1986), 276–7. See also W. H. C. Frend, *The Rise of the Monophysite Movement: Chapters in the History of the Church in the Fifth and Sixth Centuries* (Cambridge: University of Cambridge Press, 1972), 124–5.

32. Uspensky, 155. See also note 38 below.

33. E-mail correspondence via Robert Taft, May 20, 2002.

34. Joseph Jungmann, *The Mass of the Roman Rite,* Vol. 1 (New York: Benziger Bros., 1951), 120ff. See also Robert Cabié, *History of the Mass* (Washington: The Pastoral Press, 1992), 75–84.

35. See Theodore Klauser, *A Short History of the Western Liturgy* (Oxford/New York: Oxford University Press, 1979), 135–40.

36. See Mitchell, 19–29.

37. D. Holeton, "The Communion of Infants and Young Children: A Sacrament of Community," in *And Do Not Hinder Them: An Ecumenical Plea for the Admission of Children to the Eucharist,* Faith and Order Paper 109, ed. G. Müller-Fahrenholz (Geneva: World Council of Churches, 1982), 63.

38. Cf. George Bebis, *Symbolai eis ten peri tou Nestoriou Ereunan (ex Apopseos Orthodoxou),* (PhD diss., University of Athens, 1964), 320–2; and Chrestos Androutsos, *Symbolike,* 2nd ed. (Athens: 1930), 285–9ff, and 339ff. I owe these references to my doctoral student Deacon Stefanos Alexopoulos.

39. Pontifical Council for Promoting Christian Unity, *Guidelines for Admission to the Eucharist between the Chaldean Church and the Assyrian Church of the East* (Rome: Catholic Church, 2001), para. 3.

40. Peter Fink, "Eucharist, Reservation of," in *The New Dictionary of Sacramental Worship,* ed. idem. (Collegeville: Michael Glazier, 1990), 428.

41. Session XIII, VI, in Schroeder.

42. "Eucharist," III., 32, *Baptism, Eucharist, Ministry* (Geneva: World Council of Churches, 1982).

43. Robert Taft, "A Generation of Liturgy in the Academy," *Worship* 75:1 (2001): 58.

*To be is to worship; human existence is inescapably
liturgical, doxological. . . . Quite simply, we become
ourselves only in the act of praising God.*

Nathan Mitchell, "The Amen Corner: Worship as Music,"
Worship 73:3 (May 1999): 254.

Catherine Pickstock
and Medieval Liturgy

John F. Baldovin, SJ

Over the past forty years, since the promulgation of *Sacrosanctum Concilium*, the Constitution on the Sacred Liturgy of Vatican II, a number of scholars have proposed serious critiques of the conciliar constitution and especially of the subsequent reform of Roman Catholic worship. Perhaps the most intriguing critique in recent years has come from the pen of the Cambridge scholar Catherine Pickstock. Bursting onto the academic scene with her powerful, if opaque, *After Writing: On the Liturgical Consummation of Philosophy*[1] in 1998, she has captured the interest of a number of liturgical scholars, not least Nathan Mitchell.[2] In this essay I intend to situate Pickstock's treatment of liturgy within her overall project and also within the movement known as Radical Orthodoxy. Second, I will offer an analysis of her treatment of the medieval Roman liturgy of the Mass and the theology that it represents. I will conclude with some consideration of her views on liturgy and society.

Pickstock's Project

Radical Orthodoxy is a theological movement begun in Cambridge in the 1990s and spearheaded by John Milbank, Graham Ward and Catherine Pickstock. These three scholars edited *Radical Orthodoxy: A New Theology*, which serves as a kind of summary of the movement.[3] In their words Radical Orthodoxy "in the face of the secular demise of truth, seeks to reconfigure theological truth."[4] In other words, these authors are self-consciously responding to the modern and postmodern critiques of power. What makes them self-conscious, and not merely restorationist, is their recognition of the place of language in construing reality. Language is unavoidable, as the deconstuctionists like Derrida and Foucault have well understood. On the other hand, Radical Orthodoxy is a direct response to the cynicism and relativism that comes in the wake of the postmodern deconstructionists. They seek to revive an Augustinian Neoplatonism as a holistic vision of the world and social order.[5] According to Russell Reno, Milbank's project fails to preserve the specific identity of Jesus Christ in favor of theological abstraction, thus sliding back into "modern" presuppositions. Reno lays this failure at the door of Milbank et al.'s Anglo-Catholicism, which he regards as an invented tradition.[6] We shall see below if a similar criticism can be applied to Pickstock's treatment of medieval liturgy.

One more general comment on Radical Orthodoxy is in order. Milbank, Pickstock and Ward are keenly aware of the place of violence and power in postmodern thought. They want to offer an alternative to the Nietzschean struggle for power so evident in the postmodern deconstructionists—a vision of peace and harmony with its foundation in the gospel.[7] I must admit great sympathy with this project. Teaching in South Africa some years ago, I came to the conclusion that the issue of violence (and of course, nonviolence) must be the starting point for foundational theology done there—so endemic and overpowering were crime and violence in that newly liberated society. Since then, especially by reading René Girard and his interpreters, I have reached the conclusion that dealing with violence must somehow lie at the heart of all theology.[8] If a struggle for power becomes the object of liturgy, for example, then Christian worship simply cannot do its work of reconciliation. Only a Christology and sacramental theology that can somehow face violence directly will be of value today.[9]

Pickstock's *After Writing* begins with a rereading of Plato's *Phaedrus* in an attempt to show why Jacques Derrida's interpretation of orality (as opposed to writing) is in error. In fact Derrida and those who think like him create "the polity of death" by isolating snapshots on the written page. Pickstock refers to this process as "spatialization" and suggests that it will have an effect on contemporary understandings of the liturgy. The deconstructionists represent the dead end of a project of mapping and dissecting reality begun by Petrus Ramus and René Descartes.[10] Losing the narrative connections that hold reality together is "asyndeton, syntax characterized by the absence of co-ordinating and subordinating conjunctions."[11] Hence we have another symptom of the frenzy to map and categorize everything by lists. Verbs lose out to nouns in the process.[12] The passion for nouns leads to what Pickstock calls "necrophilia." I will let her speak for herself:

> [M]odernity seeks less to banish death, than to prise death and life apart in order to preserve life immune from death in pure sterility. For in seeking only life, in the form of pseudo-eternal permanence, the "modern" gesture is secretly doomed to necrophilia, love of what has to die, can only die. In seeking only life, modernity gives life over to death.[13]

For Pickstock it is essential that the continuum that could be called "the great chain of being" is maintained. Along with other members of the Radical Orthodoxy "school" she argues for a return to an Augustinian Neoplatonism, which we shall see below, is vital to her interpretation of Saint Thomas on transubstantiation.

One final step in Pickstock's program must be described before I deal directly with her treatment of medieval liturgy and the question of liturgy and culture. She lays the modern problematic at the doorstep of the fourteenth-century Franciscan theologian John Duns Scotus, whose denial of the Thomistic *analogia entis* made the concept of being univocal and ultimately led to an arbitrary God (the *potentia absoluta Dei*) as well as to "occasionalism" in sacraments. In other words, instead of being able to construe a logic to the activity of God in a sacrament, we must posit God's activity on the basis of the divine will.[14] Thus Pickstock blames (and I do not think *blames* is too strong a word here) Scotus for the turn to the priority of epistemology over metaphysics—a turn which she finds disastrous for modern theology.[15] By denying the analogous nature of being, Scotus cannot maintain the real distinction between essence and existence, which for Pickstock allows for a being's "always arriving, always coming." She puts it this way:

> *The real distinction between existence and essence is therefore the inner kernel of both* analogia entis *and participation because it permits essence to be realized as essence only through the Being from which it always remains distinct: essence forever simply participates in that which alone realizes and fully determines it. This ontological difference invites the possibility of likeness and proximity, whereas univocity of Being produces unmediable difference and distance.*[16]

And so, Scotus is forced into a postulation of the divine will which can accept transubstantiation only as a locative presence. Saint Thomas had argued against such a flat-footed, un-nuanced understanding of presence in his treatment of transubstantiation.[17] The result for Scotus, at least according to Pickstock,[18] is that Christ's soul is only partially present in the eucharistic elements and "his Body is here effectively presented in the manner of a corpse. Here, therefore, in the very heart of piety, the cult of necrophilia is begun."[19] There is, after all, something breathtaking about such a sweeping claim!

I have tried in the above paragraphs to make an exceedingly long story short. I do not agree with reviewers who advise skipping over the first part of Pickstock's *After Writing* since the case she builds needs to be appreciated in order to understand what she is after in the more "liturgical" part of her work. The first part of the book is indeed very difficult—not only because of the complexity of the subject and of her logic, but also because she insists on being obscure and opaque (à la the postmodernists) when she could be much clearer.

In the end, I shall argue that Pickstock has a rather abstract notion of liturgy, but we need to postpone that suggestion until we consider what she has to say about Christian worship. For now it is important to understand that Pickstock is after rather large game in claiming that liturgy (or better, doxological language) is the true consummation of philosophy. All thought, all language has praise as its true goal. One is reminded of Alexander Schmemann's understanding of the human being as fundamentally *Homo Adorans*—the creature whose main goal is to adore,[20] or even the First Principle and Foundation of the *Spiritual Exercises* of Saint Ignatius of Loyola: "Human beings are created to praise, reverence and serve God our Lord, and by means of doing this, to save their souls."[21] Pickstock has a dynamic understanding of being that is rooted in her reading of Plato (and coincidentally very much at odds with the Heideggerian tradition represented by Louis-Marie Chauvet who understands Plato to have begun a tradition that favors Being over Becoming).[22] In any case Pickstock has provided a philosophical construct that will put liturgy at the center of life and thought. The second part of her book, titled "The Sacred Polis," is a good indication of the role

she expects liturgy to play in society. It is to that role of liturgy—
and specifically medieval liturgy—that I shall now turn.

Medieval Liturgy as Model

One of the aspects of her work that has made Pickstock well known
and which, in fact, has become a standard-bearer for conservatives,
is her criticism of the contemporary reform of the liturgy of the
Roman Catholic church. In addition to *After Writing* this critique
has appeared in a number of places.[23] For Pickstock the post–
Vatican II reform of the liturgy was fundamentally flawed in that it
did not adequately contextualize the liturgy in contemporary culture. As she puts it:

> [B]ecause the Vatican II reforms of the mediaeval Roman Rite
> failed to take into account the cultural assumptions which lay
> implicit within the text [of the pre–Vatican II Roman Rite],
> their "reforms" were themselves to a certain extent imbued with
> an entirely more sinister conservatism. . . . For they failed to
> challenge those structures of the modern secular world which are
> wholly inimical to liturgical purpose: those structures, indeed,
> which perpetuate a separation of everyday life from liturgical
> enactment.[24]

The main villains of the piece are the usual suspects: Theodor
Klauser and Josef Jungmann, the German and Austrian liturgical
historians upon whom the liturgical reformers relied so heavily.[25]
Summing up a several centuries of liturgical scholarship and nearly
a century of advocacy for liturgical reform, these scholars both
revealed how very accidental much of the development of the
liturgy actually was. These efforts have been matched for the
Christian East by scholars like Juan Mateos and Robert Taft.[26] On
the basis of the research of these great historians, the Constitution
on the Liturgy of Vatican II made the following well-known

prescription with regard to the reform of the liturgy: "The rites should be marked by a noble simplicity; they should be short, clear and unencumbered by useless repetitions; they should be within the people's powers of comprehension and as a rule not require much explanation."[27]

Much of the postconciliar reform of the eucharist and other liturgical rites took its inspiration from this call for simplification. This is precisely what Pickstock wants to call into question. It is in the very stops-and-starts, the hesitancies and impossible logic of the liturgy that she finds its deepest meaning. Moreover, she finds that the theological basis of the reform would have been more profound had it paid more attention to the thought of certain of its theologians. She writes:

> [T]he reform of the liturgy instigated by Vatican II was itself not adequate to its theology, for example, the work of De Lubac, Hans Urs von Balthasar, Yves Congar, and the influence of the restored Thomism of Etienne Gilson.[28]

Here are the main lines of Pickstock's appreciation of the Mass in the Middle Ages. (I shall save comments and questions until the end of the exposition.) Pickstock analyzes the opening rites of the Mass as a series of re-commencements and repetitions starting with the use of "impersonation" (assuming another's name) at the very outset: "In the name of the Father and of the Son and of the Holy Spirit." There is ambiguity here, for "in the name" could be understood both as "within" and "taking the name." This ambiguity is essential for Pickstock because it reveals the very impossibility of liturgy: the fact that it must be experienced both as gift and sacrifice, thereby overcoming the dead ends of modern philosophy.[29]

"I will go to the altar of God," the psalm (43) recited at the foot of the altar, is another example of this impossibility. Since the altar is by definition the place of alteration (her word, not my pun), it is always "receding," not within human grasp. Pickstock writes:

> The altar is therefore a supplementary, and, in worldly terms, destination which is also a beginning, the place towards which we must travel in order to be able to offer our sacrifice of praise. It follows that the liturgy of our text is always about to begin, not in a "hollowed out" sense, but as a necessarily deferred anticipation of the heavenly worship towards which we strive. Our liturgy in time can only be the liturgy we render in order to be able to render liturgy. . . . And one can only ever have begun; there is no other way to be than to be on the way.[30]

Thus Pickstock argues for the eschatological nature of the liturgy so strongly emphasized by a number of contemporary theologians.[31] In her reading of the medieval Roman Mass the approach to the altar forms yet another beginning, followed by the request for purification in the *Confiteor*, the incensation and the subsequent *Kyrie eleison* chant. From there we impersonate the angelic voices in the singing of the hymn *Gloria in excelsis Deo*. Still another request for purification comes with the priest's prayer, *Munda cor meum* (Cleanse my heart), in preparation for the Gospel.[32] Here Pickstock perceives a play on the word *munda*—both *cleanse* (the meaning of the verb) and *"worlded"* from the Latin noun for the world, *mundum*, as in "mundane." By the end of her treatment of what we now refer to as the liturgy of the word, Pickstock can write:

> The same dialectic of exaltation and subsidence or self-abasement occurs throughout the rite. . . . [T]he passage of the worshippers' advance is not construed as universally progressive, nor as under-taken by one worshipping voice alone, but as stuttering, constantly retracing its syllables, and calling for aid by means of many voices.[33]

By the same token Pickstock finds that contemporary liturgical criticism of the offertory prayers and repetition of offering in the Roman Canon is misdirected in that it fails to appreciate how we are constituted as liturgical subjects by the constant re-entering into God and in the dialectic of giving and receiving.

An important feature that she finds in the language of the liturgy is that of the "apostrophe": "a rhetorical figure used to signify vocative address to an absent, dead or wholly other person, idea or object."[34] For Pickstock such apostrophizing language dispossesses the subject so that the worshiper receives him- or herself from God, and the nominalization characteristic of the modern mania for mapping and categorizing is thereby countered. Her example is the address made to the incense in the initial incensation of the altar: *"Ab illo benedicaris in cujus honorem cremaberis* ("May you be blessed by him in whose honor you will be burned"). Of course the incense only becomes its true self when it goes up in smoke. Moreover, the absence of the one to whom prayers are addressed requires that the Mass be "rehearsed" again and again "in the hope that there might be worship."[35]

One final comment on Pickstock's treatment of the medieval Mass: The fact that a multiplicity of genres is employed in the Mass is crucial to her argument that the liturgy is not a simple linear progression. Rather, the Roman rite is "polyphonal"; it uses "narrative, dialogue, antiphon, monologue, apostrophe, doxology, oration, invocation, citation, supplementation and entreaty."[36] In other words, it always keeps us on our toes and prevents us from becoming self-satisfied.

An Analysis of Pickstock's View of the Liturgy

So what are we to make of this analysis of the medieval Mass whose aim is to demonstrate that the contemporary Roman rite (and its cousins in the Anglican communion, for example) is inadequate to the task of providing a form of worship that can stand up to secular society? In the first place we need to note that the phrase "medieval liturgy," while handy, is not terribly useful. One can begin treatment of the medieval Roman rite in fifth-century Rome and follow it through an immense number of permutations and variations both temporally and geographically up until the end of the sixteenth century—perhaps even to the last third of the twentieth. For example, as Bryan Spinks points out, the Sarum rite did not begin the Mass with the Prayers at the Foot of the Altar, which Pickstock cites as so significant.[37] A cursory glance at a synoptic chart of offertory prayers in the various medieval usages shows a good deal of variety, which even Pickstock notes.[38]

Second, Pickstock makes a plea for understanding the medieval liturgy in its context, but this apparently does not include taking a hard look at the development of the text itself nor its surroundings— for example, the church building in which it is performed.

Third, Pickstock fails to note that although the eucharist is clearly the high point of medieval worship, it is also part of an enormously complex system of services including the Divine Office, processions and other sacramental rites.

In the fourth place, many of Pickstock's textual analyses are playful, in much the same way that some postmodern theorists play with language. A good example is the priest's prayer before the Gospel, *Munda cor meum,* cited above. In the context of the prayer there is only one meaning that can be sustained by the word: "cleanse." The idea that the use of the word implies a "request to be *worlded*" is utterly fanciful, even though claiming that the Gospel makes us more citizens of the world is a wonderful idea. One begins to realize that many of Pickstock's interpretations are a template imposed upon the rite, much like the medieval allegorical interpretations of Amalar of Metz (ninth century) or William Durandus (thirteenth century). They make for excellent material for meditation but do not really do justice to the rite.

Fifth, Pickstock is fond of taking the plural "we" of the Roman rite seriously. For example, she writes of the entrance rite: "But as soon as we arrive at this state of purity, sufficient to bless one another in this way (the dialogue 'The Lord be with you . . .') we must again repeat our request for purification."[39] This is fine until one asks just who exactly is this "we" she is speaking of. Corporate understanding of the text of the liturgy came to an end as soon as Latin was no longer the common language of the people. Many of the prayers of the Roman rite that Pickstock finds so meaningful entered the liturgy after the people no longer understood and, in any case, were recited *sotto voce*.

Sixth, Pickstock acknowledges the necessity of liturgical reform during a period when receiving holy communion had become infrequent, devotional practices individualistic, and the liturgy itself a kind of spectacle.[40] The latter two features did indeed arise rather late in the Middle Ages and flourished in the period of the Baroque right through to the early twentieth century. But the first, which one can argue is the most important, is a problem that began in the sixth century at the latest. All this is to say that Pickstock's "medieval Mass" is a construct that seems to have little to do with the actual performance of the rite.[41] Just as the Middle Ages were romanticized in the novels of Sir Walter Scott and the Gothic style of architecture "revived" in the early nineteenth century, so too in Pickstock's writing we have a view of medieval liturgy which is alluring but not quite the case in reality.[42]

Liturgy, Theology and Society

All this is not to say that Pickstock is completely off the point. On the contrary, much of what she has to say is brilliant, and there is no rule which says that the historical-critical interpretation of the liturgy is the only one allowed. Just like the scriptures, the liturgy is open to the fourfold historical, spiritual (allegorical), moral (tropological) and eschatological (anagogical) analysis. This does not mean, however, that each of these forms of analysis provides an adequate basis for reforming the liturgy.

But Pickstock is also clearly on the right track in suggesting that a certain linear rationality has informed the contemporary liturgy of the Roman rite eucharist. The model for reconstructing the eucharistic liturgy was pretty clearly the seventh-century Roman Mass described in the *Ordo Romanus Primus*. Yet only the bare structure of the rite was taken as a model, not the no-longer-relevant court etiquette that is so meticulously laid out in the earlier rite. Perhaps since she is not a liturgical scholar (nor does she claim to be), Pickstock can be forgiven for ignoring the wise observations of Anscar Chupungco and others that what we have in the books of the reformed Roman rite is the basic script for the liturgy, not the liturgy itself as it must be adapted in various cultures. At the same time, Pickstock's notion of the liturgical "stuttering and stammering" of the medieval rite is an important reminder that putting the liturgy into understandable language does not make God understandable. Liturgical language still needs to point to the transcendent.

In this vein Pickstock's notion of "asyndeton" is also useful. In an article contrasting the translation of the Nicene Creed in the 1980 *Alternative Service Book* (ASB) of the Church of England with the previous translation in the *Book of Common Prayer* of 1549, Pickstock attempts to show how contemporary translators have bought into the modern use of "asyndeton," the literary practice which tends to multiply and shorten sentences, and in particular to eliminate subordinate and relative clauses. Thus she writes: "It converts six sentences into thirteen, twenty coordinating conjunctions into nine, and five subordinating conjunctions into one."[43] Her point, although worked out in twenty pages of extremely dense prose, is relatively straightforward. The Nicene Creed is not a list of true doctrinal statements about God but rather a doxological hymn, which *enacts* or *performs* the Holy Trinity by its intricate conjunctions and references that leap over one another and entwine with one another. The modern translation smoothes these complications out, but at the cost of losing the performativity of the Creed itself. In doing so it also (unwittingly) surrenders to a capitalist notion of desire as "lack," rather than the Christian/Augustinian notion of desire as "excess."

I have long resisted the idea that the Nicene Creed employed at the Sunday eucharist is a "loyalty oath" or a series of doctrinal statements that ought to be recited instead of sung, if it is to be recited at all. To be sure, the Creed's native home is the baptismal liturgy and entered into the eucharist in the East as a reaction against its polemical use by the Monophysites, who claimed Nicea/Constantinople I as their own but refused to accept the doctrinal conclusions of the Council of Chalcedon. Be that as it may, the Sunday eucharist is fundamentally the weekly renewal of Christian initiation and the Creed is more doxological than it is informational. Pickstock is right on the money: The value of the Creed is in the enacting of the Trinity as relation, and the ICET translation does blur that enactment to some extent. Moreover, Pickstock's point that short sentences mimic the disorientation of modern society is an idea worth pondering, though I cannot go more deeply into it here.[44] As she puts it,

> *Since meaning resides in the connections between things, readers of asyndetic texts have much more work to do in supplying what is absent. The several elements of salvation history are related as isolated units, devoid of syntactic or lexical indication of their purpose, or connection with the text as a whole. . . . This would-be "accelerated" narrative is not one that is continuous, but one that starts and stops with every clause. It effects a reification of singular verbal units, a list of semelfactive actions, the arbitrary disjunctive components of a catalogue.*[45]

Pickstock goes on to analyze the asyndetic nature of the institution narrative of the eucharist, coming to the opposite conclusion, namely that it is useful in throwing the hearers off-balance in their inability to control the words of Christ.

This leads us to a second aspect of Pickstock's interpretation of medieval liturgy and the theology which accompanies it. Her interpretation of Saint Thomas Aquinas is extraordinarily insightful. She understands the difficulty that arises in a Counter-Reformation understanding of the eucharist that "fetishizes" the elements, that is, turns them into objects subject to the gaze of human beings. Contrary to such a position, and following Jean-Luc Marion and Henri de Lubac, Pickstock insists that Christ's body and blood are present in the passing of time as a gift as opposed to being objects under the gaze of human beings. Thus she argues that transubstantiation is a certain kind of presence.[46] To stay with de Lubac for a moment, Pickstock also recognizes that the gift of the sacramental body and blood of Christ are at the same time the gift of the church to itself—an Augustinian notion that actually begins to fade from the picture in High Scholasticism.[47] Once again to make an extremely ingenious and complex argument short, the key to Pickstock's interpretation is the idea of desire—desire for the body and blood of Christ, which are given and yet (eschatologically) reserved at the same time, so that there is no possibility (short of heaven) of a perfect eucharist, one that need not be repeated.[48] Technically, Pickstock finds the rationale behind her interpretation in a Neoplatonic participationist understanding of the role of the accidents of bread and wine. In other words, Saint Thomas cannot be tagged with the label "poor Aristotelian," since he uses his Augustinian categories to recognize that the accidents after the consecration are miraculous because they can nourish without being substantive. Thus, says Pickstock, "the operation of matter in a *normal* fashion has been rendered miraculous."[49] Since they manifest the pure (and absurd) gift of Christ himself these material elements become *more* of what they were before. In other words, transubstantiation represents the *telos* of all things. Pickstock puts it this way: "Rather, to exceed the contrast between substance and accident is to attain to createdness as pure transparency, as pure mediation of the divine."[50] She goes on to quote Saint Thomas to the effect that it is not so much that this food is incorporated into us as that we are incorporated into this food.[51] In the end for Pickstock, the eucharist becomes the ultimately trustworthy sign, one that confounds or "outwits" the conundrum of presence and absence and thereby transcends postmodernist skepticism. Finally, for her, the eucharist *is* desire.

Conclusion

Finally I would like, by way of coming full circle, to discuss Pickstock's understanding of the relation between liturgy, art and politics. After all, her project is not so much aimed at liturgical renewal or sacramental theology, as it is to argue the necessarily doxological element in society. In a recent essay entitled "Liturgy, Art and Politics,"[52] Pickstock attempts to show how liturgy holds the worlds of art and politics together. Pickstock understands liturgy to fuse "the most realistic with the most ideal."[53] For her, liturgy stands as the foundation of society because "it relativises the everyday without denying its value." It can critique society from within and at the same time refer it to a transcendent dimension. It enables the person to be him- or herself without ever resting complacently in that identity. It enables art and real life to be held together, which is something the modern world cannot do.[54] The person becomes self-realized only by entering into the liturgical role. This understanding has implications for the individual as well as communal dimension of human being. Finally, liturgy has direct consequences for economics since the liturgical act is meant to deal with surplus wealth in public festival. No doubt Pickstock has the traditional cultural phenomenon of "potlatch" in mind.[55] She also points to a modern pseudo-liturgy, which uses spectacle to induce order. One is reminded of Leni Riefenstahl's horrifying portrayal of the Nazi Nuremberg rallies of the 1930s in her film *Triumph of the Will*.

There are a number of other powerful insights in Pickstock's essay on liturgy, art and politics, but those cited here will suffice to show that Pickstock has valuable insights into the role that liturgy can play, not only in religious life as such, but with regard to society and culture in general. Her work will be of little use to those who want to know how to reform the liturgy. She offers no specific pre-scriptions, only critique. It is doubtful that we could simply return to a translated form of the medieval Roman rite, though I suppose Pickstock could be read as advocating such a return. In fact, Pickstock is rather more radical than that, for her critique goes to the very roots of capitalist economics, and the conservatives for whom she has become a hero might well want to rethink their position, just as they would have to do if they took the economic writings of Pope John Paul II seriously.

At the outset of this essay I referred to Catherine Pickstock's critique of the liturgy as intriguing. I hope that these few pages have inspired the reader not only to agree with the assessment, but also to read her work and judge it on its own merits. In some ways her thinking shows how important it is to do the hard scholarship of liturgical history without falling into vague and superficial gen-eralities. On the positive side, however, it shows just how signifi-cant liturgy truly can be in the hands of a brilliant mind.

◆————————————————————————————

1. Catherine Pickstock, *After Writing: On the Liturgical Consummation of Philosophy* (Oxford: Blackwell, 1998).

2. Nathan Mitchell, "The Amen Corner: Worship as Music," *Worship* 73:3 (1999): 249–59, esp. 254–59; idem., "The Amen Corner: That Really Long Prayer," *Worship* 74:5 (2000): 468–77.

3. *Radical Orthodoxy: A New Theology,* eds. John Milbank, Catherine Pickstock, Graham Ward (London: Routledge, 1999). See also John Milbank, *Theology and Social Theory: Beyond Secular Reason* (Oxford: Blackwell, 1991).

4. Ibid., 1.

5. See the perceptive analysis of Russell Reno, "The Radical Orthodoxy Project," *First Things* 100 (2000): 37–44.

6. Ibid., 40–1.

7. Ibid., 38.

8. See René Girard, *I See Satan Fall Like Lightning,* trans. J. G. Williams (New York: Orbis, 2001); Gil Bailie, *Violence Unveiled: Humanity at the Crossroads* (New York: Crossroad, 1995); James Alison, *The Joy of Being Wrong: Original Sin through Easter Eyes* (New York: Crossroad, 1998); Raymund Schwager, *Must There Be Scapegoats? Violence and Redemption in the Bible* (New York: Crossroad, 2000); Anthony Bartlett, *Cross Purposes: The Violent Grammar of Christian Atonement* (New York: Crossroad, 2001).

9. See my own attempt to address these issues especially via the eucharist, in "Lo, the Full Final Sacrifice: On the Seriousness of Christian Liturgy," in *Antiphon* 7 (2002).

10. *After Writing,* 49–61.

11. Ibid., 95.

12. Pickstock perceives a good example of this process in the contemporary English translation of the Creed: "Asyndeton: Syntax and Insanity. A Study in the Revision of the Nicene Creed," *Modern Theology* 10 (1994): 321–40.

13. *After Writing,* 104.

14. Ibid., 132.

15. Ibid., 127.

16. Ibid., 129.

17. Thomas Aquinas, *Summa Theologiae,* trans. Fathers of the English Dominican Province (New York: Benziger, 1914), IIIa, 76, a 5.

18. I must disclaim direct knowledge of Scotus. See the critical remarks of Pickstock's reading of Scotus in Bryan Spinks, "Review of *After Writing,*" *Scottish Journal of Theology* 51 (1998): 510. Also the review by Regis Duffy, in *Theological Studies* 60 (1999): 175.

19. *After Writing,* 134.

20. *For the Life of the World: Sacraments and Orthodoxy* (Crestwood, N. Y.: St. Vladimir's Seminary Press, 1973), 15.

21. George E. Ganss, *The Spiritual Exercises of Saint Ignatius: A Translation and Commentary* (St. Louis: The Institute of Jesuit Sources, 1992), 32.

22. See Louis-Marie Chauvet, *Symbol and Sacrament: A Sacramental Rereading of Christian Existence* (Collegeville: Liturgical Press, 1995), 26–33.

23. Catherine Pickstock, "A Sermon for St. Cecilia," *Theology* 100 (1997): 411–8; idem., "Medieval Liturgy and Modern Reform," *Antiphon* 6 (2001): 19–25; idem., "A Short Essay on the Reform of the Liturgy," *New Blackfriars* 78 (1997): 411–8.

24. Pickstock, "A Short Essay," 56.

25. Theodor Klauser, *A Short History of the Western Liturgy,* trans. John Halliburton, 2nd ed. (New York: Oxford University Press, 1979); Josef Jungmann, *Missarum Sollemnia: The Mass of the Roman Rite,* 2 vols., trans. Francis Brunner (New York: Benziger Bros., 1950).

26. Juan Mateos, *La célébration de la parole dans la liturgie byzantine* (Rome: Pontifical Oriental Institute Press, 1971); Robert Taft, *A History of the Liturgy of St. John Chrysostom,* 6 vols., (Rome: Pontifical Oriental Institute Press, 1975). See especially Taft's apologia for the method of comparative liturgy in "Anton Baumstark's Comparative Liturgy Revisited," in *Comparative Liturgy Fifty Years after Anton Baumstark (1872–1948),* eds. Robert F. Taft and Gabriele Winkler (Rome: Pontifical Oriental Institute Press, 2001), 191–232.

27. *Constitution on the Sacred Liturgy,* 34, in *Vatican II: The Conciliar and Post-Conciliar Documents,* ed. Austin Flannery (Collegeville: The Liturgical Press, 1982), 12.

28. Pickstock, "Short Essay," 63.

29. *After Writing,* 169–70; see also 208.

30. Ibid., 183, 185. Thus Pickstock proves herself a worthy sparring partner for the likes of Derrida and Foucault.

31. E.g., Geoffrey Wainwright, *Eucharist and Eschatology* (New York: Oxford University Press, 1981); Joseph Ratzinger, *The Spirit of the Liturgy* (San Francisco: Ignatius Press, 2000).

32. *After Writing,* 189.

33. Ibid., 189–90.

34. Ibid., 193.

35. Ibid., 200; see also the interpretation of *Haec quoitiescumque feceritis* ("As often as you do this") from the words of institution as an example of the repetition inherent in the liturgy, 223.

36. Ibid., 213.

37. Spinks, "Review of *After Writing,*" 510.

38. See Craig Wright, *Music and Ceremony at Notre Dame of Paris 500–1500* (Cambridge: Cambridge University Press, 1989), 118. See also *After Writing,* 179.

39. Pickstock, "Medieval Liturgy and Modern Reform," 22.

40. Ibid., 21.

41. For further critique by liturgical historians, see the excellent reviews by Kenneth Stevenson, *Journal of Theological Studies,* New Series 50 (1999): 452–4; and Bryan Spinks, cited above in note 18.

42. Reno may be correct in seeing the root of this romanticism in the writer's Anglo-Catholicism. He writes: "But monuments are not living institutions, and Gothic buildings are no substitute for enduring practices. Radical Orthodoxy cannot invent the flesh and blood of a Christian culture, and so must be satisfied with describing its theoretical gestalt, gesturing in postmodern fashion, toward that which was and might be." "The Radical Orthodoxy Project," 41.

43. Pickstock, "Asyndeton," 325. The ASB translation is in fact the ecumenical translation of the International Consultation on Common Texts (ICET) and is used as well in most contemporary English versions of the liturgy, including the Roman Catholic. With very few alterations the same version appears in the text of the Roman Catholic eucharist employed in the United States. Pickstock's analysis corresponds to the connections and clauses not only in the 1549 *Book of Common Prayer* but also in the Greek and Latin versions of the Creed. See Heinrich Denziger, *Enchiridion Symbolorum: The Sources of Catholic Dogma* (St. Louis: Herder, 1957), #54, 86.

44. I am not as sure that I would agree with her argument about the replacement of the traditional Latin form of the Creed: "I believe" *(Credo)* with "We believe." The latter reflects the Greek of the Creed handed down from Nicea and Constantinople I. See Pickstock, "Asyndeton," 333.

45. Ibid., 331–2.

46. Catherine Pickstock, "Thomas Aquinas and the Quest for the Eucharist," *Modern Theology* 15 (1999): 164. This essay parallels her treatment of transubstantiation in the last chapter of *After Writing,* 253–66.

47. Ibid., 178; see also 171.

48. As was the case with her analysis of the Mass, Pickstock follows Saint Thomas here in his rather eisegetical treatment of the unfolding of the rite. See *After Writing,* 169–71. See also Thomas, *Summa Theologiae* III:79,81,83.

49. "Thomas Aquinas and the Quest," 174. For the purposes of the present essay we can leave aside the question of the relation between the institution narrative and consecration. The recent decision by the Vatican allowing for the validity of the ancient Eucharistic Prayer of Addai and Mari *(Anaphora of the Apostles)* of the Assyrian Church of the East raises the question of whether one can point to a moment of consecration in the way that Thomas and the whole Western tradition after the twelfth century presumed. The Eucharistic Prayer of Addai and Mari contains no institution narrative. In any case liturgical

scholars and sacramental theologians have been questioning the notion of a "moment of consecration" for some time.

50. Ibid., 175.

51. Citing *Summa Theologiae* III:73.a.3. ad 2.

52. Catherine Pickstock, "Liturgy, Art and Politics," *Modern Theology* 16:2 (2000): 160.

53. Ibid., 160.

54. Ibid., 162. This is reminiscent of the categories "dramatic" and "political" that R. T. Scott pointed out in "The Likelihood of Liturgy," *Anglican Theological Review* LXII:2 (1980): 103–20. See Louis-Marie Chauvet, *Symbol and Sacrament,* 171–80 for an analysis of the tripod of Christian existence (sacrament-doctrine-ethics).

55. Pickstock, "Liturgy, Art and Politics," 166. For a similar approach to the relation between ritual and economics at the root of culture and society, see Ernest Becker, *Escape from Evil* (New York: Free Press, 1974).

Christians ancient and modern have had a hunch . . .
that something *connects all creation, embracing its*
contradictions without being destroyed by them—
something as elemental and pervasive as music,
*some*one *who can breach the barriers between beasts*
and humans, cradle and Cross, the living and the
dead. That someone, so Christian faith and worship
acknowledge, is Jesus Christ, the "firstborn of all cre-
ation . . . the firstborn from the dead" (Colossians
1:15, 18) . . . Mozart understood—better, perhaps,
than most theologians do—that the whole harmony
of creation praises God, a harmony that includes
shadows—though the shadows are not darkness, the
flaws are not failures, sorrow is not despair, trouble is
not tragedy, and unending sadness is not the last
word about life.

Nathan Mitchell, "The Amen Corner: The Life of the
Dead," *Worship* 66 (November 1992): 537, 543.

Marriage and Mozart: Ritual Change in Eighteenth-Century Vienna[1]

Michael S. Driscoll

E amore un ladroncello,	*Love's like a little thief,*
Un serpentello e amor.	*Love's a vicious little viper,*
Ei toglie e da la pace,	*He brings us peace of mind,*
Come gli piace, ai cor.	*And takes it away when he likes.*
Per gli occhi al seno appena	*As soon as he's opened up a path*
Un varco aprir si fa,	*Through our eyes right to our hearts,*
Che l'anima incatena	*He wraps his chains around our souls*
E toglie liberta.	*And deprives us of our freedom.*
Porta dolcezza e gusto	*He'll bring you sweet contentment,*
Se tu lo lasci far;	*If you let him have his way,*
Ma t'empie di digusto,	*But he'll fill you with disgust,*
Se tenti di pugnar.	*If you try to fight him back.*[2]

In the late 1770s Wolfgang Amadeus Mozart (1756–1791) began to contemplate marriage with the opera singer Aloysia Weber. In a letter to his father of 7 February 1778 he reflected about marriage in the polite society of Catholic Austria, where many people contracted marriage as a money match. Mozart wrote:

I should not like to marry in this way; I want to make my wife happy, but not to become rich by her measure. So I shall let things be and enjoy my golden freedom until I am so well off that I can support a wife and children. . . . People of noble birth must never marry from inclination or love, but only from interest and all kinds of secondary considerations. . . . But we poor humble people can not only choose a wife whom we love and who loves us, but we may, can and do take such a one, because we are neither noble, nor highly born, nor aristocratic, nor rich, but, on the contrary, lowly born, humble and poor; so we do not need a wealthy wife, for our riches, being in our brains, die with us.[3]

Although this letter does not tell us directly anything about the Catholic sacrament of marriage, it is clear that the understanding of marriage differed according to social class. In Mozart's mind, marriage and love went hand in hand.

The topic to be addressed is the Catholic sacrament of marriage in Vienna at the end of the eighteenth century. It is particularly interesting to note how the sacramental practice varied from one social milieu to another in order to determine what role the Catholic church played in this imperial city. Mozart gives some indications of this socio-religious context in *The Marriage of Figaro* and *Così Fan Tutte,* two operas concerned with romance and marriage.

Concerning Mozart's own marriage with Constanze Weber, Aloysia's sister, we have a few details that help fill out our understanding regarding matrimonial procedures. Toward the end of July 1782 it became necessary for Mozart and Constanze to obtain from the appropriate authorities several official documents in connection with their marriage. First, Mozart applied to the Vienna police administration for a waiver of the requirement that he produce his baptismal certificate, which, apparently, he had neglected to bring to Vienna from Salzburg. Also on 29 July, Constanze Weber's guardian, Johann Thorwart, successfully petitioned the senior marshal's office to grant permission for her to marry Mozart. Then on 1 August, Mozart applied to the Prince-Archbishop's Court *(Fürsterzbischöfliche Konsistorium)* of Lower Austria to allow his marriage to take place at Vienna's Cathedral of St. Stephen even though his residence in Vienna was not officially within the jurisdiction of the cathedral parish. These documents give us an insight about ecclesiastical law and practice concerning the normal procedure for marriage in Mozart's day. It is interesting to note the cooperation between civil and ecclesiastical officials for the religious ceremony. The fact that the archbishop was also a prince played a significant role in this collaboration. Concerning marriage, civil law and ecclesiastical law were one.

Marriage after Trent

To better understand Roman Catholic marriage in eighteenth-century Vienna, first we need to contextualize the sacrament in the universal church. The Council of Trent in the late sixteenth century in its penultimate session pronounced on the subject of marriage as a sacrament in response to the Protestant reformers who denied the sacramentality of marriage, claiming that it was a mere ordinance. Trent seems to have had two goals where marriage was concerned: to ensure its public celebration out of respect for the social character of marriage and to secure its reverent celebration out of respect for its sacramental character. The result was a series of prescriptions concerning the publication of banns, marriage before the church in the presence of the parish priest, the ascertaining of the couple's consent to the marriage, and the exchange of vows in the presence of a priest. In addition, the priest was to seal the marriage with a formula such as "I join you together in matrimony . . . " (from Rouen, fourteenth/fifteenth century) or some local equivalent. Records of all marriages were to be kept in parish churches. Moreover, the couple was exhorted not to live together before marriage, but to confess their sins and to receive the eucharist three days before the wedding or at least three days before they consummated their marriage.[4] However, the Council of Trent, in a note reproduced in the Roman ritual itself, stated that "if any provinces have herein any praiseworthy customs and ceremonies besides the aforesaid, the holy Synod earnestly desires that they be by all means retained." Given this option, and given the extreme sparseness of the service provided in the ritual, what we have here is less a nuptial liturgy than a formula for ensuring that all the conditions for a clearly valid marriage are met, and one must doubt that it was ever intended to be used as it stood. Indeed, the use of the ritual itself, unlike the other liturgical books, was not originally mandatory, but was merely to serve as a model for the reform of local rites. Where it was eventually adopted in place of customary forms of marriage, there was considerable impoverishment, but the *Rituale Romanum* did not begin to supplant local rituals on any scale until the second half of the nineteenth century. Even then many local communities, such as Roman Catholics in Austria, continued to follow their own traditional rites of marriage into which the Roman requirements were simply incorporated.

Marriage in the Austrian Empire

Until the late eighteenth century, jurisdiction over marriage in Austria rested with the church. A regulation of 20 September 1753 responded to the question of the purely civil effect of marriage. Still these cases were submitted to the religious courts for adjudication. Essentially through the reign of the Austrian Empress Maria Theresa (1740–1780) the church had jurisdiction over marriage. Her son and successor, Joseph II (1765–1790), continued his mother's policies as co-regent of Austria, but when he became emperor in 1780 he introduced radical reforms, especially in the domain of ecclesiastical jurisdiction. This lead to the dissolution of "inactive" orders

(1,300 monasteries), the establishment of public education controlled by the government, control over the salaries of priests, the organization of welfare institutions (hospitals and orphanages, institutions for the mentally ill and the blind), and the introduction of civil marriage. Marriage was thus transferred to the control of the state, according to paragraph 1 of the marriage law of 16 January 1783. If a legal difference arose between religious and civil marriage, the state would intervene to resolve the dispute through the national courts of justice. Fundamentally the precondition of a valid marriage contract was regarded as a prerequisite for the sacrament, whereby Joseph II deviated from the national regulation of marriage insisting more upon the civil status of marriage than the sacramental status, although the liturgical rite remained the same. Additionally the Josephist legal reform on marriage recognized the possibility of divorce in certain cases. The marriage law of Joseph II was transferred to the published civil law book on 1 November 1786 and was received with only slight deviations into the general civil law book in 1811.

What Joseph II intended in his legislation of 1780–90 seemed to be a reduction of the church in his empire to the functional status of a department of government. But he was not the one who innovated the effort. Already Gallicanism had raised the question of non-church control over marriage, and this attitude spread well beyond the borders of France. By the middle of the eighteenth century Wenzel von Kaunits-Reitberg, chancellor to Empress Maria Theresa, was thoroughly imbued with it. He began the process of lessening the influence of the church by removing priests and religious from teaching posts in the empire, including the removal of the Jesuits from the faculties of philosophy and theology at the University of Vienna.

To understand better the Josephist reform, one needs to look to the events of the 1760s, which paved the way for it. In 1763 Johann Niklaus von Hontheim, under the pseudonym Justinius

Febronius, published *On the Position of the Church and the Legitimate Authority of the Roman Pontiff.*[5] It was a charter for the domestication of the church in the empire. Hontheim's professed intent was to suggest a way of uniting dissident Christians to the Catholic church. One of his strategies for this was to subdue the universal primacy of the papal authority by recovering for Christian princes the authority over religion in their realms that he deemed had rightly been theirs before the medieval popes usurped its exercise. Indeed his Febronianism, as it came to be known, was a species of conciliarism, since his indictment of papal usurpation included the charge that it had taken over from the other Catholic bishops authority belonging to them individually and in regional council.

Hontheim's book and its ideas gained popularity in the already sympathetic schools and clergy of the Empire. Since Rome condemned Hontheim, his ideas could not be made into a manual of teaching. But its principles were reproduced in slightly mitigated form in 1772 by J. P. von Riegger's *Instruction in Ecclesiastical Jurisprudence.*[6] This became the textbook of the universities and was imposed on all monastic and episcopal schools. When Joseph II succeeded Maria Theresa at her death in 1780, he implemented his reform. His decrees asserting civil control over marriage in the Empire were clearly inspired by the Febronian theory and were a concrete application of it. On 4 September 1781 he promulgated a law forbidding his subjects to seek marital dispensations from either the papal nuncio in the Empire or from Rome itself. Application for them was to be made to the bishop of one's diocese. Lest one think that the latter could offer dispensations by virtue of their own authority as bishops, a different source of this authority was made clear to them in a letter of 28 March 1782 written by Joseph's minister, Philipp Cobenzl:

> *Marriage being a matter which is first and foremost civil, and in which the religious element is only accessory, the impediments to*

*it are similar in character. Hence it is primarily for the civil
tribunals to judge the necessity or utility of a dispensation. This
being admitted, your Majesty held that the diocesan bishop and
his Consistory are now as formerly more than competent to
decide the cause in accordance with the sacred canons of the
Roman Church.*[7]

While asserting the right of the state to adjudicate marriage
cases, he maintained the *status quo* of the ecclesiastical courts. A year
later, in 1783, Joseph took his campaign a further and more drastic
step. He issued a constitution withdrawing marriage cases from the
church courts altogether. He claimed exclusive jurisdiction over
them. He assumed that marriage is a civil contract, and therefore it
belongs to the state to decide the condition of its validity.

An even clearer indication of how far Joseph's plan for secu-
larization reached came when Archbishop Migazzi of Vienna
explained to his clergy in a pastoral letter that the new constitution
touched only the civil aspects of their Catholic people's marriages,
and that the church's canon law remained otherwise in force.
Joseph's reaction to this was to claim that the prescriptions of this
constitution regarding marriage abrogated those of canon law, and
that in the future his Catholic subjects were to be ruled in marriage matters by the state alone.

Compliance with the Febronian removal of marriage into the
civil domain was almost universal among the people and clergy of
the Empire. Few seemed to suspect in what direction and how far
the removal was to lead. Like the Protestant Reformers three centuries earlier, comfortable in their vision of themselves as permanently Christian, the Austrians were comfortable in their vision of
themselves as permanently Catholic. Their real concern was to loosen
the tether of papal control over their lives generally. The regulation
of marriage was merely the most opportune point at which to
begin the loosening. A political-religious arrangement dating back

to the early Middle Ages enhanced the desire for religious independence and simultaneously tranquilized any anxiety about a secular takeover. A number of major bishoprics were held by prince-bishops. Among these were Cologne, Trier, Mainz and Salzburg. Their bishops were civil as well as ecclesiastical rulers of their dioceses. It was difficult for them to oppose the Emperor's will to exclusive jurisdiction over marriages in the Empire because they knew they were to be the semi-independent instruments of this will and could therefore guarantee the Catholic character of marriage regulation. They were sure that the anti-religious extreme to which civil regulation went in France during the revolutionary terror would never be reached in their territories.

The Febronians were accurate in this self-assurance. But their independence from Rome led to a different destiny than the one they anticipated. They did establish marital impediments at their own discretion and dispensed from them in their dioceses. In 1788 they even asked Pope Pius VI to remove his nuncios from the dioceses in the interest of religious peace. They enjoyed their free exercise of jurisdiction, always against papal objection, for about two decades. But the Napoleonic wars and their aftermath tore up and redrew the political map of Europe. The ecclesiastical principalities of the Empire were abolished. At the Congress of Vienna, Cologne, Trier and Mainz were parceled out in pieces among Prussia, Nassau and Hesse. Salzburg was taken into the Austrian Empire. Thereafter marriages in these places were regulated by secular princes far less Christian than the prince-bishops.

The papal reaction to these Gallican and Josephist campaigns to take Catholic marriage away from ecclesiastical authority was swift and decisive. Pope Pius VI (1775–1799) resisted energetically the incursion on papal authority. In his brief *Super solidate petre* of 28 November 1786 he solemnly condemned the book *Was ist der Papst?* of the Viennese canonist Josef Eybel (1782), which embodied the principles of Febronianism as these had been laid out in

Hontheim's *On the Position of the Church and the Legitimate Authority of the Roman Pontiff.* Two years later, on 16 September 1788, Pius aimed his counter-fire more exactly. In his letter *Deesemus nobis*[8] to the bishop of Motola, near Naples, he laid down the correct interpretation of Canon 12 of Trent's decree on marriage: "If anyone says that marriage cases do not come under the competence of ecclesiastical judges, let him be anathema."[9]

Before surveying the ritual books dealing with marriage and the ritual itself, it will help to note the theological and legal premises concerning Catholic marriage. The most common premise is that in the marriages of Christians the contract is the marriage in substance; that the sacrament is so distinct from it as to be separable; that the contract is a civil entity and therefore comes by nature under civil jurisdiction. The sacrament, which is the priestly blessing, is administered by the authority of the church. That the civil authority would be in the hands of Catholic princes was assumed as part of the design.

The Ritual Books for Marriage

Concerning the administration of sacraments in the church at Vienna we are fortunate to have five printed liturgical books from the eighteenth century. Two ritual books, both dating from 1774, would certainly have been in use in Mozart's day in Vienna. Both books were the work of the printer Johannes Leopold von Ghelen of Vienna. The first is the large Viennese Ritual (424 pages), accommodated to the Roman use and containing the sacramental rites to be performed in parishes in the archdiocese of Vienna. Four copies of this book survive in Austrian and German public and seminary libraries.[10] Judging by its size and weight this was the stationary altar book.

The second book, although much smaller in size (84 pages), is of greater value to this study since it contains specifically the rite of marriage along with the order of baptism and the last rites. It also was published for use in the archdiocese of Vienna, but only two copies have survived: One is conserved in the diocesan library at Pölten and the other in the Major Seminary of Vienna (I 8417). This ritual book seems to be a reworking of an older Viennese ritual from 1670, of which only one copy has survived and is conserved at the archbishop's library in Vienna (ms. 2564). It is a diocesan ritual accommodated to and melded with the *Rituale Romanum* of 1752.

A third ritual, which is not from Vienna but rather from St. Pölten, is of special interest since it is from 1787 and reflects the legislative reforms introduced by Emperor Joseph II. Despite the ecclesiastical prohibition of the vernacular language in the administration of the sacraments, Joseph granted greater latitude to the German language. Although there is a more intensive use of the German language, the short form for the rite of marriage ceremony does not deviate from the contents as found in the earlier diocesan rituals. The only Latin is found in some of the directions (rubrics), but only occasionally.

Certainly other diocesan rituals exist for Austrian and German dioceses. A recent book by Klaus Keller provides a lengthy and detailed study of the rite of marriage in the Enlightenment period, including the time of Mozart.[11] In the interest of brevity and precision, however, this study will limit itself to these aforementioned liturgical books which existed in Vienna during the life of Mozart.

The Rite of Marriage

Here in schematic form is the rite of marriage as it appeared in the *Roman Ritual* of 1752:

> Introduction *(praenotanda)*
> Questions regarding consent
> *Confirmatio:* Exchange of vows
> Acknowledgment by the priest

Blessing and presentation of ring
Versicle
Our Father
Concluding prayer followed by remarks

The *praenotanda,* usually written in Latin, prescribes that banns of marriage are to be published three times to ensure the public nature of the event. It also states that the priest should vest in a surplice and white stole and that he should be accompanied by a server, also vested in a surplice, who carries the book and the vessel of holy water and its *aspergilium* with which to sprinkle. Then in the presence of two or three witnesses, in the church, the priest asks the man and woman separately, preferably in the presence of their parents or relatives, the question about the consent to the marriage, using the vernacular tongue.

The rite begins with the sign of the cross, either in Latin or German; then the priest asks each member of the bridal party, "N., will you take N. here present to be your lawful wife (husband), according to the rite of holy mother church?"

This questioning is intended to be public. In the rubrical note we read, "The consent of one does not suffice, it must be of both. And it must be expressed in some sensible sign, either by the parties themselves or through an intermediary." Clearly the intention is to avoid clandestine or arranged marriages, since the marriage is to be public and the consent of both is required for the validity of the sacrament.

Once the mutual consent has been received the priest invites the couple to join right hands, saying, "I join you in matrimony, in the name of the Father + and of the Son and of the Holy Spirit."[12] This formula was first used in fifteenth-century Rouen and indicates the active role of the priest in the act of marriage. This was the formula still used in 1774, around the time of Mozart, printed in both Latin and German. Other words may be used according to the received rite of each province.

Afterwards the priest sprinkles the couple with holy water and then blesses the ring with holy water, sprinkling it in the form of a cross. From the prayer it is evident that the ring is to be worn by the bride:

> Bless + O Lord,
> this ring which we bless + in your name,
> so that she who shall wear it,
> remaining faithful to her husband,
> may remain in peace and in your will,
> and live always in mutual charity, through Christ, etc.

Following the blessing and the giving of the ring accompanied by a trinitarian invocation, the priest prays, "Confirm, O God, what you have wrought among us." This constitutes his declaration or confirmation of what has taken place, and according to Trent had juridical value.

The rite of marriage continues with a versicle, "From your holy temple, which is Jerusalem," into which is inserted the *kyrie eleison,* and the Our Father, which is prayed silently. The rite concludes with an oration prayed by the priest where he implores God to look down upon the couple and assist them in their ordinance for the propagation of the human race.

When all this is done, and if the marriage is to be blessed, the priest celebrates the Mass of the Bride and Groom, as found in the Roman Missal, observing everything that is prescribed there. The Nuptial Mass consists of the chants, prayers and readings for the eucharistic celebration. In the larger Viennese ritual book of 1774 there is a *"Missa pro sponso et sponsa."*[13] This fact suggests that the two books of 1774 were intended for tandem use. The large book was left stationary on the altar while the smaller 84-page book, which was more portable and less cumbersome, was used when the priest stands before the couple asking for their consent and blessing them and the rings.

When everything has been completed, the priest enters in the register, in his own hand, the names of the couple and of the witnesses and the other things required, and that he or some other priest delegated either by him or by the ordinary has celebrated the marriage.

Of all the post-Tridentine liturgical books, the *Rituale Romanum* was the only one to be "commended" rather than "imposed." Some countries took liberties with this instruction, abbreviating or expanding it according to local custom. In the case of the church at Vienna and elsewhere in the Austrian Empire it is interesting to note the title of the rite. Prior to the reign of Emperor Joseph II, the liturgical books identify the rite as the *Ordo administrandi sacramentum matrimonii in ecclesia* (order for the administration of the sacrament of matrimony in church). After the Josephist reform, the rite does not change significantly except that it appears largely in German rather than Latin. The title of the rite, however, indicates a shift in understanding. In the Latin it reads *Ordo benedicendi matrimonium,* or something similar, and in the German *Einsegnung der Ehe,* or its equivalent. Clearly the priest after the Josephist reform sees his function as simply *blessing* the marriage, since it is the state which assures the civil dimension. There is a shift away from the understanding of marriage as a contract administered by the church to a more sacramental understanding. Although the church's administration of the civil dimension of marriage is called into question, the sacramental aspect is maintained and thus marriage is still performed in the context of the eucharistic liturgy.

Two images that date from the lifetime of Mozart and which served as souvenirs of imperial weddings illustrate graphically the changes in the rite of marriage and the customs surrounding imperial weddings. The first image (figure 1, next page),[14] a large commemorative painting, depicts the wedding of Isabella of Parma and

figure 1

Archduke Joseph in Augustinerkirche. On 6 October 1760, the nineteen-year-old crown prince, who later became Joseph II, wed Princess Isabella of Bourbon-Parma in the Hofkirche (Augustinerkirche). The Hofkirche was a long Gothic hall church begun in 1327. During the sixteenth century it was declared a court church and given over to the charge of the Augustinians. Celebrations of holy days when processions were demanded and liturgical ceremonies when large numbers of people were to be accommodated, such as weddings of the heir to the throne and state

figure 2

funerals for members of the imperial family, were generally held in this building.

The commemorative painting may have been the group effort of the workshop of Martin van Meytens, the imperial court painter, and it was destined to be hung at the Schönbrunn Palace. In the depicted scene Maria Theresa and Francis occupy the canopied imperial oratory, with their numerous progeny assembled to their right. Before the high altar three bishops unite husband and wife. The central role of the bishops is clear—they conduct the service and receive the consent of the couple. The imperial parents (indicated by the arrow) do attend the ceremony, but more as spectators. The altar is sparsely adorned, with the only image being a Christ on the cross. The image illustrates graphically the role played by the bishops as the designated officials who preside over the event, including the exchange of consent and rings.

The second illustration (figure 2, previous page)[15] is an anonymous print also depicting a wedding within the imperial family that took place almost 28 years after the imperial wedding. This ceremony took place in the Hofkapelle in 1788 with Emperor Joseph II (arrow) witnessing the marriage of his nephew Francis with Elizabeth of Württemberg in 1788, before the assembled court and clergy. This particular church had undergone a major renovation, converting it from a pure Gothic style to a more classical style in conformity with changing tastes. Gone are the frilly Gothic traceries around the arches, gone are the Baroque altars, to be replaced by a single main altar with no sculpted saints, only the four-fold crucified Christ (including the cross of Lorraine on the Gospel side). One of the curious features of the rebuilt chapel is the proliferation of boxes above the ground floor, just as in the theater. The curvilinear shape of three of the boxes corresponds in fact to the boxes in the Burgtheater at this time. Mirrors were hung behind the candelabrae, which must have heightened the dramatic effect. More light was able to enter through the windows as well because of the way they were redesigned.

This image is valuable from a liturgical perspective because it illustrates the newfound role of the emperor within the rite of marriage. The bishops are clearly in the scene but more like supernumeraries on the stage of an opera. The principal protagonist is the emperor himself, who accepts the vows of the bridal party. He could have arranged for the marriage to take place in a larger church, such as the Hofkirche (Augustinerkirche) where he was married in 1760 and where his parents were married in 1736, but he must have desired a simpler affair.

Liturgical Integration and Fusion

The churches of the Reformation denied marriage its sacramental status but, with few exceptions, framed new rites based on the view that marriage is an ordinance to be celebrated publicly in a liturgy centering on the consent of the couple to live a Christian marriage, together with the reading and exposition of the word of God and solemn prayer.

Meanwhile, medieval Catholicism continued for a time with its considerable liturgical variety. For example, in France there was an Anglo-Norman synthesis with its rite of consent at the church door. This rite eventually reached Rome through the Norman invasion of southern Italy. Thus, the thirteenth-century Pontifical of Sora has this new addition to the marriage liturgy. The French rites continued to develop, dividing into various groups, some of which had the consent at the church door, while others held it inside. The most interesting rite, however, is that of Metz (1543), which incorporates the marriage within the nuptial Mass, so that consent and the priestly joining formula occur at the offertory, and the ring giving and short marriage prayers follow the post-communion. This has the advantage of bringing the Mass and the marriage into closer union. Also the consent is separated from the ring giving, which makes for considerable clarity. The Metz tradition provides inspiration for modern revisions for this reason and is therefore worth noting now.

When the Council of Trent discussed the marriage liturgy in its penultimate session in November 1563, however, it decided to make the consent of the partners essential. It also required a priestly formula to be recited immediately after the consent. It was clear that marriage is a sacrament and that the consent of the partners effected the sacrament. The Tridentine decree on marriage, *Tamestsi*, is in some respects the liturgical exception, for it overtly encourages local marriage customs to be observed:

If certain locales traditionally use other praiseworthy customs and ceremonies when celebrating the sacrament of matrimony, this sacred synod earnestly desires that these by all means be retained.[16]

The Fathers of the Council of Trent clearly saw no need to impose a rigid uniformity on the Catholic church regarding this sacrament, and subsequent service books demonstrate that the older customs did, in fact, continue, with the noticeable difference that a priestly formula was usually introduced where it had been absent.

If the marriage rite is to vary from one country to another, then it must clearly belong to a special kind of liturgical book—the ritual locally accepted. On the other hand, the nuptial Mass is part of the missal and it had to be standard.

Particular Customs

The rite of marriage in its skeletal form is extremely spare. It begs for accessories! It is little wonder that it is prone to adaptation to local custom. Since Trent was not opposed to the introduction of local customs, it is plausible to envisage marriages celebrated in different ways in the various locales where it took place. The various classes in society also would celebrate marriages in their own particular ways, just as we witness today. But customs change according to fashion and mode, and often they are not recorded in any definitive way. Thus the particular aspect of liturgical inculturation of the rite of marriage is somewhat difficult to ascertain.

One of the local customs unknown to the Roman ritual but seemingly practiced widely in German-speaking lands was the blessing and giving of the wedding feast wine. The Viennese Ritual of 1774 incorporates this custom following the prologue of John's gospel. The prologue marks the beginning of the gospel and lends itself to the beginning of the wedded life. The reference of the wine gesture is to the wedding feast of Cana, also from John's gospel.

Another ritual element which falls under the category of local custom is the blessing of the bridal chamber or the *benedictio thalami*. The *Rituale Romanum* of 1614 provides a prayer for this occasion, which asks for God's blessing and joy for the place of slumber. The Viennese ritual incorporates this prayer based upon the Roman prayer, but with great liberty, asking for God's blessing on the nuptial bed and home.

The element of custom is more difficult to ascertain than the ritual elements because these do not always appear in the liturgical books and they tend to come in and out of vogue in different places and at different periods. But since the ritual in its stripped-down form almost demands elaboration, it is easy to see why and how these customary elements were added. By way of modern example, two regional customs whose origins are unknown are still practiced in Austria. It is conceivable that similar customs existed at the time of Mozart, but this has not yet been proven. The first is the sawing of a log by the bridal couple as a show of solidarity and unity. The two-handled saw can only be operated when there is cooperation. This custom would obviously appeal to country dwellers, but it is doubtful that it ever appeared in the high society circles of Vienna. A second custom that also indicates an Alpine origin is the honor guard with ice picks. One wonders if this custom is not a parody of a military honor guard, which would certainly have been a part of the military society of the empire.

Conclusion

Mozart raised a question in 1778, when he contemplated a union with Aloysia, concerning the manner in which marriage was celebrated at the different strata of society. Not wanting to marry like the upper class for money, he desired to marry for love. What is Mozart's attitude toward the wedded life? One place where the answer is resolved is in his operatic works, particularly *The Marriage of Figaro* and *Così Fan Tutti*.

Cherubino, at the close of Act I in *The Marriage of Figaro*, provides a clue about Mozart's take on marriage and love. These lines are not in Beaumarchais' text but were added by Da Ponte and Mozart:

Parlo d'amor vegliando,	*I talk about love when I'm awake,*
Parlo d'amor sognando . . .	*I talk about love in my dreams . . .*
E, se non ho chi m'oda,	*And if there's no one to hear me*
Parlo d'amor con me.	*I talk about love to myself.*

Bliss does not require marriage or even a partner, but love is the essential ingredient. In the end, however, wedded bliss is preferable to the solitary life. Possibly in his early love affairs and in his wedded life, Mozart caught a glimpse of felicity and would never forget it, let alone give up its "promesse de bonheur."[17]

---

1. This paper was originally prepared as a talk destined for a Symposium on Mozart and Marriage, which took place at the Kennedy Center, Washington, D.C., June 26, 1999.

2. *Così Fan Tutte*, Act II, scene X, n. 28 Aria (Dorabella singing to Despina and Fiordiligi about their situation), *The Metropolitan Opera Book of Mozart Operas,* Paul Gruber, executive ed., trans. Judyth Schaubhut Smith, David Stivender, and Susan Webb (New York: Harper Collins, 1991), 471.

3. Emily Anderson, *The Letters of Mozart and His Family,* 7 February 1778 (n. 285), 3rd ed. (New York: Macmillan Press Ltd., 1985), 467.

4. Trent, session 24, chapter 1, *Enchiridion Symbolarum: Detinitionum et Declarationum de Rebus Fidei et Morum,* Heinrich Denziger and Adolphe Schönmetzer, eds. (Herder: Barcinone, 1973), n. 1814, 418. See Martina Kronthaler-Schirmer, *Die Aussagen des Österreichischen Episkopats zu Ehe und Familie in der Ersten und Zweiten Republik unter besonderer Berücksichtigung der Hirtenbriefe* (Vienna: Ehe und Familie, 1996).

5. Johann Nicolaus von Hontheim (Justini Febronii Jcti), *De Statu Ecclesiae et Legitima Potestate Romani Pontificis. 1701–1790* (Bullioni: Apud Guillelmum Evrardi, 1765–74).

6. Paul Joseph Ritter von Riegger, *Institutiones iurisprudentiae Ecclesiasticae* [Pars I–Pars IV] (Vienna: Typis Joan. Thomae Nob. De Trattnern, 1774).

7. George Joyce, *Christian Marriage,* 2nd ed. (London: Sheed and Ward, 1948), 202, note 3.

8. Denziger and Schönmetzer, n. 2598, 517.

9. Ibid., n. 1812, 417.

10. Cf. Manfred Probst, *Bibliographie der katholischen Ritualisndruche des deustschen Sprachbereichs* LQF 74 (Münster: Aschendorff, 1993). The four locations where this ritual is conserved are as follows: Major Seminary of Vienna, Bayrische Staatsbibliothek, Maria Laach, and the Katholische-Theologische Seminarbibliotheken of the University Library of Bonn.

11. Klaus Keller, *Die Liturgie der Eheschliessung in der katolischen Aufklärung,* Münchener Theologische Studien 51 (St. Ottilien: Verlag Erzabtei, 1996). See Leopold Schmidt, *Hochzeitsbrauch im Wandel der Gegenwart* (Vienna: Verlag der Österreichischen Akademie der Wissenschaften, 1976).

12. *"Ego conjungo vos in matrimonium. In nomine Patris, et Filii, et Spiritus Sancti, Amen."*

13. Klaus Keller, *Der Liturgie der Eheschliessung in der katolischen Aufklärung.*

14. Used with permission of Kunsthistorisches Museum, Vienna, Austria. See Daniel Heartz, *Haydn, Mozart and the Viennese School 1740–1780* (New York: W. W. Norton and Co., 1995).

15. Heartz, 9.

16. *Concilium Tridentinum,* Sessio XXIV, Caput I (Mechlen: Van Elsen and Van der Elst, 1847), 238.

17. Maynard Solomon, *Mozart: A Life* (New York: Harper Collins, 1995), 176.

Our hands are not only beautiful, they are also superb technological tools with an eloquence all their own. Clenched, they form fists—defiant, dangerous weapons. Cupped, they cradle heads and comfort crying kids. Stretched out and held open, their fingers form the five radiant points of a star, rotating at the end of that magical wand we call an "arm." Quite literally, we hold knowledge, art, and soul in our hands. . . . Liturgy unfolds in the language of the hands.

Nathan Mitchell, "The Amen Corner: Toward a Poetics of Gesture," *Worship* 75:4 (2001): 359–360.

Re-Attaching Tongue to Body: The Aesthetics of Liturgical Performance

Edward Foley, CAPUCHIN

The most recent stage of liturgical reform has revealed an almost obsessive concern with officially published texts. Issues of translation have been a particularly neuralgic source of concern, as demonstrated by the high-profile debate over principles for translation of official texts. This debate has been fueled by a dramatic reversal of translation principles issued by the Vatican itself. In 1969 the Consilium for Implementing the Constitution on the Sacred Liturgy published a set of principles for translating liturgical texts that repeatedly recognized the difficulty of literal translation,[1] and noted the appropriateness of what has been deemed "dynamic equivalency" in the translation process.[2] Then in a dramatic about-face, the Congregation for Divine Worship and the Sacraments issued a very different set of translation principles in 2001, stressing the need for literal translation without paraphrase or marked by any such "equivalency."[3]

One of the more fascinating yet baffling aspects of these directives for texts and their translations has been the virtual absence of any parallel directives on how such official texts are to be performed by the various members of a worshiping community. Rather, this concern for proper praise seems narrowly focused on correctly defining and then all but cementing a liturgical text—preferably in perpetuity—in the belief that such a fixed text will ensure orthodox belief and produce orthodox believers. At its core, this is a narrowly defined concern about disembodied words on a page.

Such regard for textual disembodiment seems not only to overlook the performative nature of liturgical language, but the embodied mediation of all things liturgical, including speech. It is as though the liturgical tongue—especially the tongue of any selected to proclaim the church's official liturgical texts—has been metaphorically severed from the ecclesial body in the act of worship. The modest goal of this brief essay is to contribute in a small way to re-stitching the liturgical tongue to the ecclesial body. More specifically, my hope is to underscore the import of the embodied performativity of the liturgy by moving beyond texts and speech to a consideration of the aesthetics of liturgical performance. In so doing I hope to at least balance, if not partially mute, the textual myopia of the current era.

The inspiration for this essay—as for so many other ventures, pastoral and scholarly—is the work of teacher and friend Nathan Mitchell. His ruminations on metaphor, performativity, embodiment and particularly his reflections on "a poetics of gesture"[4] are the springboard for this enterprise. If there is any error or obscurity here, it belongs to this author and not to the source of my inspiration, whom I dearly wish to honor in these pages.

Embodying the Speaking Subject

One of the major developments of modern Western philosophical thought is the so-called "turn to the subject." This turn is announced in the writings of René Descartes (d. 1650) who—in counterdistinction to the epistemologies that dominated medieval philosophy prior to him—gives a first-person slant to the theory of knowing, summarized in his famous dictum "I think, therefore I am" *(Cogito ergo sum)*. This first-person approach to knowing, while critiqued and reshaped over the following centuries, came to dominate modern philosophy and continues to be a tenacious trend in postmodern philosophy.

What did not survive, however, was Descartes' dualism, with its separation of mind and matter. While Descartes rejected the reliability of the senses and experience, Immanual Kant (d. 1704) and others argued that knowledge begins in experience. Empiricists like John Locke (d. 1704) would go even further and hold that all knowledge arises out of experience. An extreme representative of this empirical approach was John Stuart Mill (d. 1873), who maintained that knowledge of all truths was actually derived from experience. While there are many important differences between the theories of knowledge held by these giants of modern Western philosophy, one general trend in post-Cartesian philosophy in the West that they signal is the search to reconnect mind and body in the act of knowing.

One strand in this reconnective movement is reliant upon an increased interest in language not simply as text but as event. This linguistic turn is evident in the writings of Martin Heidegger (d. 1976), for example, who in his "Letter on Humanism" (1947) speaks about language as "the house of being."[5] Similarly, Maurice Merleau-Ponty (d. 1961) in his *Phenomenology of Perception* (1945) emphasized that we are not so much beings who have speech as we are speaking entities. From his perspective language is not so much an instrument or means to an end but "a manifestation, a revelation of intimate being and of the psychic link which unites us to the world and our fellow men."[6] Heidegger's student, Hans-Georg Gadamer (d. 2002), went even further in his *Truth and Method*

(1960) when he argued for the "linguisticality of experience." By this Gadamer meant that language is not separated from reality but an integral part of human experience, and that there are no categories of experience apart from language.

This movement from the "knowing subject" to the "subject who comes to knowledge in the speaking act" next leads us to a consideration of embodiment as an essential aspect of this coming to knowledge in speaking. Similar to the linguistic turn, this *corporeal turn* in contemporary philosophy recognizes that we do not simply have a body; rather, we are a body. The French philosopher Henri Bergson (d. 1941) is generally credited as the first contemporary thinker to place the body at the center of the human process of recognition. In his *Matter and Memory: Essay on the Relationship of Body to Spirit* (1939), Bergson speaks about the "intelligence of the body," the "logic of the body" and what he called "bodily memory."[7] Bergson's insight is enhanced by the work of Merleau-Ponty who recognizes that to be a person is to be a "body-subject" for whom mind and body are linked dialectically; one cannot exist without the other. In Merleau-Ponty's opinion, our body establishes a necessary linkage to and unavoidable perspective on the world in which we live.

This corporeal turn has been taken up by numerous other philosophers, specialists in linguistics, and political scientists. Feminist scholars from various disciplines have been particularly concerned not only to erase the duality of mind and body, but to give priority to embodiment in constructing a feminist hermeneutic.[8] This embrace of embodiment across a wide spectrum of disciplines and by an array of unlikely allies has led to a new way of thinking about the "embodied mind." Moving away from the body as "container," there is a growing emphasis on the individual as a "social body" that exists as a primary and irreducible element of being.[9]

Giving pride of place to the social body in the process of human perception and knowing means that language itself cannot be properly understood except as an embodied act. Considering language as the "house of being" is no longer sufficient. Language itself—whether silently rehearsed in the frontal lobes of the cerebral cortex, rendered in pen or digitized format, or spoken out loud—requires embodiment.[10] Leland McCleary pointedly illustrates the corporeality of speech in this reflection on children:

> *Evidence for the corporality of language, even oral language, can be found in the practices of children during the process of learning to read: touching the book, tracing letters or lines of print with their fingers, touching a reader's lips, accompanying a word with a gesture, pronouncing a word out loud. Naturally these bodily supports are gradually suppressed as the child gains invisible, silent control over the mediation of the written language, but they are always available to fall back on, even by adults, when particularly difficult words or passages are encountered. It is as if the language is stored, not only in the mind, but just as surely—perhaps more surely—in the body.*[11]

Language is not only stored in the body, it is an embodied way of knowing.

Speech-Embodiment in Ritual and Sacrament

The importance of this *corporeal turn* for grasping something of the dynamics of ritual in general—and liturgy in particular—cannot be overstated. In his recent overview of liturgy and the social sciences, Nathan Mitchell suggests a shift in thinking from what he calls the "classical consensus" to "new directions in ritual research."[12] Mitchell characterizes the classical consensus as a position assumed by scholars heavily influenced by anthropology which assumes that ritual's primary purpose is the social construction of meaning through a culturally conditioned system of symbols. Meanings are authoritatively encoded in invariable rites and ultimately lie beyond the participant's power to manipulate or control them. While consisting of variable ritual messages, purveyors of this position hold that, at the deepest and most stable level, ritual meanings are never invented or encoded by participants, but are found or discovered as already given in and by the rite.[13]

In contrast, Mitchell—reckoning with the *corporeal turn*—demonstrates how some contemporary scholars are less inclined to think about ritual as the enactment of a series of invariable actions in order to discover the ritual's core, and more inclined to think of ritual as a type of "technology of the self." *Technology* may seem an unwelcome term here, with what some may consider its impersonal or economic overtones. Mitchell employs the term, however, as it appears in the later works of the philosopher Michel Foucault (d. 1984). For Foucault, "technologies of the self" was a useful framework for speaking about the many ways in which individuals "effect by their own means or with the help of others a certain number of operations on their own bodies and souls, thoughts, conduct and way of being, so as to transform themselves in order to attain a certain state of happiness, purity, wisdom, perfection, or immortality."[14] From this perspective ritual is not fundamentally a symbol system aimed at the production of meaning but a process for acquiring or embodying an aptitude or skill. Ritual in this sense is a way of inscribing the body, where the ritual process is the ritual content.

Ritual thus conceived is not simply an instrumental agent for imparting information or shaping someone in a predetermined social identity, but is a strategic way of acting that effects by signifying in and on the body. Ritualization so defined actually gives rise to corporeal knowing. And, of course, there's the rub in this turn to the embodied technologies, for in this framework ritualizing does not create what we hope or what we intend, but only what we inscribe on the body.

Contemporary sacramental theologians such as Louis-Marie Chauvet thoroughly embrace this corporeal turn. Chauvet holds not only that the body is important for understanding sacraments, but that it is essential for the entire theological enterprise. Thus he can state that "the anthropological is the place of every possible theological."[15] Consequently, even Chauvet's own concern with rethinking symbols in terms of language "is accompanied from end to end by the body, the *body-being*."[16] As for sacraments, Chauvet considers them to be expressions of the "corporality" of our faith. Consequently, in his view, to become a believer means learning to consent—without resentment—to this corporality of our faith.[17] Chauvet believes that there is no faith unless it is somewhere inscribed in a body from a specific culture and with a concrete history. Thus, he believes that one cannot even become a Christian except by allowing the church to "stamp its 'trademark,' its 'character,' on one's body."[18]

The Aesthetics of Faith Inscription

If, as Chauvet would have it, our worship is a key way in which faith is inscribed on the individual bodies of believers and on the social body we call the church, then the "how" of that inscription assumes new prominence. Sacraments in this framework are not a prepackaged *lex orandi* that delivers some canonized and invariable *lex credendi*—but an embodied cause in, on and of the body. *Lex orandi* has thus become *lex corporalis* so that our always embodied praying actually gives rise to believing or disbelieving in a unique, corporeal, contextualized way. And, of course, the parallel implication in this turn to the embodied technologies of liturgy is that liturgy—like any other ritual—does not necessarily create what we hope, what we intend, or even what is inscribed in the official books, but only what is inscribed on and through believers' skin. This is no guaranteed delivery system of prepackaged, orthodox salvation, but a salvific exploration in skin-mode. And since, over time, this kind of skin-inscription has an indelible nature to it and is virtually impossible to erase, there must be particular attentiveness that we inscribe carefully each time we ritually enact.

There are certainly many difficulties that arise when attempting to establish criteria for what appropriate liturgical inscription might look like. The cross-cultural realities of Roman Catholic worship in the United States alone would seem to mitigate against such generalizing. Criteria for embodiment, for the faith-inscribing act we call worship, if acknowledged at all, often hover at the level of taste and personal preference. The aesthetic approach of Alejandro García-Rivera, however, could provide another way.

In his *The Community of the Beautiful*, García-Rivera compellingly argues for a strong link between aesthetics and ethics.[19] Among other contributions, García-Rivera demonstrates the possibility of a dynamic relationship between the Beautiful, the Good and the True. He also believes that one key characteristic of a community deemed True, Good and Beautiful is that community's willingness and ability to embrace difference.[20] This "loving of difference," according to García-Rivera, also characterizes the Beautiful, Good and True God who created us. A community that loves difference in imitation of the Holy One is a community that, in García-Rivera's opinion, follows the theological aesthetic norm of "lifting up the lowly." He elaborates:

> [T]he glory of the Lord is a community that has caught sight
> of a marvelous vision, a universe of justice emerging from a com-
> munity's experience of divine Beauty, the "lifting up the lowly."
> Such a community counts as members the sun and stars, the
> dead and the living, the angels and the animals, and, of course,
> the marvelous yet lowly human creature. Together, in their splendid
> differences, these individuals give witness of God's power not
> only to give life but also to ordain it. . . . Redemption, in light
> of God's ordaining power, is less a state of mere existence or
> an invisible inner reality than an ordained existence, a common
> reality in the midst of marvelous differences, a community where

*the invisible becomes visible by the power of a bold and daring
spiritual imagination which makes manifest communities of
Truth, Goodness, and, above all, the Beautiful.*[21]

"Lifting up the lowly" as an aesthetic norm might seem a little
obtuse, but when brought into dialogue with the skin-inscription
we call liturgy, concrete examples easily emerge. For example, in
any given Sunday assembly assess the embodied diversity of that
assembly. Where are the racial, ethnic, age, gender and class differences incorporated into the ritual? And what ritual space do they
occupy? We might not think of it as liturgical inscription, but
sequestering children and their long-suffering parents in cry rooms
at the edges of the assembly inscribes disenfranchisement on the
skin. And where do we make space in the ecclesial body for those
with physical and mental disabilities? Even if the hearing-impaired
hold a physical place at the heart of our worship, if they cannot
enter the acoustic space with ease and the sounds of the liturgy do
not resonate for them with clarity, then the ensuing silence or gar-
bled reception virtually erases them from the sonic action. Such
embodiment would not seem to meet García-Rivera's criterion of
"lifting up the lowly."

Another way to consider the aesthetic norm of "lifting up the
lowly" in embodied worship is to consider the lead agents (that is,
ministers) in the skin-inscription activity we call liturgy. It is true
that from a phenomenological perspective every worshiper is a
body-being in the worship event and, consequently, is a key agent in
their own faith incorporation process. At the same time, however, it
is not difficult to recognize that certain liturgical moments draw
the attention—or at least occupy the time—of the majority of
worshipers more than others. In Roman Catholic eucharist, for
example, the vast majority of worshipers sit when the first reading is
read, stand when the gospel is proclaimed, and join the procession
for the distribution of communion. Focal in these activities is some

lector, presider or minister of communion who at that moment holds a privileged position in socially embodying the worship event.

Recalling García-Rivera's aesthetic norm, consider to what extent the lead agents in such inscription moments incarnate diversity? Is it only the bifocaled and gray-haired who read and proclaim? Is it only the able-bodied who greet us as we cross the threshold of the church? Is it only those whom society has judged to have achieved some arbitrary measure of intelligence who distribute the eucharistized bread and cup? Even if an assembly embraces a rich diversity in its membership, the inscription power of such diversity can be muted if there is a homogenization of the leadership. Receiving the consecrated cup from a young adult with Down syndrome stamps a distinctive character on the body of Christ, as does being greeted at the church entrance by a minister in a wheelchair or having the word proclaimed by someone for whom the dominant language of the community's worship is clearly a second language.

Considering who exercises the power of inscription in our worship leads us to a final consideration about the assembly itself. In one of the most celebrated directives of the *Constitution on the Sacred Liturgy* (1963), the conciliar authors noted that the standard by which the reform would be judged was the full, conscious and active participation of the people (n. 14). Often such participation has been evaluated at the linguistic level, that is, to what extent people have said or sung various responses. Making the corporeal turn, however, compels us to ask to what extent the people who comprise our liturgical assemblies are not simply disembodied tongues, but engaged in active embodied worship. Do they have the freedom to act in the worship, or are they only acted upon? Do they gather at the font, embrace the neophytes, feel the spray of the water, smell the chrism during the body anointing, or are they mute onlookers whose embodied inscription is passive rather than active? And when they do act, are they marshaled into common activity where individuality is discouraged or are they free, for example, not only to join in having their feet washed but also to wash the feet of others if they choose? Taking the aesthetic norm "lifting up the lowly" too literally could suggest that it only is applicable as a kind of liturgical "affirmative action" plan for those members of the assembly perceived to be outside some local norm. Given the way we have corporeally erased some of our assemblies, however, it could be a timely motto for all the faithful.

Conclusion

This essay began with the assertion that much of the focus in the current stage of the liturgical reform is a narrow concern about official texts as disembodied words on a page. One result of this textual disembodiment is what I characterized as the severing of the liturgical tongue from the ecclesial body in the act of worship. In an effort to help stitch tongue and body back together, I attempted to underscore the import of the embodied performativity of the liturgy by moving beyond texts and speech to a consideration of the aesthetics of liturgical performance. This was done by briefly considering a series of moves in contemporary thought. These included (1) the turn to the subject, (2) attempts to diminish the division between mind and body, (3) the linguistic turn, and (4) the corporeal turn which allowed us to assert the primacy of embodiment in human experience and perception, and the embodied nature of speech itself.

Moving to a consideration of ritual, liturgy and sacraments, we agreed with Mitchell that ritual is appropriately understood as a skin technology and affirmed Chauvet's insight that our worship is a key way in which faith is inscribed on the individual bodies of believers and on the social body we call the church. Consequently the performativity of that inscription is unavoidably important. Because of that, in need of some criteria by which to evaluate the embodied faith inscription of worship, we borrowed the aesthetic framework of García-Rivera. While aesthetics are often limited to the realm of the pleasurable, García-Rivera provides a link between the Beautiful-Good-True and to that end offers as criteria the embrace of difference and the theological aesthetic norm of "lifting up the lowly." Finally we exercised that norm in a consideration of public worship in order to heighten our awareness of what kind of faith inscription is actually performed in our worship Sunday after Sunday.

Given the power of embodiment, the corporality of being and the way that even our speech is a form of skin inscription, expending untold energies in the liturgical reform fixing words on a page with virtually no parallel attention to the performative nature of the words and their liturgical context seems at least questionable if not ineffectual. Believers in a God-Incarnate need to be committed to principles for worship that take incarnation seriously at every level. This means appropriate attention to texts, to be sure, but especially in a performative framework and not to the exclusion of parallel considerations of the wider embodiment of worship. It is only in attending to the aesthetics of this wider liturgical embodiment that, I believe, we will come to discover how, in "performing the Body of Christ,"[22] we more fully become the Body of Christ.

◆ ———————————————————————————————

1. For example, "The prayer of the church is always the prayer of some actual community, assembled here and now. It is not sufficient that a formula handed down from some other time or region be translated verbatim, even if accurately, for liturgical use. The formula translated must become the genuine prayer of the congregation and in it each of its members should be able to find and express himself or herself." *Comme le prévoit,* n. 20, *Notitiae* 5 (25 January, 1969): 3–12, reprinted in *Documents on the Liturgy 1963–1979: Conciliar, Papal, and Curial Texts* (Collegeville: The Liturgical Press, 1982), 284–91.

2. "Among the separate elements are those which are essential and others which are secondary and subsidiary. The essential elements, so far as is possible, should

be preserved in translation, sometimes intact, sometimes in equivalent terms." Ibid., n. 28.

3. For example, "It is to be kept in mind from the beginning that the translation of the liturgical texts of the Roman Liturgy is not so much a work of creative innovation as it is of rendering the original texts faithfully and accurately into the vernacular language. While it is permissible to arrange the wording, the syntax and the style in such a way as to prepare a flowing vernacular text suitable to the rhythm of popular prayer, the original text, insofar as possible, must be translated integrally and in the most exact manner, without omissions or additions in terms of their content, and without paraphrases or glosses." *Liturgiam authenticam,* n. 20, *Origins* 31:2 (May 24, 2001): 21.

4. Nathan Mitchell, "Toward a Poetics of Gesture," *Worship* 75:4 (2001): 356–65.

5. Martin Heidegger, "Letter on Humanism," in *Martin Heidegger, Basic Writings: From Being and Time (1927) to The Task of Thinking,* ed. David Farrell Krell (San Francisco: Harper & Row, 1993), 189–242.

6. Maurice Merleau-Ponty, *Phenomenology of Perception* (London: Routledge & Kegan Paul, 1962 [1945]), 196.

7. Henri Bergson, *Matter and Memory,* trans. Nancy Margaret Paul and W. Scott Palmer (New York: Zone Books, 1988 [1941]), 137, 139 and 197 respectively.

8. See, for example, *Gender/Body/Knowledge: Feminist Reconstruction of Being and Knowing,* eds. Alison M. Jaggar and Susan R. Bordo (New Brunswick, N.J.: Rutgers University Press, 1988).

9. Catherine Bell, *Ritual Theory, Ritual Practice* (New York–Oxford: Oxford University Press, 1992), 96.

10. On the embodied nature of language see David Abram, *The Spell of the Sensuous: Perception and Language in a More-than-Human World* (New York: Vintage Books, 1996).

11. Leland McCleary, "Technologies of Language and the Embodied History of the Deaf," *Currents in Electronic Literacy* 4 (Spring 2001): http://www.cwrl.utexas.edu/currents/spr01/mccleary.html

12. Nathan Mitchell, *Liturgy and the Social Sciences,* American Essays in Liturgy (Collegeville: The Liturgical Press, 1999).

13. Ibid., 32–3.

14. *Technologies of the Self: A Seminar with Michel Foucault,* eds., Luther H. Martin, Huck Gutman and Patrick H. Hutton (Amherst: The University of Massachusetts Press, 1988), 18, as cited in Mitchell, *Liturgy and the Social Sciences,* 65.

15. Louis-Marie Chauvet, *Symbol and Sacrament: A Sacramental Reinterpretation of Christian Existence,* trans. Patrick Madigan and Madeleine Beaumont (Collegeville: The Liturgical Press, 1995), 152.

16. Ibid., 140.

17. Ibid., 152–3.

18. Ibid., 154–5.

19. Alejandro García-Rivera, *The Community of the Beautiful: A Theological Aesthetics* (Collegeville: The Liturgical Press, 1999).

20. García-Rivera, 39–40, 72–3, 119, 183–4, and passim.

21. Ibid., 195.

22. A phrase taken from William Cavanaugh, *Torture and Eucharist: Theology, Politics and the Body of Christ* (Oxford: Blackwell, 1998), 253.

Poetic images . . . create a disequilibrium, *a thrilling sense of vertigo, a shuddering disturbance deep at the center of things that speeds outward to apprehend the whole range of reality and to alter our experience and perception of it. Because of this, poems have a power to change us that exceeds even the finest sermons and theologies. A poem does not "make sense"; on the contrary, it often urges you to "stop making sense." . . . In the deepest sense, a poem delivers "meaning" not by gripping the intellect, but by gripping the hearer's whole being—and so by demanding a total change of life, a* conversion.

Nathan Mitchell, "The Amen Corner: The Renewal That Awaits Us," *Worship* 70:2 (1996): 171.

Let the Poet Speak

Gilbert Ostdiek, OFM

One of the most alluring aspects of Nathan Mitchell's style of writing and teaching about the liturgy is his constant care and passion to let poets speak to the topic at hand. Readers of his "Amen Corner" in each issue of *Worship* can readily attest to this. Quotations abound from the poetry of Emily Dickinson, Rainer Maria Rilke, Edith Sitwell, Anne Sexton, Robert Blake, Alfred Lord Tennyson, Ezra Pound, Dylan Thomas, Gerard Manley Hopkins, John Milton, George Herbert, T. S. Eliot—the roll call could go on and on. The voice of the poet, Mitchell insists, must now become a priority for the liturgical renewal:

> *If the postconciliar generation belonged to reformers—to planners and librarians, text critics and translators, archivists and historians—* the next generation must belong to the poets. *In saying this . . . I mean that we must rediscover within ritual both the poetry of words and the poetry of motion. We need, for the new millennium, a poetics of word* and *gesture, song* and *dance. We need to learn (or re-learn) that images arise before thoughts, that poems precede sermons, that dance is older than speech.*[1]

In the same spirit that pervades Mitchell's "Amen Corner," this essay will be a series of musings, somewhat random and free-flowing, inspired by insights woven through his columns.

Ars Poetica, Ars Liturgica

"If every poem is an *ars poetica,* perhaps it can also be said that every act of public worship is an *ars liturgica,*" Mitchell has written.[2] But why should liturgists sit at the feet of the poets? What is their art? What is it that they can unveil for us?

A poet is one who knows better than any others that:

> *Words strain,*
> *Crack and sometimes break, under the burden*
> *Under the tension, slip, slide, perish,*
> *Decay with imprecision, will not stay in place,*
> *Will not stay still.*[3]

The tools with which poets ply their art are words—most often very ordinary words. But in the mouth of the poet these words no longer sound like ordinary speech. We too easily assume that the words we ordinarily use have fixed and firm meanings and "stay in place," that ambiguity and imprecision hinder clear communication and are to be avoided at all cost. Our words, we believe, are under the complete control of our thoughts. But poets know that even ordinary words used ordinarily will "strain, crack . . . slip . . . will not stay still."

What, then, of words that would dare to speak of deeper realities hidden within and beyond the ordinary? It takes a poet to ask a question we liturgists rarely entertain: "How to say God?"

> *Awake and listening*
> *—moonrays drilling the dark—*
> *I try to speak: What words*

can we cry? What sound is given to us?
Meager alphabet, sounds
   warmth of body-language.
How to say God? I have fallen
   in love with the bleeding roots
   of his life, and I am shaken
   and loosened from my sleep.

It is late in the year: words
   in their ripe innocence, burst
   around me like seeds. If we don't hear
   their resonance, hear them
   clear through with our brain, veins, flesh
   what about that other name, God?
How can it leap alive
   out of the tomb of dead signs?[4]

There is much for liturgists to reflect on here. Poets know instinctively that words spring not so much from carefully reasoned thought, but from other ways of relating to things. "Look, see, touch" is the refrain de Vinck sings in her poem. There is a resonance in things, an interconnectedness, a mystery beyond human naming. These things are heard "with brain, veins, flesh" in breathless silence, are known first in the flash of a vivid image, and the words that name them burst forth in "ripe innocence" before reason can marshal its thoughts. Gathered into poems, such words are more exclamation and song than prose.

The art of the poet, then, is to give new voice to such moments of keen awareness and revelation, to subvert what our words ordinarily say. Or better, to re-root our words in that experience out of which they were first born, to let them again become full of the untamable awe, ambiguity and plurisignation originally theirs. Words whose meaning has become desiccated and entombed in tedium of daily speech are brought back to life. And in the process our sense of how we, others and God are woven together in a great web of belonging is transformed and given new life.

Mitchell sums up the art of the poet in these ways. Human speech has its origin in "poetic outcry." The images the poet voices are based not on an ontology of cause and effect, but on a rever-beration set in motion by the "sonority of being." Poetic images create a "disequilibrium," a dislocation in our sense of reality which demands "a total change of life, a conversion." And above all, poetic expression is creative, it is a doing and making of the world.[5] In the end, it is the poets who are able to sense the sacramentality of the world and to bring to speech the awesome beauty and terror of a world "charged with the grandeur of God."[6]

To be sure, the artistry of the poet makes use of skills and techniques—rhythm, flow, meter, imagery and metaphor (to which we shall return later)—but those are not what matter in the end. They serve a deeper purpose. They invite us to set aside the homage we pay rational analysis and to hear and attend as the poet does, with imagination, veins and flesh. They engage our emotion, invit-ing us to be moved out of and beyond ourselves (the root meaning of the word *emotion*), into our race's best dreams of what the world could be and should be. That is the greatest gift of the poet's art.

That is the art Mitchell would have us infuse into the liturgy. He writes:

> *If every poem is an* ars poetica, *perhaps it can also be said that every act of public worship is an* ars liturgica, *an essay on the etiquette embodied and the energy aroused by the assembly, corporate and converting. For liturgy too is a field of dreams, where communities enact meanings and embody beliefs through ritual symbols, remembered traditions, and renegotiated patterns of power. Like a poem, worship invites participants to negotiate anew their relations with self, others, God and world. For these*

reasons, indeed, I have often argued that liturgy is poetry and,
hence, that its texts and utterances must be poetic.[7]

It is to the texts of liturgy that we now turn.

A Poetics of the Word

It is no secret that the words to be used in the liturgy have become
a source of great contention during the past decade. Should translators of the Latin texts of the Roman Rite strive for literal or
dynamic equivalence?[8] Should the language of prayer be contemporary and accessible or "sacral" and borderline archaic? Should we
or should we not use inclusive language for humankind and the
assembly? Should God preferably be named "Father" and always
referred to with masculine pronouns? In the course of these debates
(and too often to the detriment of the prayer and unity of the worshiping assembly) liturgical texts have become the rope in a tug-
of-war. Who can free us from this fruitless, no-holds-barred,
wrestling with words?

> *Wrestling with Words. In liturgy as in life, the stakes are high.*
> *Perhaps we are at a point in our social and ecclesiastical history*
> *when we need to recognize once more the indispensable place*
> *of the poets among us—poets who guard and multiply the vital*
> *force of language, who make speech a dam against oblivion.*
> *Perhaps the poets are the ones who can remind us that our*
> *language does, after all, have a future tense. . . . Above all, the*
> *poets are those who know that the frontiers of language, real as*
> *they are, border not on nothingness, but on three other great modes*
> *of statement—light, music and silence, proofs of a transcendent*
> *Presence in the fabric of our world. Where the word of the poet*
> *ceases, a great light begins.*[9]

The poet would have us learn a measure of humility and ret-
icence about the adequacy of our prayer words. How to say "God"

in a world marked by constant upheaval and torn by evil and violence is not as easy as it once seemed. "I believe in God the Father almighty" may be hard words for those who have suffered abuse at the hands of humans who bear the name "father." Prayers in our ancient tradition regularly begin with "Almighty and eternal God." Week after week our ears and minds take in those customary ritual words with little if any notice; any other way of naming God jars us into discomfort, if only for the moment.

Listen to how the poets would have us "guard and multiply the vital force" of that holy name. In a delightful poem on how things came to be named, Catherine de Vinck muses

> *A name was found*
> *in the maze of connections*
> *the child in us*
> *inventing it:*
> *"God," we say, wrapping the word*
> *around our life*
> *a garment of mist*
> *a cloudy fleece to ward off*
> *the chills of perennial pain.*[10]

Or from the pen of Rainer Maria Rilke:

> *I live my life in widening circles*
> *that reach out across the world.*
> *I may not ever complete the last one,*
> *but I give myself to it.*
>
> *I circle around God, that primordial tower.*
> *I have been circling for thousands of years,*
> *and I still don't know: am I a falcon,*
> *a storm, or a great song?*[11]

Such words have indeed reached the frontiers of speech and border on the realms of light, music and silence. Together these poems capture something of what Rudolf Otto called the *mysterium tremendum et fascinans*. God is awe-inspiring mystery, that "primordial tower"[12] and pillar of strength, awesome and serene, around which all life circles and wraps itself in search of whether to name itself "falcon, storm, or great song." But there is the other half of Otto's equation. God is also an alluring mystery in which life chilled to the bone by "perennial pain" wraps itself seeking warmth, solace and healing.

Something of that image of wrapping is also captured in one of the revised translations proposed for the Sacramentary in 1998. There the phrase *multiplica super nos misericordiam tuam* asks God to heap loving-kindness upon us in lavish abundance. But since "multiply" (a transliteration of the Latin *multiplicare,* which literally means to fold again and again) might be misunderstood today in a purely mechanical, quantitative way, the editors chose instead to have the prayer say "enfold us in your gracious care and mercy."[13] Gail Ramshaw has aptly reminded us that the strategies for our wrestling with names for God ought not be limited to nouns and adjectives; there are verbs as well.[14] The verb *enfold* can image the many ways in which parents, lovers and caregivers gather others into their embrace, wrapping them in unconditional love and care. The poets would remind us that all our words need to leave room for ever-new understandings to arise and must eventually fall silent or break into song. They also remind us that the search to name God is at the same time a search to name ourselves, that we ought not fear welcoming into our prayer new names and metaphors (or new ways of construing old names and metaphors), either for the mystery of God or for the mystery of ourselves.

These musings can be taken a step further. Metaphor lies at the heart of each of the poems just cited. They name God a "primordial tower" that centers one's life and searching, or again, a fleecy garment one gathers about oneself "to ward off / the chills of perennial pain." Traditionally, we have been taught that metaphors are picturesque figures of speech, rhetorical flourishes used by poets and such like. These embellishments, it was thought, are dispensable; in fact, plain speech could make the meaning more accessible and intelligible. More recently some scholars have come to hold rather that all thought is essentially metaphoric; that is the way the human mind works.[15] We come to know through a parallel process of comparing and distinguishing. Metaphors insist that we can move from what is known to what is unknown, but also that something is inevitably lost in the process and must be left unsaid. Metaphoric ways of thinking and speaking are second nature to the poets—how else can something of what they see and touch be carried over to hearers and readers, while reverencing the unspeakable mystery and uniqueness of all that is?

In passing we might note the parallel to a difficulty which besets the work of translation. The Greek root of the word *metaphor* is *metapherein*. Literally, this means "to carry across or transfer" and by extension "to transform or change"—implying that there is both a legitimate likeness and an irreducible difference to be taken into account. *To translate*, derived from the Latin root *transferre*, has that same dual meaning. Like poets, translators of liturgical texts are truly engaged in the work of metaphor, carrying over something from the original even while they are forced to leave something behind. In the absence of exact equivalences, every translation is of necessity an act of interpretation. Translations always run the risk of misinterpretation; but they also open the text to new nuances of meaning only dimly anticipated in the original. What complicates the task even more is that the Latin liturgical texts were composed at a time of what Walter Ong calls "primary orality." That is, for most people of that time language was spoken; literacy was at a minimum. We now live in a time of literacy, or secondary orality, when language is first and foremost inscribed. Words stored for later retrieval do not have the same living power as words that live momentarily and survive in memory only.[16] It should come as no surprise that the language of public prayer, by nature more akin to the language typical of primary orality, sits uneasily in a culture where inscribed language holds sway. And as Mitchell has noted, the movement from the earlier oral cultures into modern literary cultures has huge consequences regarding power and authority, our sense of belonging, the public vs. private character of words, and the understanding of community.[17] Mitchell concludes: "This, ultimately, is the pernicious danger posed by *Liturgiam authenticam;* in the name of preserving accuracy and fidelity, its proposed rules for 'translation' will actually guarantee the final erosion of 'the Roman liturgical tradition.'"[18]

To return to the newer approach to metaphor, Mitchell sums it up more technically in these four statements: (1) metaphor works not on the level of individual words or phrases, but on the level of discourse, where the sentence is the basic unit; (2) the basic strategy of metaphor is logical absurdity; that is, metaphor puts things together that do not seem to belong together; (3) metaphor discloses new meaning by abolishing or canceling literal reference; and (4) metaphor has a heuristic value. "What metaphor discloses is thus not a picturesque glimpse of the world that already exists, but a new *world* (one that can't be manipulated or controlled by ordinary means of measurement and analysis)—and *a new way of being in the world.*"[19] Metaphor, at the core of all human thought and speech, is a way of saying what cannot otherwise be said. The *ars liturgica* surely has much to learn from the *ars poetica.*[20]

The point here is not to suggest that all liturgical texts should be poetry.[21] Rather, those who would craft prayers for the assembly need to learn from the *ars poetica* to attend not only to theological precision and literal fidelity to a Latin original, but also to the poet's way of weaving words. Words that both reveal and hide, words that are open to a rich layering of meaning, words that resonate with the world of the hearer,[22] words that subvert their own ordinary and often impoverished meanings, words that bring one to the giddy precipice of both knowing and not knowing, where no alternatives remain but song, silence and gazing on the light. That is also the point at which liturgy's inarticulate languages such as gesture and space join in the poetics of liturgy and have a unique role to play. It is to these that we now turn with a few brief musings.

A Poetics of Gesture

Mitchell offers these provocative suggestions for a poetics of gesture:

> [L]et us focus here on what may be called "the poetics of gesture." To understand what is meant by "poetics," consider this: Our human cognition is a complex, richly layered reality. We "know" not only with our intellects, but also with our imaginations, our bodies, our hearts and souls, our feelings and emotions, our dreams and fantasies. A poetics deals with the myriad ways our artful, embodied imaginations "know." Similarly, a poetics of gesture deals with the limitlessly imaginative ways our bodily movements, positions, and postures (e.g., the lifting of a hand to take, break, give) read reality, read the world.[23]

To say that we "know" not only with our intellects, but also with our bodies and embodied imaginations is intriguing. The "Amen Corner" from which this quotation is taken tells of a treatise by Bede the Venerable (d. 735) entitled "on speaking with fingers" (De loquela digitorum), inviting us to focus our musings on the hands. Think for a moment of the many ways we use our hands to "read" the world around us. Children instinctively explore things by touching them. Tailors and shoppers feel cloth to know its quality. Sculptors and wood carvers judge the progress of their work more by feel than by sight. Mothers and doctors diagnose with their hands. We also "speak" with our hands—instinctive gestures, an unguarded reaching out to another, the gentle touch on the cheek of a grieving child, holding the hand of one suffering, clasping hands to seal an agreement or welcome someone home. Hands have their own way of knowing and speaking.[24] "Next to the face, the part of the body fullest of mind is the hand."[25]

The use of hands also plays a significant role in liturgy. A number of years ago, Godfrey Diekmann proposed that the laying on of hands is the most basic gesture in all the sacramental rites; each such gesture is symbolic of the gift of the Spirit.[26] Hands act as liturgical metaphors, not only in the core sacramental actions, but in other moments as well—hands raised in the ancient *orans* gesture of praise and thanksgiving, extended hands that channel peace, hands folded to hold sacred an inner silence, hands cupped to cradle the infant lowered into the waters of rebirth. In one of Rilke's poems that cupping of hands images what the Creator did in the beginning:

> *I read it here in your every word,*
> *in the story of the gestures*
> *with which your hands cupped themselves*
> *around our becoming—limiting, warm.*[27]

Examples could be multiplied.[28] After reviewing various ways in which the hands are used in liturgy, Guardini concludes:

> *There is greatness and beauty in this language of the hands. The church tells us that God has given us our hands in order that we may "carry our souls" in them. The church is fully in earnest in the use she makes of the language of gesture. She speaks through it her inmost mind, and God gives ear to this mode of speaking.*[29]

To this Mitchell comments: "Guardini is right, of course; liturgy unfolds in the language of the hands. Skin is unique, for it is the only human organ that can make direct contact with others—and so with the Otherness revealed in them."[30] The question for liturgists, then, is how can we let gesture, movement, posture learn from the *ars poetica* to embody and convey something of that holy presence, both awesome and alluring, something beyond what words can say?

A Poetics of Space

Our musings turn now to liturgical space. It, too, speaks without words. Mitchell writes:

> *There is, in sum, a poetics of space, a perfect economy of rest and motion, presence and "emptiness," light and shadow— which transfigures our experience of rooms and buildings— and landscapes. We first feel such a poetics arising within our bodies, for we are instinctively, powerfully drawn toward some spaces (a river's waters rearranged by rocks and rapids) and just as instinctively repelled by others (a refuse-filled landfill). Our bodies know which spaces welcome the human and the humane. Unfortunately, the body's wisdom is often overruled by minds which tell us that burnt-brown naugahyde is beautiful and that "what this room really needs" is another chain-lamp or a painted-velvet portrait of Elvis.*[31]

Mitchell then goes on to explore three aspects of a poetics of space: the skin's memory, the body's wisdom and the geometry of prayer. The underlying theme is that ritual is its own form of knowing, inscribed in the body.[32] Ritual actions involve the whole person; they embody beliefs, commitments, religious attitudes and aspirations in actions repeated again and again. As with musicians, dancers and athletes, the worshiper's body comes to know and remember the inner feeling and meaning without having to pause for conscious thought or put them into words. "Ritual prayer is, then, a holy geometry—of intersecting bodies, processional motion, departures and arrivals; of smoke swirling in spiraling circles from censers swung in arcs; of bodies bent, arms extended, voices lifted."[33]

In liturgy, as in all social activities, the most natural thing in the world is to set aside special places for significant activities and events, to dedicate them solely to this purpose. The place needed for worship will be

> a place for praying and singing, for listening and speaking—a place for human interaction and active participation—where the mysteries of God are recalled and celebrated in human history. . . . Such a place acquires a sacredness from the sacred action of the faith community which uses it. As a place, then, it becomes quite naturally a reference and orientation point for believers.[34]

Mitchell echoes this perspective and ties it to what he has said about a poetics of space when he writes:

> A space is "sacred," after all, because of what is done there, discovered there. Those who serve congregations in matters of "environment and art" are thus mystagogues who help an assembly negotiate its meeting with Mystery. . . . Faith is indeed a way of knowing Mystery—but it is a knowledge born of the body, bred in the bone, carried on breath and blood, buried in our singing skins. . . . To create worship space for a community of faith is to think with the skin, to remember with the body. . . . Art and architecture—like other human acts and artifacts— become avenues for knowing and naming the Holy.[35]

So the question for liturgists and church architects is this: How can we shape a place of worship where the community, gathered to do liturgy, can "think with the skin" and "remember with the body"— as the Body of Christ? What is at stake here is the need for the worshiping community to fashion for itself a space which maps its journey and sums up its story. "Every ritual act," Mitchell has said, "is a reinvention, a remaking and remapping of the world and of our human place in it."[36] The community's liturgical space, then, must by definition be at once a gathering place and a processional space, a place for hearing and remembering the story, a place for breaking bread and enacting all the rites that mark its journey of discipleship.

Ars Amatoria

This final set of musings takes its cue from the following words of Nathan Mitchell:

> I suggest, then, that we need a new understanding of ritual, one that fully embraces our complex human psychology. . . . I propose that we imagine ritual as an ars amatoria in which the inextinguishable human desire to bond or "connect" with others (including God) is negotiated in ritual patterns that are reverent and respectful, based on mutual recognition and regard. This art, I will argue, is learned (a skill acquired, just as humanity itself is acquired, by learning the ritual repertoire of the human community); but it is also rooted, more radically, in our neural physiology. In other words, the word "love"—which our liturgy uses so regularly to describe the relation between humanity and God—already has a complex neural history, long before it enters the arena of human awareness, emotion, and choice.[37]

Later in that same article he writes,

> I have defined ritual as ars amatoria, "the art of making love," because it is precisely the emotional quality of human word and gesture that lets us have relationships, that enables us to connect and form communities. Ideas are wonderful, but they do not really link us to one another; only emotions do.[38]

That is where poetry and liturgy link arms. Both serve to evoke and name afresh that deep feeling of belonging and relationship that binds all things together. Both evoke a passion that lies deep within the human heart, far below surface feelings and sentiments. Both have the capacity to move us in ways that can only be called by the name of love. The bishops of the United States said it simply but powerfully when they wrote, "People in love make signs of love."[39] In the end, that is what liturgy is about.

The final word to conclude these musings belongs by right to Nathan Mitchell. His plea to liturgists who would foster the liturgical renewal is simply this: Let the poet speak. He himself models well how we, each in our own little corner of the liturgical world, might respond fruitfully to that plea in one grand chorus of Amens.

> *Only poems can create a new being in our language by* making *us what they express. For in poetic utterance, we discover that language is more than a utilitarian tool for exploring reality or controlling it. The words of faith and worship, like those of poetry, are "words that crack,"* that constitute *(and sometimes subvert) reality.* Conceptual *language requires centralization,* the *fixing of forms and meanings. But poetry always has fluidity, life, movement; its energy, its images flow into lines of verse, carrying the imagination along with them. In a poem we do not "grasp" meaning; we surrender to it. That is also the way of Christian conversion and faith, the way of worship. And it is, I suspect, the way of renewal which awaits us.*[40]

---

1. Nathan Mitchell, "The Amen Corner: The Renewal That Awaits Us," *Worship* 70 (1996): 170. It gives me great pleasure to write this essay for the *Festschrift* honoring Nathan Mitchell on his sixtieth birthday. To count him as mentor, colleague and friend has truly been a blessing.

2. Nathan Mitchell, "The Amen Corner: God at Every Gate," *Worship* 68 (1994): 254.

3. T. S. Eliot, "Burnt Norton," *The Collected Poetry and Plays 1909–1950* (New York: Harcourt, Brace and World, Inc., 1971), 121.

4. Catherine de Vinck, "I Try to Speak," in her *A Book of Uncommon Prayers* (Allendale, N.J.: Alleluia Press, 1976), 145.

5. Mitchell, "The Renewal That Awaits Us," 170–2.

6. Gerard Manley Hopkins, "God's Grandeur," in *Gerard Manley Hopkins: A Critical Edition of the Major Works,* ed. Frank Kermode (New York: Oxford University Press, 1986), 128.

7. Mitchell, "God at Every Gate," 254.

8. See the contrasting positions taken by Congregation for Divine Worship and the Discipline of the Sacraments, "*Liturgiam Authenticam:* Fifth Instruction on Vernacular Translation of the Roman Liturgy," *Origins* 31:2 (May 24, 2001): 17, 19–32, on the one hand and, on the other, Willis Barnstone, *The Poetics of Translation: History, Theory, Practice* (New Haven, Ct.: Yale University Press, 1993) and Robert Wechsler, *Performing Without a Stage: The Art of Literary Translation* (North Haven, Ct.: Catbird Press, 1998).

9. Nathan Mitchell, "The Amen Corner: Wrestling with the Word," *Worship* 66 (1992): 456.

10. Catherine de Vinck, "The Word," in her *A Basket of Bread: An Anthology of Selected Poems* (New York: Alba House, 1996), 13.

11. Rainer Maria Rilke, *Book of Hours* I, 2, in *Rilke's Book of Hours: Love Poems to God,* trans. Anita Barrows and Joanna Marcy (New York: Riverhead Books, 1996), 48.

12. Translators of this poem often render the words *Uralten Turm* as "ancient tower," and one can easily imagine a hunting falcon circling around such a tower. Catherine de Vinck does just that in her response to Rilke in a poem entitled "Ancient Tower," *A Basket of Bread*, 11–2. In the translation above, "primordial" invites one to think of the stunning photo of the gaseous pillars in M 16–Eagle Nebula. These pillars of primordial matter are millions of light years in height. The photo taken by the Hubble space telescope and released by NASA on November 9, 1995, can be seen on the web at http://oposite.stsci.edu/pubinfo/jpeg/M16Full.jpg. In poetry, language becomes open-ended and creative, making room for one's own imagination to play.

13. Opening Prayer for Sunday XXII of Ordinary Time, *The Sacramentary,* Volume One, Part Two (Washington: ICEL, 1998), 598.

14. For fuller discussion, see: Gail Ramshaw, *Christ in Sacred Speech: The Meaning of Liturgical Language* (Philadelphia: Fortress Press, 1986), 151–213.

15. For discussion of theories of metaphor and how metaphor works in liturgical language, see: Nathan Mitchell, "Lexicon: Metaphor," *Liturgy Digest* 4/1 (1997): 94–8; Nathan Mitchell, "Metaphor in Modern American Research," *Liturgy Digest* 4/1 (1997): 46–86; Gail Ramshaw, "Liturgical Language: Keeping It Metaphoric, Making It Inclusive," *American Essays in Liturgy* (Collegeville: The Liturgical Press 1996); Mark Searle, "Liturgy as Metaphor," *Worship* 55 (1981): 98–120; John Witvliet, "Metaphor in Liturgical Studies: Lessons from Philosophical and Theological Theories of Language," *Liturgy Digest* 4/1 (1997): 7–45.

16. See especially: Walter Ong, *Orality and Literacy: The Technologizing of the Word* (New York: Methuen, 1989); Walter Ong, "Worship at the End of the Age of Literacy," *Worship* 43 (1969): 474–87. See also: Gilbert Ostdiek, "Liturgical Translation: Some Reflections," in *The Voice of the Church: A Forum on Liturgical Translation* (Washington: USCC, 2001), 28–32.

17. Nathan Mitchell, "The Amen Corner: Once upon a Time," *Worship* 75 (2001): 474–8.

18. Ibid., 478.

19. Nathan Mitchell, "Lexicon: Metaphor," 96 and *passim.*

20. See for example: Kathleen Hughes, "Some Musings on the Poetry of Prayer," in *Finding Voice to Give God Praise: Essays in the Many Languages of the Liturgy,* ed. Kathleen Hughes (Collegeville: The Liturgical Press, 1998), 105–17.

21. Ironically, a number of years ago one of the members of the NCCB stated publicly in the annual bishops' meeting, "The trouble with the ICEL prayers [referring to the 1973 Sacramentary] is that they have too much poetry and too little theology." A poet might well have said just the opposite!

22. An example of this resonance, worthy of Nathan Mitchell's poetic sensitivity, can be found in *Eucharistic Prayer A* (Washington: ICEL, 1986), an original composition that did not receive the final *recognitio* from Rome. In a haunting phrase, the prayer proclaims that Christ "offered life to sinners, / though death would hunt him down." The underlying metaphor in the second line is that death is a stalker. How true that is in today's world of drive-by shootings and senseless violence visited upon the innocent. The traditional affirmation of Christ's freedom in the face of death, which some felt this metaphor does not respect, is voiced in the next lines: "But with a love stronger than death, / he opened wide his arms / and surrendered his spirit."

23. Nathan Mitchell, "The Amen Corner: Toward a Poetics of Gesture," *Worship* 75 (2001): 361.

24. For more extended reflections, experiential and liturgical, see: Edmond Barbotin, "The Hand," in his *The Humanity of Man,* trans. Matthew J. O'Connell (Maryknoll: Orbis, 1975), 187–224; Romano Guardini, "The Hands," in his *Sacred Signs,* trans. Grace Branham (St. Louis: Pio Decimo Press, 1956), 15–8.

25. Guardini, "The Hands," 16.

26. Godfrey Diekmann, "The Laying On of Hands: The Basic Sacramental Rite," *Catholic Theological Society of America Proceedings* 29 (1974): 339–51.

27. *Book of Hours,* I,9, in *Rilke's Book of Hours,* 55.

28. Symbols and gestures inevitably have both a positive and a shadow side. Thus, hands have much to say in the presentation of gifts that can be read both positively and negatively. Bread and wine, the work of human hands, are carried forward in the hands of worshipers, handed over into the hands of the presider, who places them on the altar table and washes his hands in a purificatory gesture. These gestures speak loudly, long before the people respond, "May the Lord accept the sacrifice at your hands. . . ." Together these gestures serve to draw a vaguely felt but unspoken boundary around the central performer, actions and objects of the rite. Ralph Keifer, a colleague of happy memory, first pointed this out to me.

29. Guardini, "The Hands," 18.

30. Mitchell, "Toward a Poetics of Gesture," 360.

31. Nathan Mitchell, "The Amen Corner: The Poetics of Space," *Worship* 67 (1993): 361.

32. In speaking of ritual bodily inscription, Mitchell often cites the work British anthropologist Talal Asad has done on the *Rule of St. Benedict.* See: Nathan Mitchell, *Liturgy and the Social Sciences* (Collegeville: The Liturgical Press, 1999), 64–80; Nathan Mitchell, "Ritual as Reading," in *Source and Summit: Commemorating Josef A. Jungmann, SJ,* ed. Joanne M. Pierce and Michael Downey (Collegeville: The Liturgical Press, 1999), 161–81; On ritual knowing, see: Theodore Jennings, "On Ritual Knowledge," *Journal of Religion* 62 (1982): 111–27.

33. Ibid., 367.

34. Bishops' Committee on the Liturgy, *Environment and Art in Catholic Worship* (Washington: USCC, 1978), 39, 41.

35. Nathan Mitchell, "The Amen Corner: Believe in the Wind," *Worship* 73 (1999): 363.

36. Nathan Mitchell, "The Amen Corner: Lyrical Liturgy," *Worship* 67 (1993): 464.

37. Nathan Mitchell, "The Amen Corner: Ritual as *Ars Amatoria*," *Worship* 75 (2001): 252.

38. Ibid., 258.

39. Bishops' Committee on the Liturgy, *Music in Catholic Worship* (Washington: USCC, 1972), 4.

40. Mitchell, "The Renewal That Awaits Us," 172.

Liturgy is God's work for us, not our work for God. Only God can show us how to worship God— fittingly, beautifully. Liturgy is not something beautiful we do for God, but something beautiful God does for us and among us. Public worship is neither our work nor our possession; as the Rule of St. Benedict *reminds us, it is* opus Dei, God's work. *Our work is to feed the hungry, to refresh the thirsty, to clothe the naked, to care for the sick, to shelter the homeless; to visit the imprisoned; to welcome the stranger; to open our hands and hearts to the vulnerable and the needy. If we are doing those things well, liturgy and the Catholic identity it rehearses will very likely take care of themselves. . . . Liturgical art is our public gratitude that God is doing for us what we cannot do for ourselves. And there, perhaps, is where ethics and aesthetics together can begin to change the face of worship.*

Nathan Mitchell, "The Amen Corner: Being Good and Being Beautiful," *Worship* 74:6 (November 2000): 557–8.

Spirituality, the Imagination and the Arts

Patrick W. Collins

While the conjunction of spirituality, the imagination and the arts may not be immediately obvious, it is nonetheless of great importance. It will therefore be necessary to explore the meaning of each of these three terms in order to grasp their intimate and intrinsic relationship. Thereby believers can grasp more deeply what it means to have faith in God and be on the spiritual journey.

What Is Spirituality?

There are many definitions and descriptions of spirituality. According to Sandra M. Schneiders, for example, spirituality is "the experience of consciously striving to integrate one's life in terms not of isolation and self-absorption but of self-transcendence toward the ultimate value one perceives."[1] Spirituality, then, refers to our lived experience in the light of our faith, a faith which is both drawn from a particular inculturated tradition, and involves a personal appropriation of that tradition. This is what ultimately energizes how we humans live, move and have our being with felt truth and conviction.

A description of spirituality which I find useful describes spirituality as the living of one's life in relationship with what one considers to be "ultimate." Everyone has a spirituality—even an atheist. Why? Because everyone lives life in terms of what one considers to be ultimate. The question is, of course, how adequate is one's ultimate? How true to Truth is what fundamentally "runs one's engine," so to speak? The imagination and the arts may serve us well in our spirituality as a mirror reflecting one's relationship with the Ultimate. They can support it when it is the Truth and challenge it when it takes the form of an Idol.

Indeed, the distinctive human problem is always the need to spiritualize human life. This involves a deep desire to see and feel more than meets the eye in the very ordinariness of our experiences. This involves searching for wholeness in the midst of fragmentation and for community in the face of isolation and loneliness. It involves a never-ending quest for meaning and for values that endure the many changes that life inevitably brings to persons, societies and cultures.

Since humans are "spirit in the world"—embodied spirits in space and time—spirituality is the effort to understand and realize the potential of that extraordinary and paradoxical condition. This calls for more than thinking and more than eyesight. It demands insight. As Anaxagoras, a philosopher in ancient Athens, once asked: "Why are you here on earth?" And the reply? "To behold." This beholding is what spirituality is about.

Spirituality is not generic, however. It is specified in its understanding of the Ultimate by the cultural and religious context which shapes one's life project. Here we are considering a spirituality which functions within the horizon of the Christian tradition. But the gospel guides us not so much through instruction or argument as through revelation which "bodies forth" its truth for humans to see.

Such a spirituality will be anthropologically inclusive. In it the entire human experience will be probed for transcendence as immanent. That which is reflected upon is not only the explicitly religious dimension of experience but also those analogous experiences of ultimate meaning and value which have transcendent and life-integrating power for individuals and groups. These are embodied and enacted in the various arts which open participants' imaginations to transformative truths.

Three things happen in one's personal spiritual journey. First, a dimension of experience is described for reflection. Data is surfaced which can be seen from many perspectives, and especially the depth perspective of how "Ultimacy" is embodied there. Second, one's reflection upon this data leads to critical analysis. What is going on here insofar as the mind can grasp? Where is the Mystery breaking through? Third, a new synthesis takes shape as one appropriates the new intuitions and insights into one's lived experience. This is the transformational actualization of meaning.

Spirituality and the Imagination

The most important part of the human knowing process that is engaged in a healthy spirituality is the human imaginative system. Imagination may be the most active part of the human psyche in day-to-day existence. It is in fact what we do with our minds most often. Yet imagination is a word and a reality very easily misunderstood. As I use the word it is neither mental picture-making nor pure make-believe nor fantasy. It is not meant as a way to avoid the real world, escaping into one's dreamy desires. It is not a cop-out on reality; rather it is what Providence uses to get us deep down into what *is* the most Real and most True.

I speak of imagination as a power of human knowing, an act of the mind operating through the languages of image, symbol, story, myth, parable and ritual. What one comes to know through the cognitive functioning of imagination is that dimension of reality that is more than meets the sensible eye. It is the "mystery" in life. Human realities are re-described through imagination's cognitions in such disclosive terms that we see things differently. We return to the ordinary, reoriented to life's real possibilities.

An example may be useful. A man I know was, for many years, treated shabbily by his mother-in-law—or so he thought. At one Saturday night family gathering she had typically put him down and embarrassed him before everyone. Being the basically nice guy he was, he did not respond in kind. Instead, as always, he stuffed his feelings inside him. But that night he dreamed in images of ways in which he could "stick the witch," as he put it.

The next morning, as he was brooding over his encounter with this woman the previous evening, he and his family went to the Sunday liturgy. In the front row sat the mother-in-law. As he glared at the back of her head, he kept imagining ways he could "stick the witch." At that point the usher approached him to invite the man and his family to bring forward the gifts during the celebration. He knew the scriptures well enough to realize that one should not participate in such a ritual action if one is holding hostility in the heart. He was torn inside.

He didn't hear the opening song at all, which was, ironically, "They'll Know We Are Christians by Our Love." The first two readings also swept by his ears and his consciousness. But as the gospel was proclaimed, he heard the parable of the Prodigal Son in a wholly new way. This was not about someone else, somewhere else, long ago. His imagination had become engaged in such a way that he could walk around in that parabolic story and find his own story. He realized that if he was to participate authentically in that eucharist and bring forward the bread and the wine, he would have to stop imagining ways to "stick the witch" and begin imagining ways of reconciling with the woman.

He became that story through the engagement of his imagination; he was "hooked" toward conversion. He knew from this insight that he could not live with himself in truth unless he could attempt once again to bring about a reconciliation with his mother-in-law. And so he went out and acted upon this disclosure of truth which was brought about by the imagination functioning as a knowing power, realizing something of his own personal, psychic and relational truth. This was an example of spirituality as a "beholding" experience in a transformative way.

Such knowing through the imagination is not irrational cognition and, therefore, false. It is not delusion. It is not a kind of knowledge against reason but rather a knowing that is beyond reason yet not illogical. What is disclosed to the imagination may be inconceivable but it is not self-contradictory. It is simply more than meets the eye of mind or sense. Yet it is indeed truth—aesthetically perceived truth.

Such is the principal way in which spiritual truth is presented and perceived in every religious tradition. John Cardinal Newman contended that faith begins not in the notions or concepts which develop through the use of discursive reason; rather faith is gestated in and through images and symbols which are born in the human imaginative system. Belief involves a different kind of knowing than that provided by the "mind-knowing." The "mind-imagining" is of the essence in the act of believing as a spiritual being. Newman suggested that for an assent to be rationally adequate it must first be credible to the imagination.[2] The imagination must be engaged for a believer to come to "see" more than meets the eye of sense in this world. Imagination opens to disclose the Mystery of the Reign of God which is both in but not of this world.

Imagination's Functioning

How does that which is "more than meets the eye" become "seen," if you will? How does the imagination function? Human knowledge grows through sensations which are received in our consciousness as images. These mental representations of our experiences relate to other images from previous experiences. The new ones bind with older ones to form image clusters. These image clusters make up the material component of our imagination. The dynamic component within the structured imagination is the line of movement between the various image clusters. The arts set these movements going within us. This interplay between the freshly presented image clusters performed and our own previous culturally and historically conditioned experiences is what Gilbert Durand describes as "the structured imagination."[3]

Again, an example may be useful. In perceiving a piece of film art, none of the characters enter our consciousness free and unfettered. They are experienced in relation to the image clusters already active in our structured imagination. They are received by the knower as part of a whole field of past perceptions, swimming about in clusters in our consciousness. Because of this mediation through images, we experience a kind of immediate knowledge of feelings in our reaction to these "performed" persons before we ever come to know them or see their characters developed further in the film.

We like them because they look like someone we once loved. Or we respond negatively because they use speech patterns similar to that person who caused us to be fired from a job. Later in the film, if we allow the characters to develop, we come to relate to them through more complex image clusters. In this process our new experiences with these persons may blow apart our past clusters, creating whole new patterns of image relationships. For example, as we learn to perceive the truth beyond the stereotypes so often portrayed, we may no longer see black persons as bad, the poor as pitiful, nor gays as ghastly.

All mental images can be grouped into two general categories: light and dark. Some events portrayed in a staged drama may enter my consciousness and make me want to sing. Others may play out in way that make me feel like weeping. The experiences of light and dark images are grouped according to three human reflexes: ascending, enclosing or inviting.

Images of light assimilate as an ascending dynamism, according to Durand, while images of darkness incorporate an enclosing dynamism. Between these two composite groups we find the cyclic dynamism of inviting which operates as a unifying force. The latter allow us to maintain a kind of equilibrium or tensive balance between the light and the dark in our imaginations. "In these convergences are located the fundamentals of the Structured Symbolic Imagination, and within this basic structure many other groups of images come to be fixed in a person's consciousness."[4]

All of this aesthetic activity in the human imaginative system exists to bring about a certain balance in our consciousness—a tensive balance essential for any spiritual journey. As Søren Kierkegaard has written, the imagination is the means whereby all the faculties of the person are brought into "equilibrium" or "simultaneity."[5] Reality is seen synthetically, as a whole, rather than analyzed into its parts by the mind functioning as discursive reason. The imagination works from the many toward the one. It innately drives toward intimacy, interiorization and integration with each of the image clusters, old and new. This is what can happen in one's spirituality through imagination's engagement in the arts.

Perhaps this is why Jesuit theologian William Lynch claims that the imagination as expressed and experienced in the arts may be the best enemy of mental illness. He suggests that it is not too much but too little imagination that causes illness. Imagination allows the person to cope with the perceived collapse of his or her life and to rebuild a new inner and outer world. A new world has to be imagined when all appears dark and disparate and, as such, the imagination becomes the ally of hope. Without it we would go mad in despair.

Lynch describes imagination as "the sum total of all the forces and faculties in man that are brought to bear upon our concrete world to form proper images of it." Lynch suggests that for children and the mentally ill, only immediate experience seems real. The relationships to other experiences don't hold together. The part is absolutized. The part is made into the whole. Only the imagination can realize this absolutizing instinct so that the person

> can circle around the mountain of the human until it sees all
> that is there. Such an imagination will not basically be taken
> in by the fascination of the hopeless. It will not condemn itself
> too quickly. . . . It is precisely not foreclosing judgment on our-
> selves but leaving final judgment to God that requires imagina-
> tion and hope.[6]

Another scholar of the imagination, Matthias Neuman, OSB, contends that we need to treat the whole imaginative realm as "an integral and autonomous psychological system in human consciousness." This system interacts with perception, memory, bodiliness, conceptualization, volition and so on, yet it remains autonomous in its workings, possessing unique content, operations and goals directed toward the total person. This inner realm is "a veritable crossroads of the entire human psyche."[7] Thus the imaginative system is extremely complex, involving a thousand subterranean forces, forces which can be unearthed for reflection and emotional reaction through participation in the arts.

Spirituality and the Arts

The arts can engage the human imaginative system in ways of knowing that are more intuitive than intellectual and thus dispose those who perceive the arts toward deeper insights into faith and spirituality. While not primarily discursive in their avenues into truth, the arts are nevertheless truly cognitional—yet in a quite different mode than theology and doctrine. To grasp the distinction it is helpful to explore just what the imagination is and what it is not.

Aesthetic forms of expression have the transformative power to change our vision first of all; then our values begin to shift, and finally our behavior falls in line with what we have "beheld." The arts bring to the fore of our consciousness some facets of human experience for our pondering and our conversion of spirit. Since all human knowledge begins in experience, a slice of experience presented aesthetically in the arts enables participants to see more deeply into their own lives to where love calls for celebration and conversion of mind and heart.

One's spirituality begins and develops precisely through the inner activity that resembles what takes places in aesthetic expressions and experiences. Such imaginative engagement can take us deeper into that imageless place where Spirit dwells. Once a balance of felt truth has been achieved through aesthetic insight we are moved by our images toward an ever more creative stance in life. New modes of being-in-the-world are disclosed as projects for the imagination to envision and embody and enact. Our personal story becomes more whole and moves on in hope to a future which logic and discursive analysis alone could never bring about. Discursive reason cannot reach such disclosures.

Surely it is such imaginative functioning which enables one person to see in another person a whole new mode of being-in-the-world called friendship or to see the complementarity that draws persons into the two-in-one-flesh relationship of marriage. It is not logic that leads to love, but imagination which discloses love's possibilities. These are also possibilities brought about by the animation of the light-directed image clusters in the structured imagination which draw persons toward religious vocations and toward accepting prophetic vocations in the world.

Reason Can Block Imagination

The race to explore the meaning of imagination today in science, art, politics and religion is due to the unfortunate fact that Western culture has stifled imagination's power through an overemphasis on the rational. Imagination has not been the dominant motif of Western Christianity at least since the Aristotelian movement of the thirteenth century provided a fairly clear end to the earlier Latin theology of the image. The scholasticism of the university, while bringing system to thought, sometimes drained the richness of imagination which had been evident in earlier patristic and monastic approaches to truth.

Through an excessive tribute paid at the altar of reason, imagination's contribution to the cognitive enterprise has been impoverished. This narrow rationalism, resulting from the thought of such great rationalists as Descartes, Kant, Mill, Hume and Comte has resulted in what Owen Barfield has termed our modern "island consciousness."[8] We sit on the outside of reality as observers, without the imaginative faculty of participation in "the true" and "the real" of life. The movement away from imagination has been a movement away from life itself.

Human consciousness then becomes objective-manipulative. "Thinking" becomes a way of living to those who only bow to objective truth. Such objectivity separates the subject who knows from the object known. And it makes detached observers of us rather than participants in the on-going creative work of the Creator. In the process one loses the sense of self as part of more than the self, which furthers an unhealthy individualism. One also loses the world which is constrained to conform to the observable, not open to what might be. There is no longer any sense in which self and world may be bound together with cords of mutuality and participation. The world becomes simply a machine whose mastery is within the grasp of the subject.

Persons, too, seen as distant from the observing individual, become objects to be manipulated. We all become one grand technological invention, one large machine to be controlled by whoever best understands the powers of manipulation. What such consciousness breeds is an appreciation not of the quality and permanent value of reality but rather of its quantity and transience. This consciousness tends to ground life in the materialistic and the consumeristic.

One person who escaped the prison of alienated imagination was once dubbed Man of the Twentieth Century by *Time* magazine, Albert Einstein. As a child, Einstein did not talk until he was five years old. Later he was slow with words, had a poor memory and did poorly in any schoolwork that required verbal skills. Today we might suspect that he suffered from dyslexia. Perhaps, however, he was liberated very early from the objectivity imposed by words. His imagination remained forever free and childlike.

Einstein's biographer, Erik Erikson, described him as a "victorious child." Erikson wrote: "Einstein succeeded in saving the child in himself, even when he had to accept non-violent resistance, isolation and even punishment rather than submit to standardization. . . . The child would lead him to creativity."[9] Einstein described his own thought process in this way: "When I examine myself and my methods of thought I come to the conclusion that the gift of fantasy has meant more to me than my talent for absorbing positive thinking."[10] He "saw" more than meets the eye.

Einstein did not think in words when he was conceptualizing, according to Roman Jakobson, a Harvard University linguist. He imagined ideas. He attached words to them later. This wordless deliberation is related to Einstein's genius, Jakobson, suggested, because it is "more pleasant, standardized and leaves more liberty, more freedom for creative thought."[11]

It was through the power of imagination that one esteemed by rational science discovered new laws of gravitation more precise than Newton's. But that should not surprise us. For through the senses and reason we can only know what was, what is and what predictably can be. Only imagination can achieve what has been thus far inconceivable. And Einstein did just that.

Educating the Imagination

Rational reflection is based upon the ability of the structured imagination to mediate the experience of reality for reflection. There is no direct or unmediated intercourse between reality and reflection. Reality becomes available for reflection only through images and image clusters which are drawn from human experience. As Theodore W. Jennings, Jr., has written:

> *Imagination is the initial way in which existence and reality come to expression in such a way as to be available to human awareness and to serve as the legitimate ground of reflection. . . . The function of imagination then is the representation of the patterns of participation in and transcendence of the world in such a way as to make possible the experiencing of, and conscious participation in, reality.*[12]

It is always possible, of course, that the imagination can threaten and undermine the role of the rational when it becomes alienated from reason. In that case imagination is not grounded in the real. The arts present such disconnections, distortions and dysfunctions with great power. Through such aesthetic insight, one's spirituality can be turned from its own chaos toward integration by seeing one's own interiority with its potential disorders projected aesthetically.

Urban T. Holmes offers three criteria by which the creative imagination can be disciplined by reason without losing its unique autonomy. First, the imagination's images must be appropriate to the reality represented imaginally. Second, there must be a pattern of consistent thought in the imagination's products. And, third, we must not confuse the image with the reality, the representation with the referent.[13]

Imagination's orientation to reality is actually more fundamental than thinking. John Shea has noted:

> *It has tendencies which pull us in a certain direction; and although the mind may pinpoint the problems and try to solve them, it cannot change the direction. In another image, if the imagination has a gaping hole, thinking will not patch it for long. In a final image, imagination is the room and thinking is the furniture. We may move the furniture from corner to corner to get new and fascinating looks. But sometimes what is needed is a larger room.*[14]

When the imagination is engaged in and by the arts, "larger rooms" are made possible for perceivers. Such open and freer spaces are yielded by the imaginative system as it actively achieves the symbolic transformation of the given. We see things differently. We make connections that logic and the senses do not make. In the latter we look at reality on the surface and make causal connections, but we don't see into reality below the surface. Yet it is in those inner regions of reality, "the underside of life, and the high reaches of the ordinary,"[15] that linkages go on, and images cluster which are more than meets the eye and which keep human life truly human.

Surely it is in our imaginations that we are most the *imago Dei*. In those activities of imaging we not only respond to and understand our world, we also share in creating the world.

Imagination waits to be turned into creation. It defines and creates the human and the ever evolving cosmos and God's "new heavens and new earth." Through reason we explain reality but through imagination we explore its unseen possibilities and know more than eye can see and logic can discern. We can "know" or, better said, "realize" the unknowable Mystery.

Regrettably, children in general do not have Einstein's independence of imagination. Nor do contemporary adults who feed on the machine-oriented banalities of television images and stories. Regrettably, too, our educational systems have been co-opted by the objective-manipulative consciousness syndrome. In our society the sciences and technology dominate over aesthetics and philosophy. Sports take precedence over the arts. When a school's music program is reduced or curtailed due to budget cuts, some will lament such an action, but few will rebel. When funds are to be reduced for athletics, however, rebellion will be the order of the day and funding will be found hastily, often from private resources and donations.

Why doesn't the same thing happen for the arts? Why do we readily surrender that which engenders quality in life when educational costs skyrocket? Simply because we have been taught and conditioned to consider the arts, the imaginative ways of knowing and experiencing, as frosting on the cake. The lesson of American life is that violent competitive sports, with their stress on power, control and success, are the symbolic activities which more truly demonstrate who we are as a nation than the more "cultural" pursuits such as the arts.

Tragically, by emphasizing the rational more than the imaginative and the competitive more than the creative, our education system continues to produce what Reuben Alves calls the large dinosaur of present society which rules people and stifles creativity. A truly human world is the product of the creative arts, Alves claims. "We must start with the imagination, for this is the prerequisite of the creative act. And the creative act is the highest expression of human life."[16]

How can we educate children without stifling the creative potential within them and their ability to imagine and play? Must we always domesticate them with the bonds of pragmatism and rationalism, reducing them to the point where they become little more than copies of the machine-like people who preceded them— and, unfortunately, may be teaching them?

Jesus' words, "Unless you become like little children, you cannot enter the reign of God," speak volumes in our present situation. To become childlike, not childish, should be the goal of all education. It is also the goal and condition of prayer. Stemming from the Latin word *educare*, meaning to draw out or to lead out, education should be a drawing forth of the imagination of each person as well as the imposition of past ideas and present facts on the memory and on reason.

In the child the possibility of playfulness flows from an energized imagination which yields enjoyment in life. In a sense, this may be what is meant religiously by justification by faith. In the child "educated" to be an adult the essence of life is work, which yields production and consumption. Adult life becomes justification by works. In this adult world, play is produced for distraction. Its natural child-quality of spontaneity is suppressed. The work-oriented adult is even made to feel guilty about playing too much or too creatively. According to Alves,

> *Our society, dominated as it is by productivity, is the grave of the child and therefore the end of play, since the expansion of things produced and consumed depends on the repression of man's drive toward enjoyment. . . . Children's play ends with the universal resurrection of the dead. Adults' play ends with universal burial. Whereas the resurrection is the paradigm of the world of children, the world of adults creates the cross. . . . In play, each day begins*

with grace, not law. . . . The truth of play will become history
when impotence becomes power and when that which is now
power becomes impotence.[17]

In Alves' mind, resurrection is not merely a doctrine to be affirmed by the intellect. It is also a symbol to be received by the imagination in order to create, here and now, life in abundance.

Obviously what Alves is talking about in education is revolution, turning things upside down. I am suggesting something similar with regard to the ways the arts can contribute to a person's spirituality. The Catholic culture, which has tried to nourish and sustain itself primarily on the dark diet of rationalism from the Enlightenment in the eighteenth century and the Catholic neo-Thomist revival in the nineteenth century, has withered in the sunshine of real life.

Such products of the "mind-thinking" must be supplemented by aesthetic expressions born in the "mind-imagining." To return imagination to the forefront of Christian spirituality must not be seen as a reduction of theology, liturgy, and religion to art. It is rather to see that, as well as scientific and inferential disciplines, these are also aesthetic ones themselves. Revelation's primary expressive form is aesthetic. In fact, it is always through forms of imagination—myth, parable, symbol, myth and ritual—that God's claim upon us is expressed in scripture. And it is the imaginative response, not just the rational, that can interpret and distinguish such forms.

Our spiritual journeys are paved and opened through experiences of the arts in which a personal truth is disclosed that transcends objective observation. Truth here is communicated through personality, person to person, heart to heart. Any one of us instantly senses the difference between what Gerard Manley Hopkins terms "an equation in theology, and dull algebra of the schoolmen, or knowledge that leaves . . . the mind swinging, poised but on the quiver . . . the ecstasy of interest."[18] The difference lies in the understanding, employment and engagement of the human imaginative system that is expressed and experienced in the arts. This is the "soul" in us which is both before and after all other faculties, embracing the whole of existence and seeking intimacy with the whole through presence.

Imagination, then, as we saw earlier, is not a faculty but a crossroads, the linking point of all the faculties. It is the intuition with which one participates in experience. It is the intuition through which one drinks deeply of life. It is the seeing into reality which supersedes looking at reality. It gets behind appearance. It discloses the substances of things to be hoped for.

Hopkins made a useful distinction in this regard. He said that we look at a landscape but we see the "inscape," that is, we intuit the inner meaning and reality of Being expressed externally through the landscape. "To see is to engage the inscape, the convergence that lies behind the phenomena."[19] Without such seeing we remain outsiders to the human dimension of life. We do not participate with warmth and passion but observe with detachment. For, according to Owen Barfield, "final participation" in reality is an act of the imagination, getting beyond merely thinking about the thinker. He contends that the imagination is the person's capacity to make the material an image of the spiritual.[20] And it is this capacity which characterizes artists—and anyone on a spiritual journey. The "final participation" may be another way of describing Jesus' summary of his mission: "I have come so that you might have life more abundantly" (John 10:10).

Fear of Imagination

Spirituality is the way in which we live our lives at the deepest and richest levels. And life worth living is grounded in a rich imaginative connection with reality just as it must be well founded on rational perceptions and conclusions. Oh yes, imagination can get us into trouble. It can separate us from reality just as surely as can pure and narrow rationalism. Not all images are accurate. Some cluster in our structured imaginations in bizarre, distorting and destructive patterns. Such imagination gone awry is called pure fantasy; it is an escape from the real. It fails to live in the world of facts, truth and reality. Reason rightly restrains imagination from destructive fantasy. Healthy imagination is creative of truth and reality; fantasy is not. Healthy imagining builds on sensibly perceived facts and rationally derived conclusions. In a sense concrete reality dissolves, diffuses and is recreated through imagining as cognition. And, in so doing, imagination moves forward by a judicious selection and reshaping of the representations of the experience that make up our meaning.

Institutions have always feared the imagination. Why? Probably because imagination can unleash people into disorder, and because institutions place a high value on good order enforced by reasonable laws which provide limits. Religious institutions, in particular, while revering the imagination on the one hand, can never be totally comfortable with it on the other. Creativity will always threaten institutional order and control. Yet the creative imagination is the only way to a continuing, vibrant life within institutional churches. The tension between rational control and imaginative creativity is inevitable and healthy, although sometimes, at least temporarily, it can be very hurtful.

In Christian history many movements of the imagination were mystical in nature. The fourteenth-century mystics became popular at the very time that the system of scholasticism and ecclesiastical life in general were in decline. Mysticism seems to have been the interior spiritual reaction which retained vitality in an otherwise largely externally oriented church structure. Persons such as Catherine of Siena, Bridget of Sweden, Julian of Norwich, Giovanni Valle, Meister Eckhart, Henry Suso, John Tauler and John

Ruysbroeck made significant contributions to this spiritual renewal. And this was born of the imagination engaged in prayer.

Their new mysticism was less philosophical and more volitional, aimed at moving the will and the heart toward the Divine. Although *imagination* was not a common word in their writings, the shift from an emphasis on the intellect to an emphasis on the will is surely similar to what can be witnessed today in the development of a new piety which involves the retrieval of the imagination. A fundamental issue in ministry today is the recovery of a sense of enchantment and the ability to be enchanting. That is precisely one of the roles of the arts in our lives. Like the mystics who, while faithful to Catholic tradition, arose in reaction to a decadent scholasticism, we, too, are trying to recover from an over-dependence on the purely rational, clear and distinct ideas of Descartes. Holmes writes of the influence of Descartes: "The power of ambiguity, a sensibility to life, and the relation between beauty and goodness came to be lost to the God at the end of a syllogism."[21]

Imagination for the reformers of the fourteenth century involved taking great risks just as it does for us today. There is no guarantee in the life of the imagination. Like life itself, of which it is the soul, imagination is a risky business. As Alfred North Whitehead has written: "Imagination . . . is a dangerous gift, which has started many a conflagration."[22] In fourteenth-century Germany, the Flagellants and the Brethren of the Free Spirit fell into heresy, as did the Fraticelli in Italy. Twenty-six sentences from Meister Eckhart's writings were condemned posthumously by Pope John XXII, fifteen as heretical and eleven as rash and close to heresy. Later, however, it was seen that much of Eckhart's writings had been taken out of context and were in fact judged to be orthodox.

Part of institutional religion's problem with such mystics was that their language was aesthetic and was imbued with deep feeling. As such it lacked the precision and exactitude of the technical language of the Schoolmen. There it may well have been not fully

comprehended by authority and was arguably misinterpreted—
possibly even in good conscience.

Much of this intuitive, volitional and feeling-filled approach to
faith surfaced again in the late nineteenth century in the Roman
Catholic church as theologians began to incorporate the findings
and the methods of history and the physical sciences into their own
investigations. Among the theologians who gave an impetus to spirituality were Alfred Loisy, George Tyrell, Maurice Blondel and
Baron Friedrich von Hugel. Their way of expressing spiritual realities was condemned in 1907 by Pope Pius X under the label of
"Modernism, " which was described as "the synthesis of all heresies." And the near witch-hunt that ensued showed both the fears of
ecclesiastical institutions toward this approach as well as certain
inadequacies in the new thought itself. Although each one of these
thinkers differed from the other considerably in both theological
method and content, they shared two things in common: their reaction against the over-objectified and rationalistic character of the
institutionally supported neo-scholasticism and their concern to
show the authenticity of subjective religious experience.

Although both reason and human institutions rightly try to
curb imagination from the chasm of chaos and unreality, the person
who opens the windows of his or her soul to reality, whose images
are challenged and comforted through participation in the arts,
must personally move out of the order of their former systems of
thought and action to truly perceive the new. Revolutions are born
because someone got far enough out of the center of things to see
it all differently. And that reality, as Coleridge said so well, "dissolves
and diffuses and becomes recreated."

Conclusion

The place of imagining—the place of the arts, if you will—is at
the edge of the abyss where all of the impositions and limitations of

reason and law are held in abeyance for a time. In the center of every organized society much is taken for granted. There we live at the limited dimensional levels of feeling, common sense and thinking, but all this works against the fuller way of knowing and living which is the imaginative mode, a way of cognition which both precedes and follows knowledge gained through discursive reason. In this mode, one becomes unchained for a time from the order of reason and law, and one risks experiencing on the edge of existence a fuller insight into life and love.

There is great risk in surrendering to the power of the arts which lead us from the center toward the edge of the abyss, to the margins of chaos from which creativity can emerge. Moving from the center to the edge of our ordered existence creates the possibility of a point of no return. Out there, near the precipice, we may fall headlong into nothingness, into a reality of total loss and chaos. We may never return to the center, enriched by passing over to another different and perhaps dangerous position or viewpoint.

For those Christians who fear this kind of "anti-structure," as Victor Turner terms it, let them take heart from the example of Jesus, whose whole life was a passing over, a paschal mystery. He went alone to converse with God in the desert, the anti-structure. It was in the abyss of this desert experience after his baptism that he was tempted—and renewed. He was given a deeper insight into himself and his mission. It was in those many moments alone in quiet, out-of-the-way places that he came to terms with the cost of his mission. And it was at night, in a secluded garden, when he experienced the beginning of the abandonment of his personal, chosen support structure, that he accepted the lead toward the chaos of the cross: "Not my will, but thine be done." Crucified there on the edge of the abyss, stretched between heaven and earth, Jesus passed over to the center in the resurrection—but only because he had risked a pilgrimage into the wilderness.

I suggest that it was Jesus' active imagination that, from a human point of view, opened him to the graces given in the anti-structure. There he saw in the dark the mystery beyond sight, the power and presence of God. The risk of chaos, the beckoning abyss was, for Jesus, the pre-condition of life in abundance.

As Leonardo Boff has suggested:

> *Is it not possible that for us this category "imagination" may reveal the originality and mystery of Christ? . . . Imagination is a form of liberty. It is born in confrontation with reality and established order; it emerges from non-conformity in the face of completed and established situation; it is the capacity to see human beings as greater and richer than the cultural and concrete environment that surrounds then; it is having the courage to think and say something new and to take hitherto untreaded paths that are full of meaning for human beings. We can say that imagination, understood in this manner, was one of the fundamental qualities of Jesus. Perhaps in the whole of human history there has not been a single person who had a richer imagination than Jesus.*[23]

Let those who fear the loss of control implied in imagination's pilgrimage to the mystery at life's core be encouraged by these recollections of Jesus' own life journey. Imagination is the first and perhaps the fullest way to know God. And the place to imagine best is in the anti-structure toward which the arts lead us. The anti-structure, writes Turner,

> *confronts us with what is at the same time most frightening and potentially creative: the stuff of chaos. No one contemplates the possibility of a pilgrimage without the fear that they will never come back. Perhaps, however, the most deadly diabol is the rationalization we use for never going: the disapproval of the structures to which we have sold our soul.*[24]

Imagination is essential to spirituality. It is the human locus of holiness happening in the human. And the arts are imagination's primary expressive instruments and embodiments.

◆————————————————————————————

1. Sandra M. Schneiders, "Spirituality in the Academy," *Theological Studies* 50 (1989): 684.

2. See John Henry Newman, *An Essay in Aid of a Grammar of Assent,* intro. by Nicholas Lash (Notre Dame: University of Notre Dame Press, 1870/1979).

3. Gilbert Durand, *Les Structures anthropologique de l'imaginaire. Introduction a l'archetypologie general* (Paris: Bordas, 1969), 111–2, quoted from George S. Worgul, Jr., *From Magic to Metaphor* (New York: Paulist Press, 1980), 80.

4. Ibid.

5. Søren Kierkegaard, *Journals,* 243, and *Concluding Unscientific Postscript* (Princeton: Princeton University Press, 1941), 311.

6. William Lynch, *Images of Hope* (Baltimore: Helicon Press, 1965), 243, 256.

7. Matthias Neuman, OSB, "The Role of Imagination in Fundamental Theology," unpublished essay, 14, 18.

8. Owen Barfield, *Saving the Appearances: A Study in Idolatry* (New York: Harcourt, Brace and World, 1965), 89.

9. Quoted in William Greider, "Einstein Is Celebrated as 'Victorious Child,'" *The Washington Post* (March 22, 1979): Section A, 20.

10. Ibid.

11. Ibid.

12. Theodore W. Jennings, *Introduction to Theology* (Philadelphia: Fortress Press, 1976), 17–8.

13. Urban T. Holmes, *Ministry and Imagination* (New York: Seabury Press, 1976), 109.

14. John Shea, *Stories of Faith* (Chicago: Thomas More Press, 1980), 95.

15. Robert D. Young, *Religious Imagination* (Philadelphia: Westminster Press, 1979), 25.

16. Reuben Alves, *Tomorrow's Child: Imagination, Creativity and the Rebirth of Culture* (New York: Harper and Row, 1972), 89.

17. Ibid., 91, 98, 100.

18. John Coulson, "Belief and Imagination," *Downside Review* 90:298 (January 1972): 14.

19. Holmes, *Ministry and Imagination,* 95–6.

20. Barfield, *Saving the Appearances: A Study in Idolatry,* 137.

21. Holmes, *Ministry and Imagination,* 2.

22. Alfred North Whitehead, *The Aims of Education and Other Essays* (New York: New American Library, 1929/1963), 141.

23. Leonardo Boff, *Jesus Christ Liberator* (Maryknoll: Orbis, 1978), 90–1.

24. Victor Turner, *The Forest of Symbols: Aspects of Ndembu Ritual* (Ithaca: Cornell University Press, 1967), 93–101.

In liturgy as in life, the stakes are high. Perhaps we are at a point in our social and ecclesiastical history when we need to recognize once more the indispensable place of the poets among us—poets who guard and multiply the vital force of language, who make speech a dam against oblivion. Perhaps the poets are the ones who can remind us that our language does, after all, have a future tense . . . Above all, the poets are those who know that the frontiers of language, real as they are, border not on nothingness, but on three other great modes of statement—light, music and silence, proofs of a transcendent Presence in the fabric of our world. Where the word of the poet ceases, a great light begins.

Nathan Mitchell, "The Amen Corner: Wrestling with the Word," *Worship* 66:5 (September 1992): 465.

On the Vocation of the Preacher

John Allyn Melloh, SM

On December 4, 1963, the Second Vatican Council published *Sacrosanctum Concilium*, the Constitution on the Sacred Liturgy.[1] This document provided a clear statement of the vision of the Council regarding the renewal of the liturgy. One of its most important facets was its declaration that "[t]he treasures of the Bible are to be opened up more lavishly so that a richer fare may be provided for the faithful at the table of God's word"[2] by providing for a "more representative" portion of the scriptures to be read over a prescribed number of years. Importantly, the constitution boldly stated that the homily "is to be highly esteemed as part of the liturgy itself"[3] and that such preaching would have as a goal the expounding of the mysteries of faith and principles for living the Christ-life. SC stated in addition that preaching is characterized by "proclamation of God's wonderful works in the history of salvation, that is, the mystery of Christ, which is ever made present and active within us, especially in the celebration of the liturgy."[4]

Almost two years later, *Christus Dominus,* the decree on the pastoral office of bishops, noted that one of the "principal duties" of the bishops is "proclaim[ing] the gospel of Christ."[5] *Presbyterorum ordinis,* which appeared two months after *Christus Dominus,* identified the "first task" of priests as preaching the "Gospel of God to all," for it is the word of the living God which creates and forms the People of God. Additionally the decree notes that priests "owe it to everybody to share with them the truth of the Gospel"[6] through a ministry of the word, through exemplary living and through sound teaching.

The decree on the apostolate of the laity, *Apostolicam actuositatem,*[7] states that "according to their abilities the laity ought to cooperate in all the apostolic and missionary enterprises of their ecclesial family."[8] This stout charge is explored further in the document, which notes that the lay apostolate may take on many forms, all of which build up the church and sanctify the world, allowing the Christ-life to flourish.[9] First and foremost is a genuine witness of a life, marked by faith, hope and charity. Then follows the "apostolate of the word, which in certain circumstances is absolutely necessary, [whereby] the laity proclaim Christ."[10]

In 1979, the Committee on Priestly Life and Ministry of the National Conference of Catholic Bishops (NCCB) decided to address specifically the question of preaching in the United States for several reasons: Surveys indicated that the quality of preaching and homily preparation needed improvement, and the Committee wished to bring to the attention of bishops and priests the need for continuing education in homiletics. Additionally the Committee wished to provide useful information for improving the quality of preaching and wanted to make recommendations to the NCCB so that a higher standard of preaching would become normative at parochial, diocesan and national levels.[11]

The publication of *Fulfilled in Your Hearing* (FIYH) gave a great impetus to the ministry of the preached word and especially to the Sunday homily. In the first chapter, the preacher is identified as a mediator, one who represents both the community and Christ. The preacher voices the community's concerns and also offers the word of the Lord—a word of healing, pardon, acceptance and love.[12] FIYH states that "the preacher . . . has a formidable task: to speak from the Scriptures . . . to a gathered congregation in such a way that those assembled will be able to worship God in spirit and truth, and then go forth to love and serve the Lord."[13]

What is striking about the treatment of preaching in the aforementioned conciliar and post-conciliar documents is the language used in speaking of the ministry of the word. Although the decrees on the pastoral offices of bishop and presbyter and the apostolate of the laity provide a rich, theologically grounded spirituality for ministry in general and for the ministry of the word in particular, they do not employ the traditional Catholic language of "vocation." The terms *task* and *duty* are those used most frequently, and preaching seems to be relegated to the category of *function,* albeit an important one.

In this essay I would like to explore the notion of the "vocation of the preacher," with an eye toward discerning the subterranean foundation for the "task," "duty" and "function" of the preacher. I do not intend to offer an historical overview or even historical "soundings" from various periods, nor do I wish to examine the vocation from the viewpoint of juridic ecclesiology. Rather, I propose to examine the question of the vocation of the preacher from four vantage points: (1) systematic theology, drawing especially on the work of Catherine LaCugna; (2) liturgical theology, basing my considerations on Alexander Schmemann's sacramentology; (3) biblical theology, focusing on Walter Brueggemann's theology of the Old Testament; and (4) ritual studies, employing Victor Turner's study of liminality. This is a modest undertaking and does not intend at all to be comprehensive.[14]

Systematic Theology

In her magisterial treatise on the Trinity, *God for Us,*[15] Catherine LaCugna begins with the following statement:

The doctrine of the Trinity is ultimately a practical doctrine with radical consequences for Christian life. That is the thesis of this book. The doctrine of the Trinity, which is the specifically Christian way of speaking about God, summarizes what it means to participate in the life of God through Jesus Christ in the Spirit. The mystery of God is revealed in Christ and the Spirit as the mystery of love, the mystery of persons in communion who embrace death, sin, and all forms of alienation for the sake of life. Jesus Christ, the visible icon of the invisible God, disclosed what it means to be fully personal, divine as well as human. The Spirit of God, poured into our hearts as love (Romans 5:5), gathers us together into the body of Christ, transforming us as that "we become by grace what God is by nature," namely, persons in full communion with God and with every creature.[16]

The first part of the work treats how God's relationship to us in the economy of salvation *(oikonomia)* reveals and is grounded in the eternal being of God *(theologia)*, while the second part of the work teases out the multifaceted consequences of a revitalized doctrine of the Trinity. For the investigation at hand the last two chapters of the book are the most pertinent, since they deal with the themes of doxology and living trinitarian faith. Toward the conclusion of the book, LaCugna speaks of the "vocation of the theologian":

The vocation of the theologian is the same vocation that every creature shares: to glorify God. The theologian speaks of God on the basis of God's self-revelation in the face of Christ and the ongoing presence of the Spirit. The theologian, in other words, must hope that his or her thoughts and words are true and that they glorify God. It is quite clear that the confidence and authority for speaking in this way cannot be granted or revoked by anyone other than the Spirit of God because the Spirit is both the source and criterion for speaking of God.[17]

I want to explore LaCugna's thesis by considering first the vocation of praising and glorifying God and second some specific consequences for the life of the preacher. If one changes the word "theologian" to "preacher" in the above quotation, then what one concludes is that ultimately the vocation of the preacher is the shared vocation of all creatures, that is, to glorify God. "Praise is the duty and delight, the ultimate vocation of the human community; indeed, of all creation."[18] Paralleling LaCugna's thought, Walter Brueggemann comments:

> all of life is aimed toward God and finally exists for the sake
> of God. Praise articulates and embodies our capacity to yield,
> submit, and abandon ourselves in trust and gratitude to the One
> whose we are. Praise is not only a human requirement and
> a human need, it is also a human delight. We have a resilient
> hunger to move beyond self, to return our energy and worth to
> the One from whom it has been granted. In our return to that
> One, we find our deepest joy. That is what it means to "glorify
> God and enjoy God forever."[19]

It is God's sovereignty that makes praise a duty; it is God's compassion that makes praise a delight. Our God "evokes address of gratitude and awe, simply because of who God is."[20] Brueggemann speaks of "that *vocation* which is both duty and delight."[21]

For clarity's sake I note the following. First of all, God has no need of our praise.[22] By rendering praise to God, however, we are most fully human, since that is the purpose for which we were made: "We who first hoped in Christ have been destined and appointed to live for the praise of God's glory" (Ephesians 1:12). "This vocation to glory is rooted in God's providential plan, our election 'before the foundation of the world to be holy and blameless before God'" (Ephesians 1:4).[23] That God does not "need" our praise, however, is indisputable, for praise can add nothing to God, since God and not the creature is the cause of God's own perfection and completeness. Still it is true that God's "Godhood" is made actual or realized when all of creation glorifies God. Thus, "praise perfects perfection."[24] "Praise generates more praise; glory adds to glory. Praise works by overflow and contagion; it invites others to join in. God is made our God when creation and humanity render praise to God."[25] Thus, by praising God humanity is fulfilling its divinely appointed vocation. In so doing the community of praise is fashioning a world,[26] a socially created reality, in which God holds primacy of place.[27]

Second, lamentation should not be overlooked as a mighty expression of doxology.[28] Jesus in the Garden of Gethsemane and upon the cross models for us the power of lament. According to Mark and Matthew, "My God, My God, why have you forsaken me?" were the sole words uttered by Jesus on the cross—the cry of the righteous one abandoned by God. Yet the gospel accounts include this "scandalous" cry precisely because it was uttered as a prayer.[29] Christian lament is still genuine praise of God, for in lamenting the afflicted one cries out to God in a spirit of desperate trust, protesting and confessing God's promises so that one may be made whole again.[30]

Third, no human being, marked with original sin, achieves perfection in this life, which is marked by grace, but also by sinfulness. Sin is the absence of right relationship—with God, self, others and the world.[31] One could describe Christian theological ethics from this standpoint as whether or not acts glorify God and serve to establish righteous communion among persons. Through praising and rendering thanks to God, our relationship with God is established rightfully; so too, at least potentially, are our relationships with one another, past, present and future. When the assembly together glorifies and honors God, we may discover "the strongest of objective bonds with others: the link through the reality of God."[32] Doxology actuates a genuine communion of persons, thus creating or reinforcing a theological worldview characterized by right relationship.

As stated above, it is LaCugna's well-founded belief that the theologian speaks of God first on the basis of divine revelation through Jesus Christ and the ongoing presence of the Spirit. One effect of trinitarian doctrine is to help thinking correctly about how *theologia* and *oikonomia* are related; and the overarching purpose of any theology or any human activity is God's glorification. The thoughts and words of the theologian ought to be truthful—and thereby, are words that offer glory to God.[33] However, as LaCugna notes, "theology is not theology—*theos-logos*, discourse about God—unless it proceeds in the mode of praise."[34] To be in communion with the church is for the "inner moment" of a theologian's work to be the praise of God. In a similar fashion the thoughts and words of the preacher ought to manifest God's truth and proceed in the manner of doxology, that is the "inner core" is the praise of God.[35]

The basis then of all preaching is a doxological stance toward God. Such a stance embraces praise and thanksgiving, but also complaint and lament. Consider the fact that a survey among parishioners indicated that what the majority hoped for in the homily was "simply to hear a person of faith speaking."[36] The preacher is one who speaks about faith and life. How can the preacher speak authentically about faith and life? Such truthful proclamation can come only from one who contemplates the depths of life and the mysteries of faith. Only if the preacher is conscious of the vocation of glorifying God can he or she arrive at a fuller understanding of the genuine meaning of life. Only if the preacher "rehearses" attitudes of praise and thanksgiving, complaint and lament during the moments of life can the words spoken ring as true and authentic. Without a clear grasp of commonly shared Christian vocation, that is, the glorification of God, preaching can easily devolve into purely theological speculation, arcane exegetical exposition, or even pop psychology.

More, however, can be said about this doxological stance, since the purpose of preaching is also itself doxological. Preaching itself—

through its truthful and loving embrace of the God revealed in Christ and through the Spirit—renders praise to God. It is itself a part of the liturgical act, whose primary purpose is the worship and glorification of God. Along similar lines, FIYH notes that the liturgical homily helps the members of the assembly to recognize the saving presence of God in their lives and to turn to God "with praise and thanksgiving."[37] God's active presence among God's people leads to a response of praiseful thanksgiving.

LaCugna writes that "confessing faith is incomplete unless it becomes a form of life."[38] Authentic praiseful preaching comes from the mouth of the preacher who confesses trinitarian faith as a lived reality. This certainly does not mean that the preacher is more perfect or holier than the gathered assembly, but it does mean that the one who speaks God's truth is striving to live that truth.

If the Trinity is the perfect communion of persons—living in right relationship—then living trinitarian faith calls for living in right relationship in a communion of persons.[39] As the first sentence in *God for Us* patently states, "The doctrine of the Trinity is ultimately a practical doctrine with radical consequences for Christian life."[40] When one recognizes one's vocation as a call to praise and render thanks to God, then one is committed to living out the consequences, especially living in "right relationship," as exemplified by God's trinitarian life. LaCugna suggests that doxology is "the animating power of right relationship," which is attained when

> we give God the glory, whether in the public assembly or in the ordinary tasks of daily living. [When] we are in right relationship to other creatures including the goods of the earth, when we acknowledge that everything has its own intrinsic reason for existing (ratio), its own purpose (telos) other than to serve the needs and desires of human beings. . . . We are in right relationship to ourselves when we accept that our origin, existence and destiny belong not to ourselves but to God. . . . Finally,

we are in right relationship to other persons when we see them
not as means to an end, nor as creatures designed to meet our
relational needs, but persons in their own right who share the
same destiny of glory.[41]

If the homily in the Sunday assembly is to expound the "guiding principles of the Christian life," gleaned from the proclamation of God's word, then it is through living in right relationship that the preacher can then speak authentically of these principles.[42] Preaching out of life experiences—including not only the glory, but also the lament—makes for grounded preaching, which will be heard as both convicted and convincing speech, not as a collection of abstract notions.

Ultimately, the vocation of the preacher is the same profound vocation of the Christian—to render thanks and praise to God in all the moments of life. In the very act of preaching, the word of truth and love ought to manifest this most fundamental stance toward life.

Liturgical Theology

In 1973 Russian Orthodox theologian Alexander Schmemann wrote a gem of a book on sacramentology from the Orthodox perspective titled *For the Life of the World*.[43] This short treatise reveals the soul of one immersed in God's love and fully committed to a theology of liturgy that refuses to separate liturgy from life. Schmemann holds that the act of worship gathers together the church, the world and the kingdom of God in such a way that in it that world for which Jesus Christ the Savior was given up is offered back to God.

In this book, Schmemann shows how the paschal mystery is the cosmic fulfillment of humanity's vocation. For him, worship is an epiphany that reveals humanity's communion in the divine life because of Christ's resurrection. This divine life changes all of creation and also the church—the presence of the kingdom of God—revealing life's depths in sacramental celebration. Schmemann begins with a consideration of the eucharist as the celebration that designates the identity of the Christian as a worshiper of God through Christ and in the Spirit. He then in turn treats the other sacraments. Schmemann does not specifically treat the question of preaching or the vocation of the preacher, yet his commentary on ordination yields fruitful insights that are worth exploring.[44]

By his sacrificial death, Christ revealed the essence of priesthood to be love. In so doing, Schmemann contends, priestly *religion* died and priestly *life* was inaugurated.[45] Christ's sacrifice abolished religion "because it destroyed that wall of separation between the 'natural' and the 'supernatural,' the 'profane' and the 'sacred,' the 'this-worldly' and the 'other-worldly'—which was the only justification and *raison d'etre* of religion. He revealed that all things, all natures have their end, their fulfillment in the Kingdom; that all things are to be made new by love."[46]

Schmemann notes that Christ, the Savior, is the new Adam, the restorer of the old Adam's mission. Adam failed to be priest of the world and this failure resulted in the fact that the world ceased to be sacrament of the divine love and presence; the world became merely "nature."[47] Schmemann claims that consequently in the "natural world" (or one might say de-sacramentalized world), religion became an organized transaction with the supernatural. The priest was set apart as the "transactor," a mediator between what was natural and what was supernatural.[48] Thus, life and worship became dichotomous.

Schmemann holds in addition that centuries of clericalism "have made the priest or minister beings apart, with a unique and specifically 'sacred' vocation in the church. This vocation is not only different from, it is indeed opposed to all those that are 'profane.'"[49] The most unfortunate consequence of this opposition is that it caused the church to forget "that to be priest is from a profound point of view the most natural thing in the world.[50] Man was created priest of the world, the one who offers the world to God in a sacrifice of love and praise, and who, through this eternal eucharist, bestows the divine love upon the world."[51] To be "priest of the world" is the vocation of all humankind—it is to offer the world to God in a sacrifice of praise and love. Everything from God is good and should be received with thanksgiving, as Paul says in 1 Timothy 1:4. To be priest of the world is to receive all God's blessings with thanksgiving.[52]

Yet more is implied insofar as the "priest of the world" *offers* the world to God, as Schmemann puts it. How is it possible to "offer" the world—which God created—to God? Here the distinction between "market" and "symbolic" exchange assists in probing the question. In market exchange, whether through barter or money, value is at stake; for example, apples are bartered for kiwis, or money is given for a loaf of bread. In symbolic exchange, however, value is not the primary concern; there is a logic of gratuitousness, where one gives without counting.[53]

Symbolic exchange is less about the actual matter of the exchange, than about the relationship that obtains thereby. Thus as Louis-Marie Chauvet states, in symbolic exchange "subjects exchange themselves"; the dynamic at work is that of bonding. While the logic of symbolic exchange is that of gratuitousness and generosity, it also belongs to the domain of "necessary obligation." For instance, a dinner invitation leaves one "much obliged," but that does not imply that the same offering in kind must be made, that is, an exchange of exact value. That return exchange is outside the realm of calculation and computation; there is no parity involved.[54]

Chauvet suggests, "Whereas in the physical order the more two things are opposed the more they are different, in the symbolic order the more two subjects recognize their similitude the more they are different."[55] In the symbolic order difference is registered as otherness. Such otherness, in terms of symbolic exchange, is the mutual recognition of persons as partners. In other words, returning to the above example, the return exchange recognizes not only the gift (the dinner), but also the giver (the other).

It is only in the sense of symbolic exchange that the human being can "offer" the world to God. In such an exchange what is given and received is fundamentally the gift of the self to the other. This sort of exchange expresses a mutual recognition and mutual bonding. What the "priest of the world" offers is nothing more and nothing less than the "self." This "offering" may be symbolized as a token gift or it may be verbalized words offered to the other.[56]

I would contend, following Schmemann's thought, that the vocation of the preacher is "the most natural thing in the world," for it is to be "priest of the world," offering to God what created beings can indeed offer, namely words of grateful loving acknowledgement. Indeed it is to offer a "sacrifice of praise" through which divine love is recognized in all of creation.[57] The *Catechism of the Catholic Church* (CCC) speaks of the profound and common destiny of creation and of humanity, quoting Romans:

> *For the creation waits with eager longing for the revealing of the children of God . . . in hope that the creation itself will be set free from its bondage to decay. . . . We know that the whole creation has been groaning in labor pains until now; and not only the creation, but we ourselves, who have the first fruits of the Spirit, groan inwardly while we wait for adoption, the redemption of our bodies. (Romans 8:19–23)*[58]

All creation, the world and its inhabitants, share a common destiny, awaiting final redemption.[59] Yet, living in the "in between," the preacher recognizes this common destiny and offers thanks. "The world was made for the glory of God"[60] and the "glory of God consists in the realization of this manifestation and communication of his goodness, for which the world was created."[61] To come to this "realization" and to offer the world to God in symbolic exchange is to engage in an act rightly described by Schmemann as "this eternal eucharist."[62] Such an offering is a symbolic exchange of love, which is at the heart of the matter of Christ's unique priesthood.

The CCC expresses notions similar to those of Schmemann and solidly links creation and the eucharistic celebration:

> The Eucharist, the sacrament of our salvation accomplished by
> Christ on the cross, is also a sacrifice of praise in thanksgiving
> for the work of creation. In the Eucharistic sacrifice the whole
> of creation loved by God is presented to the Father through
> the death and the Resurrection of Christ. Through Christ the
> Church can offer the sacrifice of praise in thanksgiving for all
> that God has made good, beautiful, and just in creation and
> in humanity.[63]

Schmemann refers to an "eternal eucharist," meaning an unending sacrifice of praise and thanksgiving. The catechism refers specifically to the sacramental eucharistic celebration. Yet the CCC's specificity does not vitiate the notion of an ongoing thanksgiving by one who would preach the word of God in love.[64] In fact it is the ongoing symbolic exchange of love with God that in fact prepares one to celebrate the eucharist most fully.

To preach as a "priest of the world" is to embrace the world—cosmos and all creation—and offer it to the Creator God in loving symbolic exchange. It implies rehearsing an attitude of thanksgiving in all of life, even its imperfection and yearning for completion; this is an "eternal eucharistic attitude."

Biblical Theology

Walter Brueggemann's *Theology of the Old Testament*[65] is a tour de force in which the author succeeds in presenting a non-reductionistic analysis of Israel's faith, dealing with all its complexity. Brueggemann does not seek an easy balance among the various voices in which Israel's god-talk is disputed. In this work he looks at the Old Testament primarily as testimony—that is, the uttered account of God's deeds and doing which constantly shapes Israel's understanding of its God.

Part I of this book presents the "core testimony" about God and Israel's encounter and the speech that issues forth therefrom. The verbal testimony communicates to two different audiences; one type of testimony is geared toward reordering the internal life of Israel in ways faithful to God; the other speaks to the world beyond with an invitation for re-conceptualizing community life with reference to God.

Part II treats what Brueggemann terms the "counter testimony" of dispute and advocacy. The more settled convictions found in the "core testimony" are challenged by other biblical voices, especially voices represented in the Wisdom literature and the psalms. This sometime abrasive and defiant speech is confrontational; yet this confrontation is part of covenantal relationship, indicating a genuine mutual partnership between "a most peculiar God" and Israel which makes the Old Testament "endlessly interesting, generative and unsettling."[66]

Regarding the investigation at hand, what is apropos is the consideration of Israel's speech about God and with God. Brueggemann suggests that the largest rubric under which to consider Israel's speech about God is that of testimony.[67] The main question guiding his work is how ancient Israel actually speaks about God. Even though much of the Hebrew scriptures is constituted of words spoken to Israel by God, Brueggemann does not distinguish between the two, since both function as testimony.[68]

The most proper setting for testimony is the law court, in which witnesses are called to relate what happened, presenting their version of what is true. Evidence presented is a mixed matter of memory, imagination, desire and reconstruction. It is, however, on the basis of testimonial data alone that the court must determine what is real. In other words, "reality" is arrived at through a process of social construction of the truth.[69]

That there is a trial implies that some reality is in question. Various witnesses who allegedly had access to the event are qualified to speak on the basis of their having seen and experienced the matter in dispute. The actual event, however, is subject to many and varied retellings, some of which have only slightly differing nuances, while others are drastically different. The court has no purchase on the event, except through testimony. The testimony must be taken as the real portrayal of what happened.

Note that the witness is able to choose *how* to speak about the event. The choice of construal may be a calculated utterance based on the witness' bias or it may be one made without any vested interest. At the time when the witness utters the testimony, it is a public proclamation that "shapes, enjoins or constitutes reality." What is said causes something to be; in this sense testimony is originary. Finally when the court renders its verdict, the testimony becomes reality.[70]

"If we describe this process theologically," in terms of the practice in the Hebrew scriptures, Brueggemann comments, "we may say that testimony becomes revelation." It is the utterance that leads to reality; just as it is the uttered court testimony that leads to reality.[71] It is obvious that there are various kinds of testimony in Israel's speech about God. The author contends, however, that one must discern what is Israel's "characteristic" speech about God—not the earliest or most original—but the most usual modes of speech. Certainly quantity weighs in as a factor, but beyond that, Israel's speech in boundary or liminal situations is crucial—how Israel speaks in its "most freighted, exalted or exposed situations."[72]

As a beginning point, Brueggemann proposes the testimony of *todah,* a confessional statement of gratitude and thanksgiving, whereby Israel expresses its amazement, joy and thanks for a gift or deed that radically changes Israel's circumstances. Brueggemann's proposal is that the genesis for articulating an Old Testament theology is in the liturgical (and therefore public) acknowledgment of a new reality wrought by God. Not only the genesis, but also the full utterance today of Israel's faith is found in public acts of thanksgiving within the assembly.[73]

This public proclamation of thanksgiving serves as a polemic against the adversary, that is, the joyful identification with God puts the (defeated) adversary in a position of diminishment, often with a tone of condescension and gloating. Additionally any not-yet-committed observer of this *todah* utterance is viewed as holding a position that is at best ludicrous.[74] Brueggemann suggests that "the course of Israel's testimony about God attends to the way in which this God—full of sovereign power and committed in solidarity to the needy, and especially to Israel in need—dominates the narrative of Israel's liturgy and imagination."[75]

Brueggemann makes two significant points which impinge on the vocation of the preacher. First, the "testimony that Israel bears to the character of God is taken by the ecclesial community of the text as a reliable disclosure about the true character of God."[76] Just as the testimony of the scriptures is taken, grasped and apprehended as reliable, so too in an analogous way is the testimony of the preacher. The "court testimony" is an utterance of truth in the face of disputatious witnesses and in the presence of the adversary.[77] Put otherwise, the preaching event—the testimony of the preacher—is taken as a reliable witness within the ecclesial community, bearing witness to the deeds of God.

Second, the starting point for articulating Israel's faith is a liturgical declaration. Thus, the privileged place for the reception of the testimony of God is within the liturgical celebration. The acknowledgment of God's gifts and God's wonderful deeds is the starting point for understanding God's commitment in solidarity to all those in need.

Paul VI's *Evangelii nuntiandi* of 1975 seems to suggest that the preacher indeed should be a witness, one who bears truthful testimony. The first means of evangelization, states this Apostolic Exhortation, is the "witness of an authentically Christian life, given over to God in a communion that nothing should destroy and at the same time given to one's neighbor with limitless zeal."[78] The pope notes that the witness of detachment, poverty and freedom—in a word, sanctity—is a key to evangelization. "Modern man listens more willingly to witnesses than to teachers, and if he does listen to teachers, it is because they are witnesses."[79]

Immediately after mentioning the witness of Christian living, however, Paul VI emphasizes the importance and necessity of preaching.

> *Preaching, the verbal proclamation of a message, is indeed always*
> *indispensable. We are well aware that modern man is sated by*
> *talk . . . obviously often tired of listening and, what is worse,*
> *impervious to words. We are also aware that many psychologists*
> *and sociologists express the view that modern man has passed*
> *beyond the civilization of the word, which is now ineffective and*
> *useless, and that today . . . lives in the civilization of the image.*
> *These facts should certainly impel us to employ, for the purpose*
> *of transmitting the Gospel message, the modern means which*
> *this civilization has produced. . . . The word remains ever*
> *relevant, especially when it is the bearer of the power of God.*
> *This is why St. Paul's axiom, "Faith comes from what is heard,"*
> *also retains its relevance: it is the Word that is heard which leads*
> *to belief.*[80]

Additionally the exhortation singles out the liturgical celebration as an especially apt venue for preaching and notes that many "parochial or other communities live and are held together thanks to the Sunday homily," when it is "simple, clear, direct, well-adapted, profoundly dependent on Gospel teaching and faithful to the magisterium, animated by a balanced apostolic ardor . . . full of hope, fostering belief, and productive of peace and unity."[81] Note, too, that twice in this paragraph the pope mentions the necessity of love—a message impregnated with love and a love that produces devotion to preaching.[82]

Following the leads of Brueggemann and Pope Paul VI, I would assert that the preacher is called upon to offer testimony, to bear witness. What witnesses testify to is what their experience has been—what they have seen, heard and so forth.[83] In other words, witnesses testify to an actually posited event. Law court witnesses, at least in the United States, are not permitted to speculate nor are they permitted to offer conclusions—it is the court which makes that determination. The preacher's vocation is to be a witness to God—not to an abstract notion of God—but rather to a living God who through the outpoured Spirit is at work in the world. Preachers testify to their experience of God's active presence in their lives and in the world. If preachers need at times to testify to the thwarting of Spirit's mission in the world, let them do so, but modestly and moderately, for there are scarcely any individuals who do not know both personally and socially the ravages of sin. Let preachers, however, boldly bear witness to the experience—seen, heard, looked upon and touched—of the grace of God operating in this broken world. Let them not fuss excessively with the expounding of abstractions about God or theological niceties of doctrine, but rather present, as Paul VI suggested, concrete and real images evidencing the reign of God's hold in the world and the overcoming of demonic power.

Ritual Studies

In addition to the systematic, liturgical and biblical theological perspectives discussed, I would like to turn my attention to the work of the anthropologist Victor Turner. Turner's works have had widespread influence, but his major contribution, according to Mathieu Deflem, is his analysis of the dynamics of ritual, where his writings complement French structuralism while moving in a slightly different direction, as Turner accounts not only for what is said about ritual but also about the myriad relationships that occur during the ritual engagement.[84]

Turner really has nothing at all to say directly about preaching, much less of the vocation of the preacher. So why consider his ideas? I do so for two reasons. First, both LaCugna and Brueggemann give a privileged place to preaching within the liturgical context. This context is basically a ritual engagement.[85] Thus, in this section I will turn attention to the ritual setting of liturgical preaching. Second, a major focus of Turner's work has been on the elucidation of the notion of liminality, where he elaborated on van Gennep's discussion of liminality in passage rites. I would posit, without much formal justification, the fact that Christian engagement in liturgical rites is an experience of liminality. I hold that since Christians are living between Christ's resurrection, ascension and Spirit-sending and Christ's final return in glory, or, put another way, Christians live in the "already" and the "not yet."[86]

Anthropologist Arnold van Gennep has demonstrated that rites of passage are marked by three phases: separation (that is, detachment from an earlier fixed point in the social structure); liminality (that is, an ambiguous state with none or few of the attributes of the past or future state); and aggregation (that is, re-incorporation with a new, stable state with clearly defined rights and obligations). The situation of liminal persons is necessarily ambiguous, since these persons elude or slip through the usual cultural classifications. Turner notes that "liminal entities are neither here nor there; they are betwixt and between the positions assigned and arrayed by law, custom, convention and ceremonial."[87] Turner admits:

I have used the term "anti-structure". . . to describe both liminality and what I have called "communitas." I meant by it not a structural reversal . . . but the liberation of human capacities of cognition, affect, volition, creativity, etc., from the normative constraints incumbent upon occupying a sequence of social statuses.[88]

In the liminal period—and for our purpose of discussion within the liturgical act—there are moments in an out of time, in and out of secular social structure, which reveal a "generalized social bonding." Additionally, Turner contends, what emerges is a society "unstructured or rudimentarily structured and relatively undifferentiated *communitas,* community or even communion of equal individuals who submit together to the general authority of the ritual elders."[89]

Turner identifies three distinct components of the liminal stage.[90] The first is the communication of the *sacra,* that is, the sacred symbols of the community. These include objects (what is shown), actions (what is done) and instructions (what is said, for example, myths, stories and so forth). To ensure both unity and continuity in community, members must have a shared vision. The second component of the liminal stage is (awkwardly) termed ludic deconstruction and recombination of familiar cultural configuration. During this period the familiar can be exaggerated or distorted, the purpose of which is to force reflection on both the social and cosmological orders. Often the familiar is taken for granted; the hope—in de-familiarizing—is in service to revitalized understanding. The third component of the liminal stage is a simplification of relations in the social order. Fundamentally during liminality, there are the adepts, that is, the "instructors," and there are the submissive and obedient neophytes. Among the liminal persons, there is absolute equality. Such radical equality gives rise to *communitas* and sometimes an intense comradeship and egalitarianism among the liminal persons. During the liminal phase of ritual, ascribed status, roles, and so forth, are of no account.[91]

How does this discussion of Turner's views of liminality impinge on preaching? In the first place, as Turner suggests, in the liminal phase there is a simplification of social relations; there are the adepts and those to be "initiated." The "ritual elders" wield a general authority. Within the liturgical celebration there is but one "ritual elder," Jesus the Christ, "firstborn of creation" (Colossians 1:15) who in the power of the Spirit joins with his church so that Head and members offer worship to God. The assembled People of God form an "undifferentiated *comitatus,* community, or even communion of equal individuals," in Turner's words.[92] Thus, for the purpose of this discussion, there is the one "ritual elder" and—using Turner's terminology—the (so-termed) "neophytes." The usual social relations are "simplified."[93]

What preaching does, following Turner's notions, is ensure both a unity and historical continuity within the Christian body by presenting the *sacra*.[94] First and foremost, the word proclaimed is one of the presences of Christ in the assembly. Speaking from the scriptures, the preacher makes Christ's presence known through the recounting of the "sacred history," which binds Christians together and renews their faithful commitment through a living word that can shape their existence. In offering a vision of the landscape of God's reign, the preacher may indeed be engaged in ludic deconstruction and recombination so that the salient features of this mysterious reign may be in bold relief. If indeed the reign of God is not terribly visible in a broken world, the preacher seeks to point out where glimpses of God's action in the world is present. In a certain sense then the preacher raises a prophetic voice and points toward that which is often hidden by the trite, the evanescent and the quotidian.[95]

Thus, it would appear, judging from preaching within the liturgy, that the preacher takes on the role of adept or "instructor" in a liminal situation. Note, however, that the preacher has no monopoly on the word of God and its extrapolation. Because of the outpoured Spirit, present in all the baptized, preaching Christ in deed and word devolves upon all; yet within the ritual unfolding of the liturgical celebration, only one is appointed to speak, a "ritual adept."

It is within the liminal phase that the dynamic interplay of structure and anti-structure *(communitas)* features most prominently. The dialectical movement is considerable. The immediacy of *communitas* yields to structure; temporary release from structure into *communitas* allows the return to structure revitalized by the experience of *communitas*. This dialectic oscillation, however, is in service to a greater good, namely the unity of the group. The generic bond among individuals and its related sentiment of "humankindness" is the result of persons "in their wholeness wholly attending."[96] Yet what is at stake in the liturgical act is more than a "generic bond" of "humankindness." What is crucial is the recognition of bonding one with another through the power of the God's Spirit, which creates "a people made one with the unity of the Father, the Son and the Holy Spirit."[97]

Then, based upon Turner's notions, what is the vocation of the preacher in general? I would contend that whether within or without the liturgical assembly, the preacher is called to announce God's word in such a manner that it fosters the unity among God's people. Within the wonderful diversity of the church, the chosen People of God share a common dignity, have the same filial grace and same vocation to perfection, and possess in common one salvation, one hope and one undivided charity.[98] The preacher's vocation is to call people into unity with the trinitarian God, so that all may model the "right relationship" that animates Father, Son and Spirit, which is nothing more and surely nothing less than love.

Conclusion

What I have offered are considerations on the vocation of the preacher. I submit that the ultimate vocation of the preacher is the same as that of all creatures: to praise and glorify God in all aspects of life. This is the foundation for faithful preaching. Second, the preacher is called to offer the created world back to God in an act of "eternal eucharist," embracing the world as Christ did in an act of love. Third, the preacher is one who bears faithful witness to God's action in the world, discerning the movements of the outpoured Spirit of God. Lastly, the preacher's vocation is to speak within a community so as to raise to consciousness the spiritual bonding and unity that is present among God and God's holy people. The vocation, to borrow Karl Barth's phrase, is to be a "partisan of God." [99]

1. *Sacrosanctum Concilium* 1, in *Vatican II: The Conciliar and Post-Conciliar Documents,* new and rev. ed., ed. Austin Flannery (Collegeville: The Liturgical Press, 1975/1992) [hereafter SC].

2. SC 51.

3. SC 52.

4. SC 35, 2.

5. *Christus Dominus* 12, in *Vatican II: The Conciliar and Post-Conciliar Documents,* 564–90 [hereafter CD].

6. *Presbyterorum ordinis* 4, in *Vatican II: The Conciliar and Post-Conciliar Documents,* 863–902 [hereafter PO].

7. Interestingly, this decree preceded PO by one month.

8. *Apostolicam actuositatem* 10, in *Vatican II: The Conciliar and Post-Conciliar Documents,* 766–98 [hereafter AA]. Although this article does not specifically refer to preaching the gospel as either a task or duty of the laity, "cooperat[ing] in *all* the apostolic and missionary enterprises" certainly does not exclude proclaiming the gospel. [Emphasis added.]

9. AA 16.

10. AA 16.

11. The Bishops' Committee on Priestly Life and Ministry, *Fulfilled in Your Hearing: The Homily in the Sunday Assembly* [hereafter FIYH] (Washington: National Conference of Catholic Bishops, 1982), foreword. This short document is perhaps one of the best expositions of Roman Catholic liturgical preaching in the modern period. Preachers and congregations in the United States owe a great deal of gratitude to the Committee on Priestly Life and Ministry and especially to William Skudlarek, OSB, principal writer of the document.

12. Ibid., 7.

13. Ibid., 19.

14. For instance, I have chosen not to consider some significant contributions made by such theologians as Yves Congar, Edward Schillebeeckx, OP, or Karl Rahner, SJ.

15. Catherine Mowry LaCugna, *God for Us: The Trinity and Christian Life* (San Francisco: HarperSanFrancisco, 1991).

16. Ibid., 1.

17. Ibid., 365.

18. Geoffrey Wainwright, "The Praise of God in the Theological Reflection of the Church," *Interpretation* 39 (1985): 39. Note also that the Roman Catholic eucharistic prayers begin with phrases such as "it is our duty and our salvation . . . to give thanks and praise."

19. Walter Brueggemann, *Israel's Praise: Doxology against Idolatry and Ideology* (Philadelphia: Fortress, 1988), 1.

20. Ibid.

21. Ibid., 3. [Emphasis added.] Bruggemann continues: "to be sure, *praise* is addressed to heaven. . . . But it is equally true that praise is spoken by human voices on earth. The address to God indicates that praise is a theological act of profound dramatic importance. Praise is spoken on earth. Inevitably then, praise is not a pure, unmitigated impingement in heaven. The act also impinges on earth. That is, praise is not only a religious vocation, but it is also a social gesture that effects the shape and character of human life and human community. Inevitably praise does its work among human persons as much as it does in the courts of heaven."

22. Brueggemann comments: "As praise is appropriate to human community, so praise is appropriate to the character of God, for our praise is a response to God's power and mercy. Nothing more can be said to God. Nothing more can be added to God. Nonetheless God must be addressed. It is appropriate to address God in need, by way of petition and intercession. But address in need occurs in a context of lyrical submission in which God is addressed not because we have need, but simply because God is God and we are summoned to turn our lives in answer to God." Ibid., 1.

23. LaCugna, *God for Us,* 342.

24. Ibid., 338. The actual citation is taken from Daniel W. Hardy and David F. Ford, *Praising and Knowing God* (Philadelphia: Westminster, 1985), passim.

25. Ibid.

26. Cf. FIYH 18–9, which speaks of world construal as a sharing of "vision of the world." Cf. Peter L. Berger and Thomas Luckmann, *The Social Construction of Reality: A Treatise in the Sociology of Knowledge* (New York: Doubleday, 1972)

27. LaCugna explains: "Rendering praise to God does not mean simply directing piously exaggerated words toward God in heaven; the act of praise involves us in the very life of God-with-us. Word and gestures of praise are 'performative'; their utterance makes actual the glory of God to which they refer and which they intend. By naming God as recipient of our praise, we are redirected away from ourselves toward God, which is why doxology can be described as a kenotic or self-emptying act. In praise-giving, the 'I' or the 'we' of a people or congregation becomes other-centered, not self-centered." LaCugna, 339. Cf. Brueggemann, *Israel's Praise,* esp. Chapter I, which argues that praise is a constitutive act of world construal. See also USCC, *The Catechism of the Catholic Church* (Garden City, N.Y.: Doubleday, 1995), 2639 [hereafter CCC], which speaks eloquently about praise.

28. LaCugna, 339ff.

29. Louis-Marie Chauvet, *The Sacraments: The Word of God at the Mercy of the Body* (Collegeville: The Liturgical Press, 2001), 161–2; see also 162–4.

30. "Preaching and pastoral practice will have to fight a constant battle to convince us, to provide assurances, to make the case that God is indeed present among us, does indeed care for us, will indeed hear our prayer, and will be lovingly disposed to respond." LaCugna, 411.

31. Ibid., 343.

32. Ibid. Cf. Hardy and Ford, *Praising and Knowing God,* 11.

33. LaCugna, 365.

34. Ibid., 360.

35. SC 52 notes that the liturgical homily is to be esteemed as an integral part of the liturgy. Since the liturgy is ultimately an act of praise and thanksgiving, then the homily, too, ought to be an act of worship in and of itself, that is, directed toward the glorification of God.

36. FIYH 15.

37. Ibid., 26. "In the Eucharistic celebration the homily points to the presence of God in people's lives and then leads a congregation into the Eucharist, providing, as it were, the motive for celebrating the Eucharist in this time and place." FIYH 23. "The challenge to preachers then is to reflect on human life

with the aid of the Word of God and to show by their preaching, as by their lives, that in every place and at every time it is indeed right to praise and thank the Lord." FIYH 28.

38. LaCugna, 377. Cf. CCC 1816: "The disciple of Christ must not only keep the faith and live on it, but also profess it, confidently bear witness to it, and spread it. . . . "

39. Cf. ibid., 243–317 for a full treatment of the notion of "persons in communion." Cf. CCC 2331: "God is love and in himself he lives a mystery of personal loving communion."

40. LaCugna, 1.

41. Ibid., 346–347.

42. Cf. SC 52.

43. Alexander Schmemann, *For the Life of the World: Sacraments and Orthodoxy* (Crestwood: St. Vladimir's Seminary Press, 1973).

44. While examining the "sacraments of vocation," that is, matrimony and ordination, Schmemann specifically addresses presbyteral ordination, that is, the ministerial priesthood. His comments, however, are by extension valid for a consideration of the priesthood of all the baptized.

45. Schmemann, 93. [Emphasis author's.]

46. Ibid. See also Karl Rahner "How to Receive a Sacrament and Mean It," in *The Sacraments: Readings in Contemporary Sacramental Theology,* ed. Michael Taylor (Staten Island: Alba House, 1981), 73; and Michael Skelley, *The Liturgy of the World: Karl Rahner's Theology of Worship* (Collegeville: The Liturgical Press, 1991).

47. Schmemann does not mean that the world ceased to be sacramental, but rather that the modes of apprehending the world as God's gift to humanity were altered.

48. Schmemann, 93. He continues: "And after all, it does not matter too much whether this mediation was understood in terms of magic—as supernatural powers—or in terms of law—as supernatural rights."

49. Ibid.

50. Schmemann is not trying to eliminate or blur the distinction between the ministerial priesthood and the priesthood of the baptized. Clearly his intent is to show that these vocations spring from a common source and as such are not in opposition, but are in fact complementary.

51. Schmemann, 93.

52. Hardy and Ford note that doxology has a logic all its own; it is the logic of overflow, freedom and generosity. Cf. LaCugna, 338. The response to God's generosity is a paean of thanksgiving. To receive life itself demands a lyrical

response of praise. In so doing one offers to God what can be offered—doxological speech.

53. Chauvet, *The Sacraments,* 117–8. Chapter 6 treats symbolic exchange in detail.

54. Ibid., 119.

55. Ibid., 122.

56. Ibid., 122–3.

57. Cf. Edward J. Kilmartin, SJ, "*Sacrificium Laudis:* Content and Function of Early Eucharistic Prayers," *Theological Studies* 35 (1974): 268–87.

58. CCC 1046.

59. Even though all creation awaits the fullness of redemption, still the assembly prays in the eucharistic prayer: "Holy, Holy, Holy Lord, God of power and might, heaven and earth are full of your glory." For a poetic reflection on the Holy, cf. Annie Dillard, *Teaching a Stone to Talk: Expeditions and Encounters* (New York: Harper & Row, 1982), 31–4.

60. *Dei Filius,* canon 5: DS 3025; quoted in CCC 293.

61. CCC 294.

62. Schmemann, *For the Life of the World,* 93.

63. CCC 1359.

64. CCC 1361 states: "The Eucharist is also the sacrifice of praise by which the Church sings the glory of God in the name of all creation. This sacrifice of praise is possible only through Christ: he unites the faithful to his person, to his praise, and to his intercession, so that the sacrifice of praise to the Father is offered *through* Christ and *with* him, to be accepted *in* him." If one is "in Christ" through the sacrament of baptism, then one continually offers praise and prayer through Christ Jesus.

65. Walter Brueggemann, *Theology of the Old Testament: Testimony, Dispute, Advocacy* (Minneapolis: Fortress Press, 1997).

66. Brueggemann, *Theology of the Old Testament,* 409–10.

67. Ibid., 118.

68. Ibid. Appeal to testimony requires a radical break with positivistic epistemology. In appealing to testimony, one begins in a different place and thus arrives at a different type of certitude. Cf. Elie Wiesel, "The Holocaust as Literary Inspiration," *Dimensions of Holocaust* (Evanston: Northwestern University Press, 1977), who has understood the importance of testimony in his aphorism: "If the Greeks invented tragedy, the Romans the epistle, and the Renaissance the sonnet, our generation invented a new literature, that of testimony," 9. See also Shoshana Felman and Dori Laub, *Testimony: Crisis of Witnessing in Literature, Psychoanalysis and History* (New York: Routledge, 1992). Felman and Laub see

that testimony is urgent when truth is in crisis, that is, when there exists a crisis of evidence, such as exists in our day. [Quote in ibid., 119, footnote 6d.]

69. When, for example in a criminal trial, the jury declares "Not guilty," the defendant is *de jure* not guilty of the alleged crime, despite the actuality of the event in question.

70. Brueggemann, 121.

71. Ibid.

72. Ibid., 122.

73. Ibid., 128.

74. Ibid.

75. Ibid., 144.

76. Ibid., 121.

77. Cf. Thomas G. Long, *The Witness of Preaching* (Louisville: Westminster/John Knox Press, 1989). Under the rubric of "preacher as herald of God's word," Long treats Barth's theology of proclamation. After a balanced and gentle critique of Barth's view, Long adopts the model of preaching as "bearing witness." Cf. ibid., pp. 24–30. It strikes me, however, that the two views could be conflated.

78. *Evangelii nuntiandi* 41, in *Vatican II: More Post-Conciliar Documents,* ed. Austin Flannery (Northport: Costello, 1982), 711–61 [hereafter EN].

79. Pope Paul VI, "Address to the Members of the Consilium de Laicis (2 October 1974)," *Acta Apostolica Sedis* 66 (1974): 568.

80. EN 42.

81. Ibid., 43.

82. The "first and most necessary gift is love," which is the "bond of perfection and the fullness of the law," guides all to their final end. "It is the love of God and the love of one's neighbor which points out the true disciple of Christ." *Lumen Gentium* 42, in *Vatican II: The Conciliar and Post-Conciliar Documents,* 350–426 [hereafter LG]. Also "Love is the fundamental and innate vocation of every human being." *Familiaris consortio* 11, in *Vatican II: More Post-Conciliar Documents,* 815–98.

83. Cf. 1 John 1:1–4 where John speaks of testifying to what he has heard, seen, looked upon and touched.

84. For a fine summary presentation of many of Turner's crucial concepts, see Mathieu Deflem, "Ritual, Anti-Structure, and Religion: A Discussion of Victor Turner's Processual Symbolic Analysis," *Journal for the Scientific Study of Religion* 30 (March, 1991): 1–25; see also Mary Collins, OSB, "Ritual Symbols and the Ritual Process: The Work of Victor W. Turner," *Worship* 50 (September, 1976): 336–46.

85. Turner clearly states: "Ritual is a principal means by which society grows and moves into the future." *Dramas, Fields and Metaphors: Symbolic Action in Human Society* (Ithaca: Cornell University Press, 1974), 298. That liturgical celebrations are meant to move a social group into a future, cf. SC 2. The language of this paragraph is a theological extrapolation of the notion of ritual as a process.

86. Turner's notion of liminality extends beyond considerations of passage rites. He speaks of an "ill-assorted bunch of social phenomena," as diverse as neophytes in the liminal phase, subjugated autochthones, small nations, court jesters, holy mendicants, good Samaritans and so forth. Victor W. Turner, *The Ritual Process: Structure and Anti-Structure* (Chicago: Aldine Publishing Co., 1969), 125.

87. Ibid., 95. "Thus, liminality is frequently likened to death, to being in the womb, to invisibility, to darkness, to bisexuality, to the wilderness, and to an eclipse of the sun or moon." Ibid. Some may wish to object to my applying the notion of liminality to the assembly gathered for liturgy, since there are "positions assigned and arrayed" within the hierarchical structure of worship. I would contend, however, that that the usual societal positions and structures do not obtain. "Secular distinctions of rank and status disappear or are homogenized." Ibid.

88. Turner, *Dramas, Fields and Metaphors,* 44.

89. Turner, *Ritual Process,* 96.

90. Victor Turner, *The Forest of Symbols: Aspects of Ndembu Ritual* (Ithaca: Cornell University Press, 1967), 99–108; cf. also Jeffrey VanderWilt, "Rites of Passage: Ludic Recombination and the Formation of Ecclesial Being," *Worship* 66 (September 1992): 398–416.

91. Turner, *Ritual Process,* 95.

92. Frequently SC and the *General Instruction on the Roman Missal* [in Flannery *Vatican Council II: The Conciliar and Post-Conciliar Documents,* 148–203] refer to the importance of the assembly. See SC 7, 24 and 25 and GIRM 4, 5 and 14.

93. Neophytes in many passage rites, Turner states, "have to submit to an authority that is nothing less than that of the total community." Turner, *Ritual Process,* 103. Interpreted theologically the statement means that while at worship the assembly submits itself to the authority of God, to the *totus Christus* manifested in the Spirit.

94. In speaking of liminal persons, Turner points out that the community itself is the repository of a tradition, including the specific culture's "values, norms, attitudes, sentiments, and relationships." The wisdom imparted in ritual engagements has an ontological value: "it refashions the very being of the neophyte." Turner, *Ritual Process,* 103.

95. Turner notes that "[p]rophets and artists tend to be liminal and marginal people . . . who strive with a passionate sincerity to rid themselves of the

clichés associated with status incumbency and role-playing and to enter into vital relations with other[s] . . . in fact of imagination. In their productions we may catch glimpses of that unused evolutionary potential in [humankind] which has not yet been externalized and fixed in structure." Ibid., 128. FIYH states: "Especially in the Eucharistic celebration, *the* sign of God's saving presence among his people, the preacher is called to point to the signs of God's presence in the lives of his people [and I would add, God's presence in the world] so that, in joyous recognition of that presence, they may join the angels and saints to proclaim God's glory and sing with them their unending hymn of praise," FIYH 8.

96. Turner, *Ritual Process*, 128.

97. LG 4.

98. LG 32 states: "There is, therefore, in Christ and in the Church no inequality on the basis of race or nationality, social condition or sex, because 'there is neither Jew nor Greek; there is neither bond nor free; there is neither male nor female. For you are all "one" in Christ Jesus' (Gal 3:28)."

99. Karl Barth, *Church Dogmatics* (Edinburgh: T. & T. Clark, 1960), quoted in Brueggemann, *Israel's Praise*, 2.

When the Christian assembly celebrates, it simply erects a modest landmark, a sign along the pilgrim way that points to the limitlessness of God's grace within the infinitude of the world. Humble as they are, these Christian signs are essential, for they name and acknowledge the One whose presence makes possible our experience of this world as grace.

Nathan Mitchell, "The Amen Corner: Liturgy and Culture," *Worship* 65:4 (July 1991): 367.

Framing the Scriptures: Preaching at the Eucharist on High Holy Days

Andrew D. Ciferni, OPRAEM

In the six decades since the promulgation of Pius XII's *Divino afflante spiritu* (1943)[1] and in the three since the Second Vatican Council (1962–1965),[2] much scholarly and pastoral attention has established the need for greater attention to effective celebration of the liturgy of the word in Roman Catholic sacramental life. After the Council of Trent and for the four centuries between then and Vatican II, many Catholic theologians, reacting to Luther's indictments, retreated into the comfortable sphere of their ritual and sacramental tradition.[3] While Protestant churches reaped a pastoral bounty through new translations of the scriptures into the vernacular and ministerial formation on the word and on preaching during these centuries, the Catholic church failed to capitalize on such innovations. In this period, effective Roman Catholic preaching was largely confined to mission preaching outside the sacramental context.[4]

In the past half-century, Catholics have come to appreciate the fullness of a strong proclamation of the word and of preaching as an integral part of sacramental life and formation. Roman

Catholic liturgical theology since *Sacrosanctum Concilium* has demanded critical attention to the integration of word and sacrament.[5] If Roman Catholicism was formerly perceived as a church of the sacraments when juxtaposed to the Protestant churches of the word, *Sacrosanctum Concilium* and all post–Vatican II liturgical teaching have continued to stress the integrity of word and sacrament. In fact, even the terminology of separate "liturgy of the word" and "liturgy of the eucharist" might seem anachronistic, for liturgical theology has come to advocate the ritual *celebration* of the word and the necessity of biblically based sacramental action in one integrated liturgy of praise.[6] This unity of rite is expressed by liturgical theologian Louis-Marie Chauvet, who writes: "[T]here is something sacramental about the Scriptures, in the sense that they are the sacrament of the word of God, and that, conversely, the sacraments of faith exist only as the crystallization of that word."[7]

In a relatively short half-century, Roman Catholic liturgy, and more particularly the liturgy of the word, has been changed profoundly,[8] and formation for ordained ministry now calls for serious biblical study and an emphasis on effective liturgical homiletics.[9] Yet, perhaps influenced by the dominant Protestant scholarly traditions in the mid-twentieth century and by the fervor for the historical-critical method of biblical interpretation for preaching at that time, Roman Catholic preachers have sometimes too readily adopted a method of homily preparation that seems to result more in informational homilies about Christian life and faith in first- and second-century Palestine than in formational inspiration for the upbuilding of the church in the present.[10]

One check on an overly historical-critical biblical slant in preaching has been available to Roman Catholic preachers in the church's teaching that the "matter" of liturgical preaching is not confined to the scriptures proclaimed but may also include the other texts of the liturgy. The *General Instruction of the Roman Missal* notes:

*The homily is an integral part of the liturgy and is strongly
recommended: it is necessary for the nurturing of the Christian
life. It should develop some point of the readings or of another
text from the ordinary or from the Proper of the Mass of the day,
and take into account the mystery being celebrated and the needs
proper to the listeners.*[11]

Further, the *Lectionary for Mass* states:

*Whether the homily explains the texts of the Sacred Scriptures
proclaimed in the readings or some other texts of the Liturgy, it
must always lead the community of the faithful to celebrate the
Eucharist actively, "so that they may hold fast in their lives to
what they have grasped by faith."*[12]

Indeed, it is hard to imagine mystagogical preaching without attention to the non-scriptural texts of the liturgy.[13] Although FIYH
seems to restrict the textual sources of homiletic preparation to the
scriptures, Catholic professors of homiletics as well as liturgists in
recent years have been giving attention to a more expansive textual and ritual canon for liturgical preaching. In the words of
Edward Foley,"[e]xpanding beyond the written word, however, it is
possible to consider the 'liturgical bible' as further including the ritual actions, and even the feasts and seasons that we celebrate
throughout the year."[14] Without neglecting the scriptures, Roman
Catholic liturgical preaching looks to the other texts of the liturgy
and to the symbols, gestures and chants that are other essential elements of worship as apt sources for homiletic development.

Biblical scholars have pointed out that the books of the New
Testament are themselves the fruit of worshiping communities
of faith in the first and early second centuries.[15] The fixed canon
of scripture is, for Roman Catholics, animated when proclaimed in
living assemblies millennia after the final redaction of the texts to be
proclaimed and preached upon. Because of this, preachers need to

attend to the liturgical context in which the biblical texts are celebrated. Kevin Irwin provides a thorough method for liturgical theology that serves equally well for coming to the entire liturgical event as source for preaching.[16] Unfortunately, one often has the impression that homily preparation does not take the other texts of the liturgical event into account. This seems most evident when one hears no echo of the homily in the eucharistic prayer, "the center and summit of the entire celebration."[17]

Roman Catholic Preaching in the Eucharist

Catholic preachers often seem to use the homily as a way of concluding the proclamation of the scriptures of the first half of the eucharistic liturgy. One has the impression that in this model the homily functions as the high point of the liturgy of the word, after which there is a "break" that ends with the invitation to prayer before the prayer over the gifts. An image more fitted to a model of integrated celebration of word and sacrament word is one in which the homily is the bridge that weds pulpit and table. Although liturgical documents stress the intimate connection between the two, it is not always made sufficiently clear that it is precisely the homily that plays the principal role in leading from proclamation of the scriptures to proclamation of the eucharistic prayer. An exception to this is the section "The Homily and the Liturgy of the Eucharist" in FIYH, in which one finds that "the homily should flow quite naturally out of the readings and into the liturgical action that follows."[18]

In order to be the bridge connecting these two ritual components, however, the homily needs to ground the euchology and action at the table. If we hold that "[t]he meaning of the [eucharistic] prayer is that the entire congregation joins itself to Christ in acknowledging the great things God has done and in offering the sacrifice,"[19] then the "great things" to be acknowledged must in some way be recognized in the proclamation and preaching that precede the great prayer. These "great things" are made explicit in the preface, whose chief characteristic is thanksgiving. Awareness of this element is imperative in particular for Roman Catholic preachers in preparation for preaching on holy days of obligation, for on these occasions the pericopes might not narrate the content of the feast, while the preface supplies the hermeneutic of the whole liturgical "text"—including words, actions, symbols, objects.[20]

The deference given to the preface in preparing the rhetoric and theological nuances for the homily is a result of the theology of thanksgiving that is ever expressed in the prefaces, for "in the name of the entire people of God, the priest praises the Father and gives thanks for the whole work of salvation or for some special aspect of it that corresponds to the day, feast or season."[21] Chauvet develops the "deep structure" of the relation between homily and the eucharistic prayer in terms of the "symbolic exchange" between God and the "operating subject" of the liturgy, the assembly itself:

> In our text [Eucharistic Prayer 2] it [salvation history] is entirely
> focused on [Jesus]. But in other texts, it is either more developed
> into a main summary of salvation [creation, transgression,
> covenants, mission of the prophets, then of the Son, Jesus; thus
> Eucharistic Prayer 4] or, on the contrary, centered on one aspect
> of the mystery of Christ according to the feast and biblical texts
> of the day. . . . Whatever the case, two theological principles
> rule the initial thanksgiving of the church. On the one hand,
> it has no other object than the Scriptures, or rather than what
> God has done for humankind according to the Scriptures. . . .
> On the other hand, the thanksgiving always culminates in the
> paschal mystery of Christ.[22]

If the proper prefaces of seasons and feasts are used in the preparation and execution of the homily, preaching may better lead the assembly to the table, where all will be invited to lift up their hearts and give thanks to the Lord our God. If the community's response is to be authentic and not simply formulaic, the homily is a critical element grounding an honest response of praise and thanksgiving.

The Life of God in the Community Today

Such preparation for preaching is dependent upon the presider's ability to give the assembly a word-inspired language that enables them to recognize that the mystery proclaimed and preached is, in fact, the story of this church gathered around this table, of the "here-and-now situation," as FIYH expresses it.[23] For this reason the documents on the liturgy have insisted that the homily must "take into account the mystery being celebrated and the needs proper to the listeners"[24] and "must always lead the community of the faithful to celebrate the Eucharist actively, 'so that they may hold fast in their lives to what they have grasped by faith.'"[25] Note in the latter text the explicit connection between preaching and active celebration of the eucharist.

This consideration given to the preface for homily preparation suits well sound models for preaching in the church today. Fred Craddock, for example, maintains that preachers enable the assembly to "recognize" their stories in the story proclaimed in the liturgy.[26] This is done when preachers themselves recognize the same story in their own lives, the result of academic and pastoral study, meditation and preparation called for by the "Introduction to the Lectionary,"[27] and from daily pastoral care outside the liturgy for the same people to whom they will preach within the liturgy. FIYH teaches that the preacher brings three stories together: the story of God in the scriptures, the preacher's story from his or her own experiences of faith and the presence of God, and the assembly's story in its recognition of itself as the incarnation of the risen Christ in the world. FIYH devotes a chapter to the story of the assembly and the preacher.[28] The homily is the fruit of the wedding of these stories so that the people of God are sent forth to recognize God's presence when and where it is to be found.

To this end the homily is a moment of revelation, a moment, etymologically, of "pulling back the veil" so that God is recognized in a new time and a new place. In her masterful chapter "Preaching as the Art of Naming Grace," Mary Catherine Hilkert develops the theological truth that one's theology of preaching and one's theology of revelation are isomorphic: How the preacher believes it is possible for the revelation of the Holy One to happen outside the liturgy is clearly reflected in her or his homilies. This, in turn, deeply affects how the assembly comes to believe God is revealed again and again in its life of faith. This, among many other reasons, is why preaching is such a primary act of pastoral care. This revelation-in-preaching, this identification of "the human story and the story of Jesus"[29] justifies the liturgy's declaration that the mystery being celebrated is an event for today—the *hodie,* Latin for "today," that is so potent in the Latin liturgical tradition—not a narrative or re-enactment of the past. It is the assembly's experience of the mystery as an event today that helps people to lift their hearts authentically to the Lord and to give God thanks and praise. The challenge presented at the present stage of pastoral development is for the assembly to hear in what follows at the table an echo of what they heard from the pulpit. The homily leads the assembly of believers to word and action at the table.

The solemnities of the Roman Catholic church year, with their proper prefaces, would seem then to be a privileged place for mining the euchology as a primary source in homily preparation. Another reason for mining this source is that on some of these solemnities—for example, on the feasts of Mary—the scriptures proclaimed do not, in fact, narrate the mystery being celebrated in the eucharist, even though these feasts are central to the Roman Catholic liturgical tradition.

Preaching from the Prefaces on Holy Days:
A Pastoral Need

The church's liturgy assigns a rank to each of its celebrations. The higher the rank, the more closely the mystery celebrated is deemed to be to the heart of all Christian celebration, the paschal mystery of Christ's suffering, death, burial and rising to life transformed for the life of the world. The very title of the *motu proprio* approving the general norms for post-Vatican II calendar reform, *Mysterii paschalis*, hints at the centrality of this mystery. Sunday is at the very heart of Christian celebration.[30] It holds primacy of place, followed by the annual celebration of the Paschal Triduum. But some other non-Sunday celebrations are seen to be so central to the life of the church that they are declared to be obligatory.[31]

Despite the centrality of these solemnities in the liturgical tradition, there is in general both a massive absence of Catholics at these non-Sunday celebrations accompanied by a substantial lack of understanding concerning what is being celebrated on those days and, therefore, a lack of understanding about the pertinence of the mysteries to the life of faith.

Because such solemnities are often celebrated on weekdays, poor attendance may have much to do with issues of inculturation—work schedules, the demands of family life, education and so forth. But it may also have to do with a lack of understanding of the importance of these celebrations. This in turn may be due to less-than-effective preaching. More than for the Sundays of Ordinary Time or for the more well-attended liturgies of the liturgical year, the holy days of obligation languish for want of an informed pastoral understanding about why these mysteries are grave and of consequence for Christian life today. Homiletics professor James A. Wallace has recognized and responded to this pastoral lacuna. In *Preaching to the Hungers of the Heart* he thematizes preaching for feasts of the Lord as responses to our hunger for wholeness, and preaching for feasts of Mary as responses to our hunger to belong.[32]

Prefaces for the Solemnities of the Immaculate Conception and the Assumption of Mary

It is the contention of this essay that the preface as an interpretive frame for the scriptures to be preached contributes most effectively toward "lead[ing] the community of the faithful to celebrate the Eucharist actively."[33] If the homily is the span connecting pulpit and table, it is precisely the preface that serves to echo at the table the mystery revealed to be present in the assembly's life in the course of the homily. In this view, the preface is much less the beginning of a new section of the liturgy and much more a liturgical, poetic proclamation of the word at the table.

The preface, especially for great feasts, is an interpretive frame for the scriptures. Just as the frame of a painting radically affects our perception of the painting, so the preface that follows the proclamation of the scriptures frames the texts for that day. The specific challenge of relating the homily to the preface of the eucharistic prayer, especially on holy days of obligation, has suggested the usefulness of "framing" the scriptures for these feasts with their proper preface as one tool among others in effective homily preparation.[34]

The two major Marian solemnities—the Assumption and the Immaculate Conception, celebrated on August 15 and December 8—are not "events" narrated as such in the scriptures proclaimed. The almost total lack of a connection between the historical-critical approach to the scriptures proclaimed on these days and the mystery being celebrated makes them particularly challenging days for preaching, and therefore more apt test cases for a hermeneutic employing the preface in homily preparation. On these days particularly, preachers are tempted to preach on neither the readings nor the euchology of the day. My own experience of homilies on these days gives me the impression that the material for preaching is more frequently catechetical or devotional or both.

The Solemnity of the Immaculate Conception: December 8

Genesis 3:9–15, 20	*I will place enmity between your seed and the seed of the woman.*
Psalm 98: 1–4	*Sing to the Lord a new song, for he has done marvelous deeds.*
Ephesians 1:3–6,11–12	*God chose us in Christ before the foundation of the world.*
Luke 1:26–38	*Rejoice, favored one, the Lord is with you.*

The preface:
*You allowed no stain of Adam's sin
to touch the Virgin Mary.
Full of grace, she was to be a worthy mother of your Son,
and the promise of its perfection as the bride of Christ,
radiant in beauty.
Purest of virgins, she was to bring forth your Son,
the innocent lamb who takes away our sins.
You chose her from all women to be our advocate with you
and our pattern of holiness.*

A strong image in this text is that of Mary as a sign of favor at the church's beginning and the promise of its future perfection. Another is that she is chosen by God to be our pattern of holiness. Joining these images provides a frame implied in the text, namely, Mary as our companion on the way from the promise of innocent beginnings through life's journey intent in faith and hope of full communion with God despite disappointment and failure.

When I bring to the gospel text the question of how this companion can be a guide and support for me and for the church, I am struck by the depth of a faith that can say "yes" into darkness:

"Behold, I am the handmaid of the Lord. May it be done to me according to your word." This "yes into darkness" is the same act of faith that is made by a man and woman wedding their lives to one another. Only with faith in one another rooted in their belief that more than coincidence has brought them together would they be able to make this "yes" in the face of so much contrary evidence that living out this "yes" is a realistic possibility for them. Mary's "yes" will be echoed in the "yes" of parents bringing their children to the font of baptism or moving to adopt a child in the face of an inability to conceive. The signs of favor almost always present at new beginnings eventually meet with some disappointment, failure and perhaps the temptation to give up on God. But the great story expounded in today's feast is that the God who has chosen us and gives us signs of favor at each of our new beginnings also gives a sign of promise and the means to move from the beginning, through disappointment with perseverance.

A privileged symbol of God's favor, the gift of divine assistance and the icon of our individual and communal perfection is the mother of Jesus Christ, chosen like us before the foundation of the world. It is worth the effort to attend to how this gospel scene has been depicted in art over the ages. Time and again we see Mary surprised by Gabriel while she is seated with the text of the scriptures. Mary can say her "yes" because in the angel's voice she hears an echo of the reluctant "yes" of the prophets chosen and called like her to a life of fidelity despite seeming failure, rejection and persecution. This is the pattern of holiness we proclaim in the preface of the feast.

The Solemnity of the Assumption: August 15

Revelation 11:19a;	*I saw a woman clothed with*
12:1–6a, 10ab	*the sun and with the moon*
	beneath her feet.

Psalm 45, 10bc, 11, 12ab, 16   *The queen stands at your right hand, arrayed in gold.*

1 Corinthians 15:20–27   *As members of Christ all will be raised, Christ first, and after him all who belong to him.*

Luke 1:39–56   *He who is mighty has done great things for me; he has exalted the humble.*

The preface:
*Today the virgin Mother of God was taken up into heaven
to be the beginning and the pattern of the Church
in its perfection,
and a sign of hope and comfort for your people
on their pilgrim way.
You would not allow decay to touch her body,
for she had given birth to your Son, the Lord of all life,
in the glory of the incarnation.*

Giving birth is a strong framing image in this preface text. Giving birth leaves its mark on the bodies of mothers. Young women obsessed with modeling careers are not likely to become mothers until they reach the ripe old age of thirty. Scars, stretch marks, varicose veins and sagging abdominal muscles are often witnesses to generativity. Lovers of life are convinced that these are marks of glory. But those perennially preoccupied with tight, sleek, flawless slimness may one day awake to the sad realization that not only has their beauty faded but so has their fecundity.

Mary is a counter-cultural model in the face of the flawless physical beauty we see daily in media images that educate our desires in directions often quite different than desires intent on authentic love of God, others, self and God's good earth. Mary's full and final glory, free of all corruption or decay, is born of her lifelong birthing life. Again Mary is proposed and celebrated as the first disciple and the privileged icon for all Jesus' disciples, the fellow traveler on the pilgrimage.

The readings give a hint of how counter-cultural it is to commit oneself to continual birthing. There is always a dragon waiting to consume what is in the process of being brought to authentic life within us. God gives us a sign of hope and comfort in Mary, whose own commitment to aiding Elizabeth in her bringing forth life demanded that she (Mary) leave her own place of comfort to travel quickly over the hills to Judah.

Today we might well imagine that Mary's proclamation of praise, the Magnificat (Luke 1: 46–55), could only come to its full expression at the end of a life of discipleship that left its own unique scars upon her soul as well as upon her body. But God does not disappoint the desires of those who are channels of life for the world. God delivers them from death because of all their bringing forth of life. This is a variation on the central theme of paschal mystery at the heart of all liturgical celebration. The Risen Christ is not without the marks of his suffering. These scars are trophies of God's grace. Thinking of Mary's assumption or Christ's resurrection as discontinuous from a life of giving birth to new life at great price is tantamount to imaging God absent from the daily struggles we all face in making decisions for life.

Byzantine icons of this feast, called Mary's Dormition, depict her laid-out body surrounded by the apostles who have returned to Jerusalem from their missionary activities. One is reminded of hospital or other deathbed scenes where a beloved grandmother is surrounded by her grieving children and grandchildren. The grief is a testament to love and life. If, as the preface states, Mary is a sign of hope and comfort for us on our pilgrim way, it is because her Magnificat and her life of discipleship reveal her to be the beginning and pattern of perfection for us as individuals and communities— assemblies courageous enough to oppose the mighty, generous enough to go out of our way to be present to the needy, and in every circumstance thankful enough to give God the praise. We find that the other icon of this day, the pregnant sun-clothed woman whose child about to be born is threatened by the waiting dragon, is us. We know that whenever there is something of God about to be born of us, there waiting is the sabotage of our own resistance to conversion or our fear of change or our amnesia regarding the trophy scars of birthing life.

As these two examples demonstrate, utilization of the preface prayers of the high holy days of the church's liturgical year, both as points of departure and sources of inspiration, can elicit richly symbolic and scripturally sound images and understandings for those preaching on these special feasts. The crafting of powerful homilies capable of bridging the scriptural message, the mystery being celebrated and the lives of the community of faith is more than possible, if care is taken to situate the homily within the broader liturgical framework of the feast.

1. *Acta Apostolica Sedis* 35:10 (October 20, 1943): 297–326.

2. All references to the documents of Vatican II are cited with the title and number in the translation and edition of Austin Flannery, OP, *Vatican Council II: The Conciliar and Post-Conciliar Documents, Study Edition* (Northport, N.Y.: Costello Publishing, 1987).

3. James F. White, *Roman Catholic Worship: Trent to Today* (New York: Paulist Press, 1995).

4. Jay Dolan, *The American Catholic Parish: A History from 1850 to the Present* (New York: Paulist Press, 1987).

5. *Sacrosanctum Concilium* 56.

6. Andrew D. Ciferni, OPRAEM, "Word and Sacrament," *The New Dictionary of Sacramental Worship*, ed. Peter E. Fink, SJ (Collegeville: Liturgical Press, 1990): 1318–20.

7. Louis-Marie Chauvet, *The Sacraments: The Word of God at the Mercy of the Body* (Collegeville: The Liturgical Press, 2001): 43.

8. A helpful abbreviated history is available in Martin Connell, *Guide to the Revised Lectionary* (Chicago: LTP, 1998): 1–34.

9. The Bishops' Committee on Priestly Life and Ministry, appendix of *Fulfilled in Your Hearing: The Homily in the Sunday Assembly* [hereafter FIYH] (Washington: NCCB, 1982): 43–4.

10. For a Roman Catholic critique of the exclusive use of the historical-critical method of biblical interpretation, see, among other works, Luke Timothy Johnson, *The Real Jesus: The Misguided Quest for the Historical Jesus and the Truth of the Traditional Gospels* (San Francisco: HarperSanFrancisco, 1996).

11. *General Instruction of the Roman Missal,* fourth edition, as in *The Sacramentary* (New York: Catholic Book Publishing, 1985): 41 [henceforth GIRM]; and *Institutio Generalis Missalis Romani,* as in *Missale Romanum, Editio Typica Tertia* (Vatican City: Typis Vaticanis, 2002): 65 [henceforth IGMR]. Throughout I will indicate the corresponding number in the IGMR.

12. "Introduction," *Lectionary for Mass,* second typical edition (Washington: USCC, 1998): 24.

13. Jeffrey P. Baerwald, SJ, "Mystagogy," *The New Dictionary of Sacramental Worship:* 881–3. See also Kathleen Hughes, *Saying Amen: A Mystagogy of Sacrament* (Chicago: LTP, 1999).

14. See his "The Homily beyond Scripture: *Fulfilled in Your Hearing* Revisited," *Worship* 73 (1999): 351–8.

15. See, among other sources, the sections on "The Growth of the Tradition" and "The Shape of the Canon" in Dianne Bergant, CSA, "Introduction to the Bible," *The Collegeville Bible Commentary,* ed. Dianne Bergant, CSA, and Robert J. Karris, OFM, (Collegeville: The Liturgical Press, 1989): 3–14.

16. Kevin W. Irwin, *Content and Text: Method in Liturgical Theology* (Collegeville: The Liturgical Press, 1994); he had already applied this method in a series of seasonal guides to the eucharist and hours (New York: Pueblo Publishing Co.).

17. GIRM 54 and IGRM 78.

18. FIYH, page 23.

19. GIRM 54 and IGRM 78; note that the 2002 edition of the *Missale* adds *in Spiritu Sancto* to the former "to the Father through Jesus Christ," a shift of trinitarian theology of no mean consequence, but not one bearing directly on the matter at hand.

20. Richard McCarron, *The Eucharistic Prayer at Sunday Mass* (Chicago: Liturgy Training Publications, 1997): 134–5; McCarron gives Augustine of Hippo as an example of "Preaching from the Eucharistic Prayer."

21. GIRM 55, IGRM 79.

22. Chauvet, *The Sacraments,* 130–1.

23. FIYH, page 3.

24. GIRM 41.

25. *Lectionary for Mass,* 24.

26. Fred B. Craddock, *Preaching* (Nashville: Abingdon, 1985): 159–162.

27. See Chapter IV, "Homiletic Method," of FIYH, pages 29–39.

28. See pages 3–15.

29. See Hilkert, *Naming Grace: Preaching and the Sacramental Imagination* (New York: Continuum, 1997): 44–57, 89–107.

30. See *Norms Governing Liturgical Celebrations* (Washington: USCC, 1984): 7–9.

31. Canon 1246, as in *Code of Canon Law: Latin-English Edition* (Washington: Canon Law Society of America, 1983), page 445.

32. *Preaching to the Hungers of the Heart: The Homily on the Feasts and within the Rites* (Collegeville: The Liturgical Press, 2002).

33. *Lectionary for Mass,* 24.

34. See, for example, Adrian Nocent, OSB, *The Liturgical Year* (Collegeville: The Liturgical Press, 1977). Nocent, though consistently bringing out the essential dogmatic content of proper prefaces, does not frame the scriptures of the day, which he treats separately, within the strong images proclaimed in these prefaces.

Words are the source of both memory and forgetting, birth and decay, fact and fiction. If words are epitaphs (shorthand for events that have come and gone), they are also invitations to transcend the limits of death, recipes for surviving both time and loss. Every word is, then, a mutiny, an act of defiance, an ineradicable affirmation of the human in the face of all that is deadly and destructive. For we humans not only possess words, we are possessed by them.

Nathan Mitchell, "The Amen Corner: Wrestling with the Word," *Worship* 66:5 (September 1992): 450.

"Practice Makes Perfect": Reading as a Transformative Spiritual Practice

Raymond Studzinski, OSB

In *Zen and the Art of Archery,* Eugen Herrigel, a German philosopher, talks about his experience of learning Zen while serving as a visiting professor for six years at the University of Tokyo.[1] Zen practitioners seek enlightenment through various practices and learn Zen in the context of engaging in some art such as flower arranging or, in Herrigel's case, archery. These arts in Zen function as religious rituals, spiritual exercises in which the goal is nothing external but rather an inner change in the practitioner. Shortly after his arrival in Japan, Herrigel went to a Zen master who proceeded to train him in archery. Day after day he would practice pulling back the string on the bow, trying to find just the right moment to let go. But even after some years of practice the master would always say that it still wasn't right.

Frustrated, Herrigel tried to master the technique by using his head, sensing there was a rational approach to how to do it right. Indeed, this seemed to him to bring the needed result. But the master sensed immediately that Herrigel was cheating, not playing by the rules, and was ready to end the teaching relationship. Herrigel prevailed on him and the training sessions went on. One day, the master told Herrigel, still struggling because *he* wanted to shoot the arrow just right, "*It* shoots."[2] When Herrigel finally surrendered control and let it shoot, archery became for him the "artless art" and passed over into Zen. "Bow and arrow are only a pretext for something that could just as well happen without them, only the way to a goal, not the goal itself, helps for the last decisive leap."[3]

This story can lead us to wonder about the proverb "practice makes perfect" and ask what becomes perfect through practice or what does practice do for us or to us. In light of the Herrigel story, to shoot the arrow perfectly in Zen is no longer to be shooting the arrow. The practice accomplishes its goal by shifting the sense of agency, the sense of who is really in charge. In this essay I intend to explore what it is that ritual practices do as Christians engage in them. Taking as a departure point Nathan Mitchell's thesis in his essay "Ritual as Reading" that ritual is a form of religious reading,[4] I will examine in detail what happens in the spiritual practice of reading that impacts on the reader and a community of readers. I will look at the elements of the art of religious reading, called in the monastic tradition *lectio divina,* and how people learned the proper way to engage in that practice.

Practices and their role in religious or spiritual development are the subject of an increasing number of investigations.[5] Undergirding these contemporary explorations is the recognition that people deepen their connection to the Transcendent through activities in which they engage regularly and purposefully and that there is a pressing need to articulate the shape and form of such practices for contemporary believers. Robert Wuthnow has suggested on the basis of sociological analysis that what society is in need of is a practice-centered spirituality that has a foundation in a tradition and community and yet is flexible enough to respond to an ever-changing world. Such a spirituality would overcome the problems associated with what he calls a "spirituality of habitation," where there are clearly demarcated places for the sacred and the human but also a tendency to the static because of a strong focus on a stable, ordered world, and a "spirituality of seeking" where flexibility is a highlight but accompanied by a proclivity to be too fluid and eclectic.[6]

The historical theologian Margaret Miles, concerned like Wuthnow about an appropriate spiritual response to the dilemmas of the contemporary world, argues for noticing how Christians through the centuries have lived out their beliefs. She claims that such practical arrangements arose not from the study of theology but from the need to direct and order daily life in a way that gave expression to faith and ensured meaning. Many of the tools employed in the past can be reappropriated and put to service today. "Our creativity—a real creativity—can be exercised by finding and pressing into service tools that are unused or underdeveloped in Christian tradition."[7] What often remains unexplored is how these faith-based tools accomplished their goals. As Michel Foucault once remarked: "People know what they do; they frequently know why they do what they do; but what they don't know is what what they do does."[8]

William Spohn has thrown some light on how Christian spiritual practices do what they do.[9] Approaching practices as the ordinary means that Christians use to shape their lives in the pattern of Christ, Spohn directs attention to how they train the imagination as well as form dispositions that give rise to a vibrant moral life. These practices are both pedagogical and transformational. Their power is related to their ability to form character and tutor the affections, thus leading people to acting in virtuous ways. "Both oral and spiritual practices set us up for the right dispositions. They channel good intentions into habitual behavior, and those habits evoke and train the dispositions of the heart."[10] Central among these practices, according to Spohn, are those that entail a prayerful engagement of the scriptures. Reading, particularly reading done slowly and meditatively as in the early centuries of Christianity, transforms the reader.[11] Christians read the scriptures but also become more adept at reading God's other book, the world around them. Reading represents a way of construing a text and all reality in the light of the revelation of God in Jesus Christ.

In his essay "Ritual as Reading" Mitchell proposes that we approach ritual "as a way of 'reading' reality."[12] The reading in ritual is an activity which engages the whole person of the reader. In contrast to contemporary ways of thinking about and doing it, reading here is not a retreat into private mental spaces but a venture outward, a full-fledged engagement of reality. What is read is lived, is performed. The meaning of what is read is not thought out so much as lived out. This practice of reading that Mitchell sees as so integral to vital liturgical activity is profoundly transformative for, to paraphrase Eugen Herrigel's experience, "it reads," or better, "the Word reads us" and schools us in reading all reality. This type of reading, *lectio divina,* however, is eclipsed today by more consumer-oriented ways of engaging words—texts, words are used as commodities to satisfy an insatiable need for information and distraction. George Steiner, Ivan Illich and a chorus of others call for a return to the classic, sacramental approach to reading.[13] Furthermore, contemporary analyses sharpen appreciation for what transpires in such reading and how the practice of this reading "makes perfect."

Transformative Power of Ritual Reading

To read in the manner of the ancients and monastics who saw reading as a pathway to transformation is to read with a deference to what is read and with a care and attention that often are lacking in contemporary approaches. J. A. Appleyard has suggested that people in the course of life and at various moments embrace different styles of reading with corresponding attitudes, intentions and responses. He describes the reader as at times a player, hero/heroine, thinker, interpreter and pragmatist. These varying styles remind us that reading is complex and evolves as one grows older and more experienced.[14] To approach reading as a spiritual practice is to be ready to give full attention to what is read, to enter into a special mindset.

Paul J. Griffiths has given special thought to the type of reading found in various religious traditions.[15] In contrasting religious reading with more usual contemporary practice, he notes: "It's possible to read religiously, as a lover reads, with a tensile attentiveness that wishes to linger, to prolong, to savor, and has no interest at all in the quick orgasm of consumption."[16] The need for religious reading Griffiths links to the need to give a religious account of things, a comprehensive story that responds to central questions of life in a compelling way and thus is capable of providing an organizing frame for living out life.[17] This account, if it is to serve adherents of a particular tradition, must be learned, and religious reading is one avenue for mastering the story.[18]

Religion, as Griffiths describes it, is a craft involving various skills. These skills Christians acquire as they engage in three practices: worship, prayer and reading. For dedicated believers, the Bible holds central place and plays an important role in all three practices. In reading the Bible, Christians are presented with tools and skills they can then use to interpret the world around them. The world is, as it were, written into the margins of the Bible. The scriptures are the norm par excellence and learning to draw out the riches of the sacred texts in reading impacts on other skills such as reorienting will and appetites.[19]

As Griffiths explores the specifics of religious reading, he attends to the special relationship that the religious reader has with the work. Involved in this particular relationship are a set of attitudes, a distinctive way of knowing and a consequent way of acting. Christian believers as well as other believers approach what is read as a rich and stable treasury that is never exhausted. "Reading, for religious readers, ends only with death, and perhaps not then: it is a continuous, ever-repeated act."[20] Furthermore, from the standpoint of faith, people are made to be readers; they are equipped with an ability to draw forth nourishment from the sacred text.[21]

The reader's relationship with what is read is further deepened through the effort to retain the words in memory. In the early church and during the monastic centuries, reading, *lectio,* included meditating, *meditatio.* As Carol Zaleski observes, meditation was not so much a matter of thinking over what was read as focusing attention on the scriptural words through assimilation and the storing of the words in memory.[22] Frequent rereading facilitated memorization. The scriptural example for what should take place is Ezekiel's eating the scroll (Ezekiel 3:1–3). The words were to be internalized and become part of the reader. Just as the scriptures were a storehouse of riches, so the memory became itself a treasury of scriptural riches. The storage in memory further intensified the power of the scriptures. "A memorized work (like a lover, a friend, a spouse, a child) has entered into the fabric of its possessor's intellectual and emotional life in a way that makes deep claims upon that life, claims that can only be ignored with effort and deliberation."[23]

Inasmuch as reading in the earlier Christian centuries was seldom silent but vocalized, memory was memory of muscular movement and of sounds. Words were associated in memory with gestures and activities. The reader's body was inscribed with the text.[24] Such close identification with the scriptural word arose from the desire to let the word completely shape one's life. Elaborating on this identification, Griffiths links reading with composing and refers to the term *lectature* as capturing this further dimension of reading. *Lectature* has to do with the desire to create, to "compose" in one's life following the pattern of the words read. The term accentuates that the religious reader is not concerned with information or even with learning to write better. Rather religious reading "is done . . .

for the purpose of altering the course of the readers' cognitive, affective and active lives by the ingestion, digestion, rumination, and restatement of what has been read."[25]

Religious readers are selective in what they read. Only certain works are accorded authority and become the verbal nourishment of believers. Such works constitute what is known as a canon, whereas works that are construed as radically antithetical to religious ends are relegated to an index. "Commitment to some body of works as an endlessly nourishing garden of delights is essential to religious reading; and authoritative decision as to which works are of the right sort is a necessary condition for religious engagement with them."[26] The scriptures for Christians comprise the canon in the strict sense and are the primary focus for Christian life. Religious reading is not done in isolation but depends on community and tradition for authorizing the what and how of religious reading. It is the community that introduces new members through a process of catechesis to the sacred books and the practice of reading them.[27] It is the community that must rally now, according to Griffiths, to ensure that religious reading does not meet extinction as the consumer mentality pushes people farther and farther away from the venerable practice.

Perspectives from the Phenomenology of Reading

Investigations into the phenomenology of reading further illuminate the way reading, including religious reading, impacts on the reader. Georges Poulet indicates the manner in which reading affects the sense of an "I" who is reading. It is as though an "invasion" takes place that suddenly brings into the reader's inner world thoughts, images, ideas that were previously alien but now have taken up residence within. It is a dramatic experience that leads Poulet to observe: "Reading, then, is the act in which the subjective principle which I call I, is modified in such a way that I no longer have the right, strictly speaking, to consider it as my I, I am on loan to another, and this other thinks, feels, suffers, and acts within me."[28]

Wolfgang Iser also elaborates on the interaction of the reader and the text and the changes that are wrought. He emphasizes how different reading is from simply deciphering signs on a page. "The fact that completely different readers can be differently affected by the 'reality' of a particular text is ample evidence of the degree to which literary texts transform reading into a creative process that is far above mere perception of what is written."[29] Rereading, with its revelation of hitherto unnoticed connections and insights, is yet another illustration of the creative dimensions of the reading act.[30] Because texts inevitably have gaps—they can never tell the whole story—they invite in each reading the reader's unique creative efforts to fill in the blank spaces, to make connections. Each time a text is reread, different efforts to fill in the gaps can be pursued. Thus a text has no end of possible realizations; it is in this sense inexhaustible.[31] As a person reads, there is both a sense of anticipation about what lies ahead and a sense of retrospection regarding what has already been surveyed. The reader is busy making connections among past, present and future. In this way reading the text provides the reader with a real experience, and through that experience he or she can view life differently. Of course, the transformative potential of reading depends on the willingness of the person to leave behind his or her own experience in order to engage and participate in the adventure the text offers.[32] Reading holds the possibility of conversion, and in religious reading, *lectio divina,* that is a desired consequence of such reading.

Religious Reading as Deep, Intensive Reading

Yet another contrast between contemporary secular approaches to reading and religious reading has to do with extensive versus intensive reading. Extensive reading came into prominence at the end of the eighteenth century when the focus was on reading broadly and independently so as to satisfy one's curiosity. With this approach came a more casual attitude toward books and a more superficial and hasty manner of reading.[33] All this stood apart from the older intensive way of reading which itself received further emphasis during the Reformation. Here the focus was on reading and rereading a small number of books, of which the Bible was the centerpiece. At the time of the Reformation, with its principle of *sola scriptura,* readers approached the Bible as a self-interpreting document and gave it repeated attentive rereadings. The Bible elicited from devout readers a reverence and a firm belief that its logic would become clear to them.[34] In some ways this Reformation approach reclaimed attitudes toward the scriptures that were central in the monastic movement.

Introducing a term similar to intensive reading and yet going beyond it, Richard R. Niebuhr writes of "deep reading."[35] This is a way of reading the scriptures that is attuned to the language and word patterns leading to the innovative rather than the conventional, a way of reading that challenges rather than affirms the status quo. It is an experiential reading in which readers allow their experience and the passage to interconnect. Niebuhr describes it in this way: "In deep reading we do not have a text 'before' us as much as a 'presence' of voices, of living words and symbols, around us. . . . Reading of this kind is similar to living in a sprawling house, in which we climb up and down and explore adjoining rooms, halls, and yard."[36] Continuing the spatial analogy, he notes: "But deep reading is still more lively and complex; for we are continuously stepping in and out of this voluminous space, now regarding its written symbols from the 'outside' as though inscribed on a façade and now living and exploring in their midst."[37]

Robert Mulholland, like Niebuhr, wants to accentuate the power of the scriptures to break into lives and to suggest new and daring possibilities.[38] He explains that the scriptures are able to do this because they, as it were, break the crust that keeps us insulated and resistant to change. By shifting our usual perceptual focus they open us to the possibility of a new slant on things.[39] Paralleling the distinction between extensive and intensive reading, Mulholland speaks of informational and formational reading. In the case of informational reading, the text is perceived as an object to be mastered and the knowledge gained as something that will have practical benefits for us. A major difference in formational reading is the willingness of the reader to let the text shape him or her and work in its own way.[40] The crust that prevents the entrance of the word into one's life is, as Mulholland sees it, the culturally reinforced tendency to approach everything from a functional, informational standpoint, to see all things in terms of what they can do for us.[41] With their crust intact, readers are imprisoned in a cold, factual world, kept from fully imagining a world filled with the surprises and innovations of grace.

Reading, Imagination, and Play

Charles Dickens's novel *Hard Times* opens with a chapter entitled "The One Thing Needful" in which the narrator claims that *facts* are that one thing needful.[42] Facts form the heart and center of the schooling children receive in the industrialized society of Coketown, where the novel is set. "Teach these boys and girls nothing but Facts. Facts alone are wanted in life. Plant nothing else, and root out everything else."[43] Thomas Gradgrind, "a man of facts and calculations," is the proud sponsor of this approach and his own children suffer because of it. Their starved imaginations are the consequence of such obsessive focus on the world of facts. "Murdering the Innocents" is the apt title for the chapter that details the operations of Gradgrind's school where children are known by a number rather than a name. A government spokesperson announces to the students: "We hope to have, before long, a board of fact, composed of commissioners of fact, who will force the people to be a people of fact, and of nothing but fact."[44]

Dickens is out to protest a society that no longer nourishes the imagination. He laments, too, that religion, a stimulus to hopeful imagining, is given short shrift as materialism becomes the all-encompassing creed. As one commentator notes, "Religion too is perverted and slighted, yet emerges fitfully as one of the few forces that can save men from the living death which is Coketown."[45] The children of Coketown are not taught to appreciate the mystery of life or to stand in awe of creation and the wonders of nature. Life is desiccated, devoid of meaning or any deep purpose apart from production and accumulation. Martha Nussbaum observes:

> The novel shows in its determination to see only what can enter the utilitarian calculations, the economic mind is blind; blind to the qualitative richness of the perceptible world; to the separateness of its people, to their inner depths, their hopes and loves and fears; blind to what it is like to live a human life and to try to endow it with a human meaning. Blind above all, to the fact that human life is something mysterious and not altogether fathomable.[46]

The concern with facts in Dickens' novel resonates with the contemporary preoccupation with information. It is easy to conclude that the students in the Gradgrind school were taught only to read for facts, for information. They were not encouraged in letting their reading tutor their imaginations. Consequently, unlike religious reading, their reading probably would not excite or inspire, would not provide purpose. In their environment imagination was foolish and so not tapped. Yet imagination plays an important role in religious or any deep reading and opens up visions of possibility in the one who reads.

Where the Coketown children were not supposed to venture was the world of creative imagining, the world of play that would enable them to break out of the stagnant and dehumanizing world they inhabited. Ritual reading is a doorway to that world as it calls people to play, to imagine differently about themselves and life around them.

The psychoanalyst and pediatrician D. W. Winnicott saw the ability to live creatively as related to a type of experiencing which moves beyond hard facts and imagines and approaches reality as charged with significance. To live creatively is to enter a world of illusion, a world that first takes shape in early childhood but has lifelong significance.[47] To live creatively is to take the mundane and make it into something enriching and consoling. Illusion here is not a falsification of reality but rather a penetration below the surface of reality in order to grasp it more fully. Iser has noted the importance of illusion in the reading process. "Without the formation of illusions, the unfamiliar world of the text would remain unfamiliar; through the illusions, the experience offered by the text becomes accessible to us. . . ."[48] There is also a processing of illusions that goes on. "As we read, we oscillate to a greater or lesser degree between the building and the breaking of illusions."[49] Through this activity the text becomes a living event for us. "Through this entanglement the reader is bound to open himself up to workings of the text and so leave behind . . . preconceptions."[50]

Niebuhr has approached biases such as these preconceptions as "pre-perceptions" which he relates to "usurping images."[51] Images operative within our psyches shape and guide our attention to what is before us. "There can be no disclosure of a richer reality, no widening of our sensible hearts, unless we welcome images into the eye of attention that are fitting and expansive, capable of bringing the larger world to birth in us."[52] He goes on to point out how Jesus in his ministry put forward new images that broke down the usual perceptual schemes of his listeners. Calinescu, building on the formulations of Winnicott, sees reading as having a playful dimension and as providing scripts for imagining.[53] Such scripts absorbed in religious reading tutor the affections as Spohn has suggested. Studies on affects further substantiate this position.[54] Thus, as Mitchell observed, monks who gave themselves faithfully to *lectio* would find themselves becoming humble, hospitable, loving, and reverent. The sacred words they read would displace their former ways of imaging and acting and conform them to a new pattern.[55]

Michel de Certeau has introduced some concepts which further advance thinking about how reading leads to transformed behavior.[56] In a frequently quoted passage de Certeau wrote: "Readers are voyagers; they move across lands belonging to someone else, like nomads poaching their way across fields they did not write, despoiling the wealth of Egypt to enjoy themselves."[57] For him reading is a "tactic," a way of operating, empowering individuals to seize an opportunity, to manipulate events to particular advantage. Tactics stand in contrast to strategies, which have a more clearly defined place and create structured relationships by casting others in roles such as customers or adversaries. Strategies are the operations of the powerful, those who occupy privileged positions.[58] De Certeau expands on the tactical nature of reading. Throughout he emphasizes the active dimensions of reading over against a view of it as passive:

> To read is to wander through an imposed system (that of the text, analogous to the constructed order of a city or a supermarket) . . . The reader takes neither the position of that author nor an author's position. He invents in texts something different from what they 'intended.' He detaches them from their (lost or accessory) origin. He combines their fragments and creates something un-known in the space organized by their capacity for allowing an indefinite plurality of meanings.[59]

Related to de Certeau's distinction between strategies and tactics is his contrast of places and spaces.[60] A planned city constitutes a place but it becomes a space for walkers who move through it. Applied to reading, the text is the place that the reader turns into space.[61] It is the space where the innovative emerges. DeCerteau associates Christianity with both tactics and practices, at least if it is true to the originating impulse. After Jesus' resurrection, the community turned to a host of practices, which, following Jesus' own practice, are to make room, to create space, to allow for the creative to emerge. The community is to live with an ever-present awareness of the Other who called it into existence. To read religiously is to open a space within a textual place, to allow the spirit to emerge from the letter.[62]

De Certeau alludes to the effort to control the reading process within institutional Christianity. Precisely as such control declines, he noted, the freedom and creativity of the reader grows larger.[63] More readers then experience themselves called by the scriptures through the figures embodied in the scriptural texts, speaking to them and bringing them to a critical moment. The Bible does not directly prescribe what is to be done but nonetheless engenders conversion. As Jeremy Ahearne has summarized de Certeau's view of the process, "[The scriptural texts] call to us rather as figures which something in us (desire? an underlying will?) *recognizes* in the obscure mirror of a fable as corresponding to its own secret movement."[64] In a somewhat congruent position to de Certeau, Schuyler Brown writes with regard to the scriptures: ". . . a religious text arises out of a world of archetypal imagery, and a responsive reader is able to penetrate, through the surface level of the text, to those deep structures which powerfully engage his or her unconscious feelings."[65] For de Certeau, the practice of reading the scriptures touches people at a deep level and most crucially prompts them to do as Jesus did, to make space for the marginalized.

Conclusion: Reading and Discipleship

Religious reading necessarily involves the Other, both the transcendent Other and particular others; it is always social. Reading the sacred narratives brings this point home time and again. Like the art of archery in Zen, the practice of reading invites surrender to the Other. It is the surrender of the disciples who, like Jesus who calls them, leave all things behind. They and future disciples are called to a journey, to leave behind established places and venture into wilderness spaces where they are equipped with a few tactical practices for survival. They are to keep moving, not to pitch tents as they had wanted at Mount Tabor. Like their Jewish forebears in the desert, they must travel light. "Just as, after the destruction of the Temple, the Jews were deprived of a country, with no proper place . . . so believers are abandoned to the road with only texts for luggage."[66]

---

1. Translated by R. F. C. Hull (New York: Random House, 1983).

2. Ibid., 53.

3. Ibid., 7.

4. In *Source and Summit: Commemorating Josef A. Jungmann, SJ,* ed. Joanne M. Pierce and Michael Downey (Collegeville: The Liturgical Press, 1999), 161–81.

5. Among the more recent efforts are: *Practicing Our Faith: A Way of Life for a Searching People,* ed. Dorothy C. Bass (San Francisco: Jossey-Bass, 1997); *Practicing Theology: Beliefs and Practices in Christian Life,* ed. Miroslav Volf and Dorothy C. Bass (Grand Rapids: Eerdmans, 2002); Craig Dykstra, *Growing in the Life of Faith: Education and Christian Practices* (Louisville: Geneva Press, 1999); and Robert Wuthnow, *After Heaven: Spirituality in America since the 1950s* (Berkeley: University of California Press, 1998), esp. Chapter 7, "The Practice of Spirituality," 168–98. Earlier works include: Richard J. Foster, *Celebration of Discipline: The Path to Spiritual Growth,* rev. ed. (San Francisco: HarperSanFrancisco, 1988); Craig Dykstra, *Vision and Character: A Christian Educator's Alternative to Kohlberg* (New York: Paulist Press, 1981); and Margaret R. Miles, *Practicing Christianity: Critical Perspectives for an Embodied Spirituality* (New York: Crossroad, 1990). For an overview of the practices in relation to biblical interpretation, see Mary McClintock Fulkerson, "Practice" in

Handbook of Postmodern Biblical Interpretation, ed. A. K. M. Adam (St. Louis: Chalice Press, 2000), 189–98. For a social science perspective on practices, see Pierre Bourdieu, *Outline of a Theory of Practice,* trans. Richard Nice (Cambridge: Cambridge University Press, 1977). For a philosophical account, see Alasdair MacIntyre, *After Virtue: A Study in Moral Theory,* 2nd ed. (Notre Dame: University of Notre Dame Press, 1984), esp. 187–203.

6. See Wuthnow, 3–6, 15–16.

7. Miles, 13.

8. Cited in Huber L. Dreyfus and Paul Rabinow, *Michel Foucault: Beyond Structuralism and Hermeneutics,* 2nd ed. (Chicago: University of Chicago Press, 1983), 187.

9. William C. Spohn, *Go and Do Likewise: Jesus and Ethics* (New York: Continuum, 1999).

10. Ibid., 39.

11. Ibid., 136–7.

12. Mitchell, 170.

13. George Steiner, *No Passion Spent: Essays 1978–1995* (New Haven: Yale University Press, 1996), 1–40; Ivan Illich, *In the Vineyard of the Text: A Commentary to Hugh's Disdascalicon* (Chicago: University of Chicago Press, 1993), 1–7; and Margaret Miles, "Intentions and Effects: Beauty, Pluralism, and Responsibility," *Sewanee Theological Review* 41:1 (1997): 49–58.

14. *Becoming a Reader: The Experience of Fiction from Childhood to Adulthood* (Cambridge: Cambridge University Press, 1991), 14–9.

15. *Religious Reading: The Place of Reading in the Practice of Religion* (New York: Oxford University Press, 1999).

16. Ibid., ix.

17. Ibid., 3–13.

18. Ibid., 16.

19. Ibid., 19–20.

20. Ibid., 41. Griffiths notes that the relationship between religious readers and a literary work does not require that they are written down. See also Illich, 97–8.

21. Ibid., 41–2.

22. Carol Zaleski, "Attending to Attention," in *Faithful Imagining: Essays in Honor of Richard R. Niebuhr,* ed. Sang Hyun Lee, Wayne Proudfoot, and Albert Blackwell (Atlanta: Scholars Press, 1995), 138–40.

23. Griffiths, 47.

24. See Mitchell, 171–2.

25. Griffiths, 54.

26. Ibid., 68.

27. Mitchell, 158–63.

28. "Phenomenology of Reading," *New Literary History* 1:1 (October 1969): 57.

29. "The Reading Process: A Phenomenological Approach," *New Literary History* 3:2 (Winter 1972): 283.

30. Ibid., 285; see also Matei Calinescu, *Rereading* (New Haven: Yale University Press, 1993).

31. Iser, "The Reading Process," 284–5.

32. Ibid., 286–7.

33. Calinescu, 86–7.

34. Ibid., 85–6.

35. "The Strife of Interpreting: The Moral Burden of Imagination," *Parabola* 10:2 (May 1985): 39.

36. Ibid., 40.

37. Ibid.

38. *Shaped by the Word: The Power of Scripture in Spiritual Formation* (Nashville: Upper Room Books, 1985).

39. Ibid., 33.

40. Ibid., 49–59.

41. Ibid., 110–12. See also Walter Wink, *The Bible in Human Transformation: Toward a New Paradigm in Biblical Study* (Philadelphia: Fortress Press, 1973), 47–8. Using his own terms, Wink amplifies on what breaking out of one's usual frame of reference means: "Having begun . . . as the object of a subject (the heritage), I revolt . . . and establish myself as a subject with an object (the text), only to find myself in the end . . . as both the subject and object of the text *and* the subject and object of my own self-reflection. Thus there is achieved a communion of horizons, in which the encounter between the horizon of the transmitted text lights up one's own horizon and leads to self-disclosure and self-understanding, while at the same time one's own horizon lights up lost elements of the text and brings them forward with relevance for life today," 66–7.

42. *Hard Times: An Authoritative Text, Contexts, Criticism,* ed. Fred Kaplan and Sylvère Monod, 3rd ed. (New York: W. W. Norton, 2001).

43. Ibid., 5.

44. Ibid., 9.

45. Robert Barnard, "Imagery and Theme in *Hard Times*," in ibid., 394.

46. "The Literary Imagination in Public Life," in ibid., 436–7.

47. D.W.Winnicott, *Playing and Reality* (London:Tavistock, 1971), 1–6; Raymond Studzinski, "Tutoring the Religious Imagination: Art and Theology as Pedagogues," *Horizons* 14:1 (1987): 24–38.

48. Iser, "The Reading Process," 290.

49. Ibid., 293.

50. Ibid., 296.

51. Niebuhr, 43–4.

52. Ibid., 46.

53. Calinescu, 159–60.

54. See Silvan S.Tomkins, "Script Theory: Differential Magnification of Affects," *Nebraska Symposium on Motivation* 26 (1979): 211–21; and Gershen Kaufman, *Shame: The Power of Caring,* 3rd ed., rev. and expanded (Rochester, Vt.: Schenkman, 1992), 192–5.

55. *Liturgy and the Social Sciences,* American Essays in Liturgy (Collegeville: The Liturgical Press, 1999), 71–5.

56. *The Practice of Everyday Life,* trans. Steven Randall (Berkeley: University of California Press, 1984).

57. Ibid., 174.

58. Ibid., xix–xxi; see also Roger Silverstone, "Let Us Then Return to the Murmuring of Everyday Practices: A Note on Michel de Certeau, Television and Everyday Life," *Theory, Culture & Society* 6 (1989): 81–2.

59. De Certeau, 169.

60. Ibid., "Walking in the City," 91–110, where de Certeau begins by describing the view from the top of the World Trade Center towers.

61. See Frederick Christian Bauerschmidt, "The Abrahamic Voyage: Michel de Certeau," *Modern Theology* 12:1 (January 1996): 6–7; and also Graham Ward, "Michel de Certeau's 'Spiritual Spaces,'" *South Atlantic Quarterly* 200:2 (Spring 2001): 501–17.

62. Bauerschmidt, 13.

63. De Certeau, 172.

64. "The Shattering of Christianity and the Articulation of Belief," *New Blackfriars* 77 (November 1996): 497.

65. *Text and Psyche: Experiencing Scripture Today* (New York: Continuum, 1998), 26.

66. Michel de Certeau, "The Weakness of Believing," trans. Saskia Brown, in *The Certeau Reader,* ed. Graham Ward (Oxford: Blackwell, 2000), 236.

To create worship space for a community of faith is to think with the skin, to remember with the body. . . . It is to understand that faith must be embodied in a world of our making—in the stories we tell, in the scriptures we read, in the rituals we rehearse, and in the objects, forms and spaces we create for habitation and celebration. Art and architecture—like other human arts and artifacts—become avenues for knowing and naming the Holy. . . . Buildings become sacred not because they reflect a particular period or style or "look," but because of the actions and embodied memories of the communities that use them.

Nathan Mitchell, "The Amen Corner: Believe in the Wind," *Worship* 73:4 (July 1999): 363–4.

In the Celtic Tradition: Irish Church Architecture

R. Kevin Seasoltz, OSB

Throughout the ages, the design of temples and churches has profoundly influenced the development of architectural forms. With the exception of the family dwelling, no other building has offered architects such ample opportunities to exercise their talents. Architectural and engineering concerns, however, have not been the only sources of influence on the shape of church buildings. Worship patterns and spirituality have also played dominant roles in church design. Often the shape of the buildings has conditioned or determined liturgical possibilities, but especially since the Second Vatican Council, it has been the shape of the liturgy itself which has influenced the style of architecture employed in the building of new churches and the renovation of extant buildings. The Vatican II reform and renewal of the liturgy have necessitated the development of new liturgical spaces which might better facilitate worship patterns more in keeping with the new theology of worship set out by the Council.

The Middle Ages

Historians of church architecture in Ireland tend to concentrate their attention on three main periods: the Middle Ages, the nineteenth century and the twentieth century, for these periods reflect significant differences not only in architectural style but also in liturgical practice and spirituality. This history provides a background against which one can view the major accomplishments that have been achieved in the design and appointment of Irish church buildings in the last forty years.[1]

During the Middle Ages, it was in churches that the most creative architecture was to be found. In Ireland most church buildings from the early period survive only in ruins, but at least from the tenth century onward, remains reveal a reasonably accurate impression of what was accomplished architecturally. Churches took various forms, ranging from small oratories, like the one at Temple Benen on Aranmore, to complex monastic churches, like those at Graiguenamanagh in Kilkenny and Athassel in Tipperary. The churches reflect the fact that Christian worship varied markedly from the eremetic style of the early Irish saints to the complex ritual patterns of the later Middle Ages.[2]

Until the twelfth century, Ireland was scarcely influenced by the Roman methods of building that characterized Christian architecture in most parts of Europe. This changed dramatically in the twelfth century, when the Irish church was brought firmly within the realm of Western Christianity, resulting in the introduction of diocesan boundaries, more than thirty bishoprics and the establishment of new religious orders from the continent, especially the Cistercians and Augustinians. These changes revolutionized church architecture so that for the first time large churches with aisles, transepts and separate chancels were introduced, and monasteries were built in an orderly fashion around square or rectangular cloister garths. These large complex ecclesiastical structures, however, were often viewed as foreign intrusions, not in keeping with the architectural simplicity associated with the early Irish saints.[3] The Irish version of Romanesque is illustrated at Cormac's Chapel on the rock of Cashel (1127–34), where there is a well-defined chancel, sculptured tympana and traces of twelfth-century paintings.

Following the invasion of Ireland in 1169–70, large parts of the country were settled by Anglo-Norman colonists who brought with them the English Gothic style of church building, so well reflected in the two Dublin cathedrals, Christ Church and St. Patrick's. The most active church builders of the later Middle Ages were the friars, especially the Dominicans and Franciscans, whose ministry focused above all on the common people through preaching and pastoral care. The friars themselves celebrated the Liturgy of the Hours in a long narrow chancel almost completely separated from the nave where there were various side chapels to accommodate private Masses and popular devotions. The most elaborate late Gothic church is that at Holy Cross, in Tipperary. This Cistercian abbey attracted numerous pilgrims who came to venerate relics of the true cross. Holy Cross is one of a number of medieval churches in Ireland recently restored for public worship. These churches, however, are not ideally suited for celebration of contemporary liturgy since the nave is usually quite unrelated to the chancel. Certainly it is rather rare that restored medieval church buildings can accommodate effectively the demands of the theology and practice of liturgy as envisioned by the Second Vatican Council.[4]

The Nineteenth Century

The development of church buildings in Ireland over the centuries was determined not only by historical, theological and liturgical factors but also by the whims of architectural fashion, reflected above all in the numerous churches built in the nineteenth century, which represented a great variety of revivalist styles. Most of the leading architects looked back to the high Middle Ages for their inspiration but some designed churches in a classical, early Christian or Romanesque style. The early decades of the century were marked by extensive church building by the Church of Ireland with the help of considerable government funding. Both before and after the Catholic Emancipation Act of 1829 the Roman Catholic Church embarked on a vast building program, including several large churches and cathedrals, among them St. Mary's Pro-cathedral in Dublin and the cathedral at Carlow. Many Catholic churches were built in a neo-classical style, chosen perhaps because the clergy acquired familiarity with that style during their continental travels and because Catholics wanted their buildings to be distinguished from those of the Church of Ireland.[5]

A Gothic revival developed in the 1840s, led by A. W. N. Pugin, who was convinced that a medieval setting was the only one suitable for Christian worship. His buildings include the Catholic cathedrals at Killarney in County Kerry (1842–50) and at Enniscorthy in County Wexford (1843–48).[6] The most popular alternative to Gothic in the nineteenth century was Romanesque, in the style of early Irish churches, some of which have an attached belfry similar to the Temple Finghin at Clonmacnoise. There is no doubt that the nineteenth century in Ireland was a period of amazing vitality in church design that was a response to the need for more worship spaces. It was also a period of exciting architectural diversity, much of it of very high quality.[7] The interior layout of these churches reflected a post-Reformation understanding of liturgy. For Protestants, that meant emphasis on preaching and a de-emphasis on the eucharist and images in the church. For Catholics, it meant a spectator church with almost exclusive emphasis on the Mass celebrated by the clergy, while eucharistic and other devotions often sustained the religious lives of the common people.

The Modern Period

In assessing the complex origins of twentieth-century church architecture, we need to keep in mind a number of factors. First of all there were widespread social and technological developments which called for imaginative architectural responses. The most outstanding example of a modern architectural approach to church design would be the Church of Notre Dame du Raincy, a spectator church near Paris designed by Augustus Perret in 1923. The plan is traditional, the structure flooded with colored light and free of monumentalism; there is a sense of openness and unity within the whole assembly.[8]

This discovery of the possibilities that could be realized in church building through the use of glass, concrete and steel was complemented by the development of a profound theology of the eucharist, seen as a corporate act of worship involving the whole assembly of the Christian faithful actively and intelligently participating in the rite. This union of sound theology and architectural expertise was given marvelous expression by the German architect Rudolf Schwarz working in close collaboration with the famous liturgical theologian Romano Guardini. The site was the Burg Rothenfels-on-Main center of the Quickborn youth movement. In 1927, the Schloss Rothenfels, a castle which served as the headquarters of the Catholic Youth Movement in Germany, was remodeled under the direction of Guardini and Schwarz. The castle contained a regular chapel as well as a large hall which was occasionally used for the celebration of the eucharist. The hall, a rectangular space with white walls, deep windows and stone pavement, was devoid of any decoration. One hundred black cuboid stools, the only furniture in the room, could easily be changed in accord with the various functions taking place in the space. When the eucharist was celebrated, an altar was set up with the assembly surrounding it on three sides. There was no sense of monumentality; it gave expression to simple beauty and flexibility; it made possible the celebration of Mass facing the community; it demonstrated the priority of persons over things and the importance of hospitality as a distinctive character of the church. The influence of this simple arrangement on the liturgical development in Germany and Switzerland (and subsequently in other parts of the world), has been enormous. It provided a clear symbol of the communal nature of the church expressed above all in the corporate dimensions of the liturgy, especially the eucharist.[9] The experience at Rosenfels inspired Schwarz to write *The Church Incarnate* (1938), an epoch-making book which set out an impressive theological foundation for church building.[10] Schwarz facilitated the harnessing of a fresh understanding of the liturgy with amazing developments in technology and engineering techniques.

Following the Second World War, major churches were built in Europe, designed especially by three distinguished German architects: Rudolf Schwarz, Emil Steffan and Dominicus Bohm. Their work, grounded in sound liturgical principles, stood in marked contrast to Le Corbusier's Chapel of Notre Dame du Haut at Ronchamp (1955), which was an important milestone in European architecture but not a structure that promoted liturgical renewal.[11]

The first modern church built in Ireland in the twentieth century was that of Christ the King at Turners Cross, Cork, designed in 1927 by the American architect Barry Byrne. Built of steel and concrete, the edifice brought a strong sense of unity between priest and people, between sanctuary and nave. In Ireland, however, the design of churches in imitation of earlier styles of architecture continued well into the 1960s; most of these buildings were adorned with artificial veneers which simply presented earlier architectural styles but used new engineering and structural techniques.[12] For example, Romanesque and Gothic buildings were constructed with reinforced concrete.

New beginnings were inspired by the Church Exhibitions Committee of the Royal Institute of Architects of Ireland and the encouragement of the Benedictines of Glenstal Abbey.[13] Their efforts, however, were overshadowed by the significant directives of the Second Vatican Council, especially those contained in the Constitution on the Sacred Liturgy. In 1965 the Irish hierarchy established an Advisory Committee on Sacred Art and Architecture whose members were either distinguished architects or specialists in theology.[14] The documents issued by the Second Vatican Council, especially the Constitution on the Sacred Liturgy, the Constitution on the Church and the Constitution on the Church in the Modern World, strengthened the liturgical movement in Ireland and inspired the creativity of some of the best architects. Hence the years after the Council witnessed a dramatic development of church building in Ireland. Naturally, the quality of the new churches was uneven, but for a relatively small country, outstanding examples of excellence were achieved.

Much of the inspiration for these remarkable buildings was provided by the Irish Episcopal Commission for Liturgy. The Irish Roman Catholic bishops were among the first members of the hierarchy to issue a directory on the environment and art of Christian worship. The first edition was published in 1966 and revised in 1972. A third edition, considerably revised and expanded, was completed in 1991 but not issued until 1994.[15] Introducing the directory, Bishop Joseph Duffy, chairman of the Advisory Committee, highlighted the importance of the assembly as the celebrant of the liturgy and stressed the vital role of a vision of faith. He writes:

> *The Directory contains basic information but always with an eye on the liturgical assembly, the ministers and people who actually use or will use the building. For this reason it spells out a vision of faith which explains the information and unifies the various*

*stages of the planning and execution. The vision is of God
gathering his people together present among them. . . . Like
any other building, a church is a piece of architecture, the result
of human intelligence and skills applied to various materials.
But it differs from other buildings in that it is first and last a
work of faith and a sign of faith. It is a sign of a world redeemed
in Christ and filled with the Spirit of God, and yet a world in
which the fruits of redemption have still to be fully recognized.*[16]

It is this emphasis on transcendence which can ensure that
the renewed liturgical space communicates a sense of awe and mystery. As Bishop Duffy notes,

*It calls for spiritual qualities on the part of those responsible for
its construction and maintenance, qualities which go beyond
technical skills and even artistic flair. They are the qualities which
surface when a true sense of the liturgy has been achieved:
reverence for the divine presence, devotion to its protection, trust
in its permanence.*[17]

Certainly the years following the Second Vatican Council saw dramatic developments in church architecture in Ireland. Though the quality was uneven, there were many outstanding achievements. The brief for a new church building set out by the Second Vatican Council and postconciliar documents was generally quite open and generous in its basic requirements, asking above all for a free-standing altar permitting the presider to face the rest of the assembly, and a gathering of the community around the table of the word as well as the eucharistic table. Since the Council various plans for church building and reform have emerged in Ireland as well as in other parts of the world. They can be broadly divided into four general categories: (1) longitudinal shape, based on the traditional division of sanctuary and nave; (2) transverse emphasis, in which there is a careful planning of a close relationship between assembly and altar;

(3) centralized plan, giving rise to more or less circular buildings, but rarely concentric to the altar; and (4) antiphonal plan, in which the assembly gathers on two opposite sides of an axial space containing the altar at one end, the ambo at another and the presider's chair placed in close relation to both altar and ambo. These plans reflect an understanding of liturgical celebration ranging from that of spectator worship (longitudinal plan) to full, active and conscious participation by the whole assembly (antiphonal plan).[18]

With the development of new technology and materials, including reinforced concrete, steel, factory laminated wood, and new forms of colored glass, along with important advances in engineering, church architects were able to move away from the concept of a long, narrow nave, dictated by the use of stone, brick and wood, and to respond more effectively to fresh concepts of space and light, more in keeping with the modern liturgical movement.[19] In Ireland, as in other parts of the world, modern church architecture stirred up lively public debate with many people taking a vociferous dislike to what was happening in the church. Despite the challenge, traditional sanctuaries were often hastily changed, sometimes with disastrous results, simply so that Mass could be celebrated facing the people.

Longitudinal Plans

Michael Scott was the leading architect of his generation following the Second World War; he was responsible for introducing the International Style into Ireland. It was not until 1964, however, that he had a commission to build a church in Ireland. The church of Corpus Christi at Knockanure in County Kerry is a building of absolute simplicity and dignity, based on the architectural philosophy of Mies van der Rohe: Less is more. Although it rises well above the surrounding countryside, it has little in common with the rugged Kerry landscape.[20]

Between 1967 and 1977, Liam McCormick established a reputation for being the most important church architect in Ireland. During that decade he designed a number of significant churches, including St. Michael's at Creeslough and St. Colmcille's in Glenties, both in County Donegal; Our Lady of Lourdes at Steeltown in Derry; and Christ Prince of Peace at Fossa in County Kerry. His buildings show great respect for the landscape, particularly the wilds of Kerry and Donegal. He was neither philosopher nor theologian but possessed a profound sense of what was right in solving particular architectural problems. At times he achieved an expression of sheer poetry, but at other times his sanctuaries are not sufficiently generous in scale to allow for proper ritual movements.[21] Likewise the relationship between his sanctuaries and naves tends to reduce the laity to mere spectators. As is generally recognized, longitudinal plans tend to separate the altar from the people, thereby setting up a stage for the enactment of the liturgy.

Transverse Plans

One of the first plans that assembled the congregation around the altar was that for the Convent Chapel in Cookstown, County Tyrone, designed by Laurence McConville in 1965. The grouping of the sisters around the altar, a strong piece of sculpture by Michael Biggs, evoked a firm sense of community. The tabernacle, however, was placed on the main altar even though the chapel was completed after the Second Vatican Council. The space was enhanced by handsome contributions by young Irish artists, including stained glass by Patrick Pye, Stations of the Cross by Benedict Tutty, and metalwork behind the altar by Patrick McElroy. It was about this time that Irish artists were recognized as having an important contribution to make to the church environment.[22]

An appreciation for the whole assembly as the celebrant of the liturgy was also reflected in the plan for the Church of the Holy Spirit in Ballycalen, County Wexford (1971), designed by Wilfrid

Cantwell. He was convinced that a church should not be based on a static axial plan but should reflect and facilitate a sense of movement since the church is a community of pilgrim people. In Ballycalen, however, that movement gets bogged down because of the excessive weight of the beams and pillars.[23]

Effective use of new materials that allowed for flexibility is reflected in many of the churches built in the 1970s. This is evident in the church of St. Fintan in Sutton, County Dublin (1973), designed by Andrew Devane, who had worked in the firm of Frank Lloyd Wright in the United States. The emphasis is clearly on the honest use of materials and the development of organic forms.[24]

From 1975 onward there was a general effort to incorporate the demands of the liturgical movement and the directives of the Second Vatican Council and postconciliar norms into the design of church buildings in Ireland. There was an effort to break out of the mold of what a church should look like and to take account of the social and cultural context in which a church building would function. The church of Our Lady of the Nativity in Newtown, County Kildare (1975), designed by Tyndal, Hogan and Hurley, put an emphasis on the interiority of the church and its domestic character.[25] In this regard it reflected the liturgical theology of Frédéric Debuyst, set out in his *Modern Architecture and Christian Celebration.*[26] Emphasis was placed on community and the close relationships experienced in the modern house.

In 1976 a church architecture competition was held in the Archdiocese of Dublin, which was then in the midst of a major diocesan expansion. A number of good churches resulted from the competition, but the quality of most of them was considerably hampered by budgets totally inadequate to cover quality design construction.[27]

Another competition was held for a Chapel of Reconciliation at Knock in County Mayo. The commission was awarded to DeBlacam and Meagher. The building contributes a modern presence in an otherwise rather dreary architectural landscape, dotted with various crosses, statues and buildings of indifferent quality. Surrounded and covered with grass, the building appears to be an extension of the landscape. There are 65 confessionals and counseling rooms around the interior walls. The inner space moves from a dimly lit periphery to bright light over the sanctuary area, which is rather an anticlimax because the furnishings lack a strong sense of presence. A number of competent artists, including Eric Pierce, James McKenna and Lorna Donalon, contributed to the appointment of the space.[28]

Circular Plans

Circular buildings have a very long history in Ireland. That basic plan can easily be accommodated to the desire for a church in which the assembly encircles the altar on three sides with the church walls encircling the community. It was this background which inspired Liam McCormick to design the church of St. Aungus in Burt, County Donegal, in 1967. This building is considered to be McCormick's most important contribution in the development of Irish church buildings. He abandoned his former predilection for a rigid rectangular plan in favor of a circular structure, which allowed freedom in locating subsidiary spaces within a double circle. The building stands as a piece of sheer poetry in the midst of a gorgeous landscape.[29] The crucifix, altar and font were designed by Imogen Stuart, one of the most distinguished artists who has contributed many pieces to modern churches in Ireland.[30]

Another example of a fan-shaped church is Saint Paul's Church in Mullingar, designed by Meehan, Levins, Delaney, Kavanagh and Associates. The simple shape of the building is broken to accommodate a sunken baptismal area and a chapel for the reservation of the eucharist. The baptistry, designed by Christopher Ryan, was intended for total immersion—a rarity in Ireland.[31]

In September 1979 Pope John Paul II visited the shrine at Knock and designated the Church of Our Lady Queen of Ireland a basilica. Designed in 1970 by Louis Brennan, Brian Brennan and Daithí Hanly, it is the largest worship space in Ireland, accommodating 7,500 people. It is estimated that a million and a half pilgrims visit Knock each year. The church is a twelve-sided amphitheater with the altar at the center of the space beneath a vast hexagonal drum. The Blessed Sacrament is reserved in a chapel behind the sanctuary. There is ample open space to allow easy movement of the large number of pilgrims, including those in wheelchairs. Behind the altar is an enormous tapestry designed by Ray Carroll.[32]

Antiphonal Plans

In the years since the Second Vatican Council, Richard Hurley has emerged not only as an exceptionally competent architect of church buildings, but also as the author of articles and books in which he has set out a profound and clear liturgical theology and its implications for the design and appointment of sacred spaces. Among his exceptionally beautiful accomplishments was the design of the National Institute for Pastoral Liturgy in Carlow (1980). The center was the brainchild of Msgr. Sean Swayne, a gifted and tireless worker for liturgical reform and renewal in Ireland. The center was designed to train priests and laity in all matters of liturgical reform and renewal, including sacred art and architecture.[33] For many years an annual seminar was held at the center for practicing architects and artists who came from all over Ireland to share ideas and gain inspiration.

The brief for the project included gutting a whole wing of an extant building at St. Patrick's College and the creation of a gathering space, a room for eucharist, a Blessed Sacrament chapel, and a sacristy. The gathering area was of special importance since it would provide a place of welcome, a place of assembly both before and after the liturgy, and would flow over into the dining room. The room for the eucharist is right off the gathering area, which is partially two stories high and contains an open staircase. Spacious and filled with light, the room for the eucharist was the great room of the extant building. Hurley planned the space so that the room is oriented toward an informal antiphonal gathering surrounding a central area focused on the altar. The presider's chair was placed at one end of the axis with the altar and ambo placed on the other side, on an axis facing up the room. Everything in the room was a shade of off-white—walls, floor, ceiling, light fixtures and carpet. The only color was added by the sap green of the large fig tree behind the presider's chair and a terra cotta Madonna and Child sculpted by Benedict Tutty. Carefully crafted vestments and altar vessels also added to the vitality of the room. In some ways the ambiance was reminiscent of Cistercian churches, which tradition-ally have placed emphasis on interiority and simplicity;[34] at Carlow the emphasis was not only on awe and mystery but also on the whole assembly as the celebrant of the liturgy. A totally different environment was created in the Blessed Sacrament chapel, an inti-mate area off the room for the eucharist, conveying a sense of peace and withdrawal, a place for personal prayer and quiet reflection. The exquisite tabernacle was designed and executed in silver by Peter Donovan.[35]

Richard Hurley was also commissioned by the Cistercian nuns at Glencairn to renovate their church in keeping with the demands of the reformed liturgy. The altar was moved from the apse to the west end of the building, and the nuns' choir was placed between the ambo and tabernacle now standing in the former apse. The nuns naturally celebrate the Liturgy of the Hours in their choir stalls and remain there for the liturgy of the word during the eucharist, moving around the altar for the eucharistic prayer and communion. Benedict Tutty designed and executed the tabernacle and processional cross, Phyllis Burke the stained glass in the apse.[36]

What was formerly a side chapel for guests was converted into a reconciliation space but it is never used. That space could have been converted into a handsome chapel for the Blessed Sacrament, but the nuns preferred the tabernacle in the body of the church.

In 1999 Richard Hurley was commissioned to renovate St. Mary's Oratory at St. Patrick's College in Maynooth, County Kildare. There are two chapels in the college, a major chapel built in 1879 and St. Mary's Chapel, originally a study hall designed by Augustus Welby Pugin but refurbished as a chapel in 1878. In 1967 the chapel was re-ordered when the sanctuary was moved from the west wall to the lengthy north wall, with the students surrounding the altar on three sides. That arrangement proved to be unsatisfactory. The latest renovation includes new woodblock flooring and oak paneling and a new pipe organ, with the addition of major artwork commissioned especially for the space as well as moveable furniture. The main thrust of the plan is the restoration of the east-west axis of the chapel and the development of an antiphonal plan with the alignment of the major liturgical furnishings along the spine of the east-west axis. The pipe organ and the ambo are at one end of the chapel, the altar stands in the midst of the assembly, and the presider's chair is located in front of a devotional space where the tabernacle is located on the west wall. Standing between two stained glass windows is a large tapestry designed by Patrick Pye. Below it is an abstract painting by Kim En Joong, which surrounds the tabernacle designed by Benedict Tutty. This latter ensemble, designed by the architect, creates a vivid splash of color and presents a strong focus for personal prayer apart from the time for liturgical celebration.[37] The space is indeed formative of the seminarians who worship there.

Cathedrals

The directives of the Second Vatican Council brought about major changes in existing cathedrals in Ireland, which had originally been constructed for a very different understanding of the celebration of liturgy. Several of the Irish cathedrals have been re-ordered quite successfully.

St. Macartan's Cathedral in Monaghan is a neo-Gothic building in the Ulster borderland diocese of Clogher in Northern Ireland. Originally dedicated in 1892, the cathedral was renovated under the wise direction of the current bishop, Joseph Duffy. In 1982 he called on the distinguished Dublin sculptor, the late Michael Biggs, to adapt the interior of the church to postconciliar liturgical needs. Originally the intention was to limit any changes to the sanctuary area and to retain existing furnishings, but that plan was fortunately rejected.[38]

The basic cruciform shape of the church and the concentration of natural light at the intersection of the nave and the transepts determined the place for the altar, which should be the focal point of any church. Four side chapels were given over to separate sacramental functions, relating them to the assembly, to one another, and to the eucharistic altar. The Blessed Mother's shrine and the Stations of the Cross were given their own special but secondary places and not treated simply as decor. A large crucifix, designed by the late Richard Enda King, rests with simple dignity against a pillar at the left of the altar and behind the ambo. A chapter room has been renovated for small group liturgies and for exposition of the Blessed Sacrament. Michael Biggs himself designed the altar, bishop's chair, and ambo, as well as lettering throughout the building. The strong, sturdy and pleasing form of the altar dominates the cathedral from every angle and proclaims clearly, "I am what this building is about."[39]

Frances Biggs, Michael's wife and a woman of many accomplishments, designed five extraordinary tapestries for the church, three to hang behind the bishop's chair, one behind the baptismal font, and one behind the tabernacle. The hanging behind the tabernacle is especially powerful, containing a large broken host symbolic of the body of Christ broken for all of us so that our bodies might be broken for one another. She also designed the Stations of the Cross, which have been executed in strong colors and very simple lines, more like cartoons for stained glass windows.[40]

In 1995 Richard Hurley was commissioned to carry out a major renovation of the Cathedral of St. Mary and St. Anne at Cork. The sunken baptistry, located immediately inside the great west door, sets up a strong axis with the altar and bishop's chair located behind it. Unfortunately it does not allow baptism by complete immersion. The new sanctuary is thrust out into the nave of the church and accommodates the altar with the assembly arranged on three sides. The bishop's chair, the stalls for the presbytery, the pulpit, the baptismal font and several other pieces were retained from the old cathedral, but they were moved to new positions in order to accommodate the new liturgical design. The work of distinguished artists has been wonderfully incorporated in the space, and includes paintings by Patrick Pye in the Lady Chapel at the back of the cathedral; stained glass by James Scanlon in the Blessed Sacrament chapel, which is located in a quiet area off the sanctuary; sculptures and shrines by Ken Thompson; a silver tabernacle by Peter Donovan; and the altar, ambo and tabernacle pillar by Richard Hurley.[41]

Since the Second Vatican Council, no building in Ireland has caused such public controversy as the proposed renovation of the Cathedral of the Assumption at Carlow. Richard Pierce, who has a sound reputation and skill in conservation, was eventually hired as architect in order to placate the town people and heal the divisions. His plan brings the altar forward as far as possible into the nave without obstructing the view of the people in the transepts. Unfortunately the tabernacle is located directly behind the main altar; it is placed in the old main altar which is embedded in a new reredos constructed of stone and located in front of the east window. The bishop's chair has been given a new location between the chancel and the north transept. Although the overall reordering in the Carlow Cathedral has brought some sense of satisfaction and relief to the various parties who disputed the reordering scheme in the first place, it is quite clear that the end result is a serious compromise.[42]

Reformed Churches

Roman Catholics constitute by far the largest majority of church-going Christians in Ireland. It is not surprising, therefore, that most of the churches built in Ireland in the last forty years have been built for the celebration of Roman Catholic worship. The major Reformed churches in the island were largely completed by the end of the nineteenth century. In the last century the building of new Reformed churches was largely confined to the Methodist and Presbyterian congregations. Two new Methodist churches attracted notice, one at Ballinteer in County Dublin designed by Edwin Squire, and one at Shankill Road in Belfast designed by Gordan McKnight in 1985. Both were built in a modern idiom. Three new Presbyterian churches were constructed: the First Presbyterian Church at Larne in 1978 by Samuel Stevenson & Sons; Lucan Presbyterian Church in County Dublin, designed by Hamilton Young Associates in 1988; and Lisnabrees Presbyterian Church designed in 1990 by Knox and Markwell for a congregation at Bangor in County Down.[43]

Some Conclusions

Irish architects and artists are certainly entitled to a sense of pride and satisfaction when they reflect on what they have achieved in the last century in the field of church architecture and the environment for worship. The best work in Ireland surely compares very favorably with what was achieved in Europe and the United States.

Developments in the liturgy and in a renewed understanding of ecclesiology have given architects and artists a rich opportunity to exercise their creativity. In reflecting on successful Irish architectural projects, we are able to draw several conclusions which have ongoing value in communal efforts to construct and appoint sacred spaces in which the whole assembly of the faithful might worship God and be transformed into vital communities of faith who are in turn transforming agents in establishing the reign of God in the world.

First, church leadership, especially on the part of bishops and pastors, is essential in encouraging and commissioning competent architects and artists for church projects. That leadership was exercised by the Irish Episcopal Commission for Liturgy in the development of the various editions of *The Place of Worship: Pastoral Directory on the Building and Reordering of Churches.* Such leadership has not been provided by most hierarchies and pastors in the Catholic church.

Second, the most competent architects are most likely to design the most effective buildings. They must, however, be capable of dialoguing with their clients and be open to the development of a deep understanding of the church's theology of worship.

Third, the best artists available should be commissioned to appoint liturgical spaces. They should be involved in the design and construction of the building early in the development of the project rather than being commissioned to create art after the design of the building has been completed. Like the architects, they must be willing to dialogue with their clients and should see their role as one of ministry to the community.

Fourth, budgetary limitations should not necessarily determine what is to be built and appointed. A master plan should be created so that long-range projects can be envisioned. The great Gothic cathedrals were not built in a day; likewise parish plans should be developed always with the future of the community in mind.

Richard Hurley has expressed well the challenge offered to Irish architects and artists who hope to minister to the church in the future; he also challenges architects and artists from other parts of the world:

> [A]s the trend towards meeting the demands of social activity within the context of church building develops, it is possible that church architecture will lose its sacred meaning, its raison d'être. It becomes more important than ever that the symbolized mood defies rationalization. That is why historians still look to the Gothic church as representing the embodiment of a sacred building. The task of finding a new inter-relation between social need and aesthetic expression still haunts the serious architect. If aesthetic ambition fades, then the star which has always been present in Christian architecture will fade with it. The Catholic Church is faced with a number of important questions relating to church architecture. Why build? What to build? How to build? Should church architecture still have as a priority the ambition to be an art form? If the answer is yes, then the church must take the matter more seriously . . . and make more funds available to achieve a consistently higher standard than heretofore achieved. And what about the liturgy, which after all is the raison d'être for church building? These matters are important, because if the liturgy is not given the attention it demands then one can hardly blame architects [and artists] if they too fail to deliver buildings suitable to their function and of high aesthetic value.[44]

1. Brian de Breffny and George Mott, *The Churches and Abbeys of Ireland* (London: Thames and Hudson, 1976).

2. Roger Stalley, "Middle Ages," in *Sacred Places—The Story of Christian Architecture in Ireland* (Dublin and Belfast: The Royal Institute of the Architects of Ireland

and The Royal Society of Ulster Architects, 2000), 6; De Breffny and Mott, 7–104.

3. Stalley, 7.

4. Ibid., 7–9.

5. Paul Larmour, "The Styles of Irish Church Architecture in the Nineteenth Century," in *Sacred Places,* 10–3.

6. See: *Pugin: A Gothic Passion,* eds. Paul Atterbury and Clive Wainwright (New Haven: Yale University Press, 1994), especially the essay by Roderick O'Donnell, 63–89.

7. Larmour, 11–2.

8. Richard Hurley, "20th Century," in *Sacred Places,* 14.

9. Ibid.

10. Rudolf Schwarz, *The Church Incarnate: The Sacred Function of Church Architecture,* trans. Cynthia Harris (Chicago: H. Regnery Co., 1958).

11. Hurley, 14.

12. Hurley, *Irish Church Architecture in the Era of Vatican II* (Dublin: Dominican Publications, 2001), 21–5.

13. Hurley, "20th Century," 14.

14. Ibid. The committee included J. J. McGarry (chairman), Wilfrid Cantwell, Ray Carroll, A. D. Devane, Austin Flannery, Richard Hurley, Cahal McCarthy, W. H. H. McCormick, Gerard Montague, James White and Brendan Devil (secretary).

15. Irish Episcopal Commission for Liturgy, *The Place of Worship* (Dublin and Carlow: Veritas and the Irish Institute of Pastoral Liturgy, 1994). For a detailed commentary see: R. Kevin Seasoltz, "The Place of Worship," *Worship* 69 (1995): 175–8.

16. Ibid., 5.

17. Ibid., 6.

18. Hurley, "20th Century," 15.

19. See Michael J. Crosbie, *Architecture for the Gods* (Mulgrave, Australia: The Image Publishing Group Pty. Ltd., 1999).

20. Hurley, "20th Century," 15. See also *Irish Church Architecture,* 45–6.

21. Ibid., *Irish Church Architecture,* 48–9.

22. Distinguished 20th-century Irish artists such as Mainie Jellett, Louis le Brocquy, Gerard Dillon, Patrick Collins and Patrick Scott, created works which might well be called "sacred," but they were not commissioned to produce work for the church. See Gesa E. Thiessen, *Theology and Modern Irish Art* (Blackrock: The Columba Press, 1999).

23. Richard Hurley and Wilfrid Cantwell, *Contemporary Irish Church Architecture* (Dublin: Gill and Macmillan, 1985), 73.

24. Hurley, "20th Century," 16.

25. Hurley and Cantwell, 94–7.

26. Frédéric Debuyst, *Modern Architecture and Christian Celebration* (Richmond: John Knox Press, 1968).

27. Hurley, "20th Century," 16.

28. Hurley, *Irish Church Architecture,* 78–9.

29. Hurley, *Irish Church Architecture,* 81. See also: Hurley and Cantwell, 65–6.

30. See Brian Fallon, *Imogen Stuart: Sculptor* (Dublin: Four Courts Press, 2002); *Stations of the Cross by Imogen Stuart* (Blackrock: The Columba Press, 2001).

31. Hurley, *Irish Church Architecture,* 79–80.

32. Ibid., 88–9.

33. Richard Hurley, "The Eucharist Room at Carlow Liturgy Center: The Search for Meaning," *Worship* 70 (1996): 238–50.

34. See Terryl N. Kinder, *Cistercian Europe: Architecture of Contemplation* (Grand Rapids and Kalamazoo: William B. Eerdmans Publishing Company and Cistercian Publications, 2002).

35. Hurley, *Irish Church Architecture,* 95.

36. Ibid., 95–6.

37. Richard Hurley, "St. Mary's Oratory, St. Patrick's College, Maynooth, Co. Kildare," *Irish Architect* (October 1999): 18–20.

38. *A Cathedral Renewed,* ed. Eltin Griffin (Blackrock: The Columba Press, 1998). See R. Kevin Seasoltz, "A Cathedral Renewed: St. Macaertan's, Monaghan," *Worship* 74 (2000): 268–70.

39. See Joseph Duffy, "Michael Biggs: Liturgical Artist," *Doctrine and Life* 44 (February 1994): 110–5.

40. Eltin Griffin, "The Cathedral Artists: A Release of Creative Energy," in *A Cathedral Renewed,* 50–5. See also: Frances Biggs and Donal Neary, *The Way of the Cross* (Dublin: Veritas, 2002).

41. Richard Hurley, "Cathedral of St. Mary and St. Anne, Cork," *Irish Architect* (March 1997): 29–34.

42. Hurley, *Irish Church Architecture,* 124–6.

43. Hurley, "20th Century," 17–8.

44. Hurley, *Irish Church Architecture,* 127.

Bibliography of Nathan D. Mitchell
(as of August 2002)

Ongoing

Editor: *Assembly* (Notre Dame Center for Pastoral Liturgy), 1989–present.

Editor: *Liturgy Digest* (Notre Dame Center for Pastoral Liturgy), 1992–present.

2002

"The Amen Corner: How We Belong," *Worship* 76:4 (July 2002): 367–77.

"The Amen Corner: Whose Liturgy?" *Worship* 76:3 (May 2002): 268–77.

"Tell It Slant: Gestures and Symbols in the Liturgy," *Liturgical Ministry* 11:2 (2002): 89–94.

"The Amen Corner: Seeing Salvation," *Worship* 76:2 (March 2002): 167–76.

"The Amen Corner: Brave New World," *Worship* 76:1 (January 2002): 67–77.

2001

"The Amen Corner: This Saving Cup," *Worship* 75:6 (November 2001): 545–53.

"How Can We Keep from Singing?" *Pastoral Music* 26:1 (October–November 2001): 44–6.

"The Amen Corner: Once upon a Time," *Worship* 75:5 (September 2001): 469–78.

"The Amen Corner: Toward a Poetics of Gesture," *Worship* 75:4 (July 2001): 356–65.

"What's Next in the Liturgical Movement? Part 3: The Loss of Catholic Cultures," *Rite* 32:4 (May/June 2001): 4–7.

"The Amen Corner: Ritual as *Ars Amatoria*," *Worship* 75:3 (May 2001): 250–9.

"What's Next in the Liturgical Movement? Part 2: Vernaculars," *Rite* 32:3 (April 2001): 4–6.

"The Amen Corner: Liturgy as Lingua Franca," *Worship* 75:2 (March 2001): 173–82.

"What's Next in the Liturgical Movement? Part 1: A Little History," *Rite* 32:2 (February/March 2001): 4–6.

"The Amen Corner: Cause for Celebration," *Worship* 75:1 (January 2001): 68–77.

2000

Table, Bread and Cup: Meditations on Eucharist—Selections from Assembly (Notre Dame: Notre Dame Center for Pastoral Liturgy, 2000).

"The Cross That Spoke," *The Cross in Christian Tradition,* ed. Elizabeth A. Dreyer (New York: Paulist Press, 2000), 72–92.

"Washed Away by the Blood of God," *The Cross in Christian Tradition,* ed. Elizabeth A. Dreyer (New York: Paulist Press, 2000), 57–71.

"The Amen Corner: Being Good and Being Beautiful," *Worship* 74:6 (November 2000): 550–8.

"Re-Membering Assembly," *Pastoral Music* 25:1 (October–November 2000): 34–8.

"The Amen Corner: That Really Long Prayer," *Worship* 74:5 (September 2000): 468–77.

"Elected Silence, Sing to Me," *Pastoral Music* 24:6 (August–September 2000): 67–8.

"The Amen Corner: Seeing in the Dark," *Worship* 74:4 (July 2000): 370–9.

"Troubling Assertions from Rome," *America* 183 (July 1–8, 2000): 20–1.

"The Amen Corner: The Rest Is Commentary," *Worship* 74:3 (May 2000): 248–56.

"God's Word: A Human Word," *U.S. Catholic* 65 (Spring 2000): 33–40.

"Jesus: The Real Thing," *GIA Quarterly* 11:3 (Spring 2000): 8–9, 36–7.

"Re-creating the World: A Meditation on the Easter Vigil," *Catechumenate* 22 (March 2000): 2–13.

"The Amen Corner: Capital Letters," *Worship* 74:2 (March 2000): 173–82.

"The Amen Corner: Life—What's Liturgy Got to Do with It?" *Worship* 74:1 (January 2000): 59–68.

"Jesus Takes the Road Less Traveled," *GIA Quarterly* 11:2 (Winter 2000): 8–9, 38.

1999

Liturgy and the Social Sciences, American Essays Series, ed. Edward B. Foley (Collegeville: The Liturgical Press, 1999).

"Ritual as Reading," *Source and Summit: Commemorating Joseph A. Jungmann SJ,* eds. Joanne M. Pierce and Michael Downey (Collegeville: The Liturgical Press, 1999), 161–81.

"Worship of the Eucharist Outside Mass," in *Handbook for Liturgical Studies,* vol. III: *The Eucharist,* Anscar J. Chupungco, ed. (Collegeville: The Liturgical Press, 1999), 263–75.

"The Struggle of Religious Women for Eucharist," *Benedictines* 52:2 (Winter 1999): 12–25.

"The Amen Corner: Reforming a Millennium," *Worship* 73:6 (November 1999): 545–55.

"It's Your Own Mystery," *GIA Quarterly* 10:2 (Winter 1999): 10–11, 36–7.

"Powers of Persuasion," *America* (October 9, 1999): 12–5.

"The Amen Corner: Eucharistic Devotion," *Worship* 73:5 (September 1999): 457–66.

"The Future Present," *GIA Quarterly* 11:1 (Fall 1999): 8–9, 40–1.

"The Amen Corner: Believe in the Wind," *Worship* 73:4 (July 1999): 359–68.

"To End is to Begin," *GIA Quarterly* 10:4 (Summer 1999): 8–9, 36–7.

"The Amen Corner: Worship as Music," *Worship* 73:3 (May 1999): 249–59.

"The Spin of Ordinary Time," *GIA Quarterly* 10:3 (Spring 1999): 10–1, 38–9.

"The Amen Corner: Eucharist without Walls," *Worship* 73:2 (March 1999): 180–8.

Book review: "*Ritual: Perspectives and Dimensions,* by Catherine Bell," *Worship* 73:1 (January 1999): 95–6.

"The Amen Corner: Back to the Future?" *Worship* 73:1 (January 1999): 60–9.

1998

Real Presence: The Work of the Eucharist (Chicago: Liturgy Training Publications, 1998); new and rev. ed., 2001.

"Liturgy and Ecclesiology," in *Handbook for Liturgical Studies,* vol. II: *Fundamental Liturgy,* Anscar J. Chupungco, ed. (Collegeville: The Liturgical Press, 1998), 113–27.

"The Amen Corner: Smells and Bells," *Worship* 72:6 (November 1998): 539–47.

"The Amen Corner: The Economics of the Eucharist (Part II)," *Worship* 72:5 (September 1998): 452–63.

"Days of Christmas Pasch," *GIA Quarterly* 10:1 (Fall 1998): 10–2.

"The Amen Corner: The Economics of the Eucharist (Part I)," *Worship* 72:4 (July 1998): 354–65.

"The Amen Corner: Becoming Eucharist," *Worship* 72:3 (May 1998): 270–80.

Book review: "*The Future of Eucharist: How a New Self-Awareness among Catholics is Changing the Way They Believe and Worship,* by Bernard Cooke," *Horizons* 25 (Spring 1998): 123–4.

"The Amen Corner: A Tale of Two Documents," *Worship* 72:2 (March 1998): 162–72.

"The Amen Corner: Rocking toward the Third Millennium," *Worship* 72:1 (January 1998): 78–86.

1997

Liturgy Digest 4:2 (Notre Dame: Notre Dame Center for Pastoral Liturgy, 1997).

Nathan Mitchell and John Witvliet, *Liturgy Digest* 4:1 (Notre Dame: Notre Dame Center for Pastoral Liturgy, 1997).

"The Amen Corner: Reform the Reform?" *Worship* 71:6 (November 1997): 555–63.

"A Place for Eucharist," *Assembly* 23 (September 1997): 36–7.

"The Amen Corner: Rereading Reform," *Worship* 71:5 (September 1997): 462–70.

"The Amen Corner: Negotiating Rapture," *Worship* 71:4 (July 1997): 350–7.

"The Amen Corner: Culture Wars II: Seeking Common Ground," *Worship* 71:3 (May 1997): 350–57.

"Love's Lyrics: The Eucharistic Prayer," *Assembly* 23:2 (March 1997): 10–1, 16.

"The Amen Corner: Culture Wars," *Worship* 71:2 (March 1997): 168–78.

"The Amen Corner: Liturgical Correctness," *Worship* 71:1 (January 1997): 62–71.

"What is the Renewal That Awaits Us?" *The Renewal That Awaits Us*, eds. Eleanor Bernstein CSJ, and Martin F. Connell (Chicago: Liturgy Training Publications, 1997), 18–31.

1996

Nathan Mitchell and John F. Baldovin, eds., *Rule of Prayer, Rule of Faith: Essays in Honor of Aidan Kavanagh, OSB,* (Collegeville: The Liturgical Press, 1996).

Nathan Mitchell and John Witvliet, *Liturgy Digest* 3:2 (Notre Dame: Notre Dame Center for Pastoral Liturgy, 1996).

_____. *Liturgy Digest* 3:1 (Notre Dame: Notre Dame Center for Pastoral Liturgy, 1996).

"Charism," "Ministry," "Ordination," "Servant," and "Shepherd," *The Collegeville Pastoral Dictionary of Biblical Theology*, ed. C. Stuhlmueller (Collegeville: The Liturgical Press, 1996).

"The Amen Corner: The Pleasure Police," *Worship* 70:6 (November 1996): 542–51.

"The Amen Corner: Real Presences," *Worship* 70:5 (September 1996): 452–62.

"The Amen Corner: The Violent Bear It Away," *Worship* 70:4 (July 1996): 335–43.

"The Amen Corner: Glory to God in the Lowest," *Worship* 70:3 (May 1996): 251–60.

"A Place at the Table," *Assembly* 22 (May 1996): 712–13, 718.

"The Amen Corner: The Renewal That Awaits Us," *Worship* 70:2 (March 1996): 163–72.

"The Amen Corner: Plenty Good Room," *Worship* 70:1 (January 1996): 63–72.

1995

Nathan Mitchell and John Witvliet, *Liturgy Digest* 2:2 (Notre Dame: Notre Dame Center for Pastoral Liturgy, 1995).

Forty short articles on liturgical topics, in *HarperCollins Encyclopedia of Catholicism,* ed. Richard McBrien (San Francisco: HarperCollins, 1995).

"The Amen Corner: Painted Prayer: Poetry in ICEL's Psalms," *Worship* 69:6 (November 1995): 556–65.

"The Amen Corner: The ICEL Psalter: A Faithful Rendering," *Worship* 69:5 (September 1995): 447–58.

"Conversion: Falling in Love with the World," *Assembly* 21 (September 1995): 680–1.

"Rituals of Recovery," *Assembly* 21 (September 1995): 682–3, 6.

"The Amen Corner: The ICEL Psalter: History and Access," *Worship* 69:4 (July 1995): 361–70.

"The Amen Corner: Ongoing Assault," *Worship* 69:2 (March 1995): 154–63.

"The Amen Corner: Caressing the Tiger," *Worship* 69:1 (January 1995): 78–87.

"Who Is at the Table?: Reclaiming Real Presence," *Commonweal* 122 (27 January 1995): 10–5.

"Baptism in the Didache," *The Didache in Context: Essays on Its Text, History and Transmission,* ed. Clayton Jefford (New York: E. J. Brill, 1995), 226–55.

1994

Eucharist as Sacrament of Initiation, Forum Essays 2 (Chicago: Liturgy Training Publications, 1994).

Nathan Mitchell and John K. Leonard, *The Postures of the Assembly during the Eucharistic Prayer* (Chicago: Liturgy Training Publications, 1994).

Liturgy Digest 2:1 (Notre Dame: Notre Dame Center for Pastoral Liturgy, 1994).

Liturgy Digest 1:2 (Notre Dame: Notre Dame Center for Pastoral Liturgy, 1994).

"The Amen Corner: Eucharistic Theology in the New Catechism," *Worship* 68:6 (November 1994): 536–44.

"The Amen Corner: The New Catechism—Some Assembly Required," *Worship* 68:5 (September 1994): 450–7.

"The Amen Corner: Liturgy Encounters Culture—Again," *Worship* 68:4 (July 1994): 369–76.

"Eight Thesis on Quality: Some Proposals for Reflection," *Assembly* 20 (June 1994): 640–1, 6.

"The Amen Corner: God at Every Gate," *Worship* 68:3 (May 1994): 249–56.

"The Amen Corner: Beat! Beat! Drums!" *Worship* 68:2 (March 1994): 157–64.

"The Amen Corner: A Mansion for the Rat," *Worship* 68:1 (January 1994): 67–72.

1993

Liturgy Digest 1:1 (Notre Dame: Notre Dame Center for Pastoral Liturgy, 1993).

"The Amen Corner: The Winter Pascha," *Worship* 67:6 (November 1993): 534–41.

"The Amen Corner: Lyrical Liturgy," *Worship* 67:5 (September 1993): 460–9.

"The Amen Corner: The Poetics of Space," *Worship* 67:4 (July 1993): 360–7.

"The Amen Corner: Silent Music," *Worship* 67:3 (May 1993): 261–8.

"The Amen Corner: Mystery and Manners," *Worship* 67:2 (March 1993): 164–73.

"The Amen Corner: The Coming Revolution in Ritual Studies," *Worship* 67:1 (January 1993): 74–81.

1992

"The Amen Corner: The Life of the Dead," *Worship* 66:6 (November 1992): 536–44.

"The Amen Corner: Wrestling with the Word," *Worship* 66:5 (September 1992): 449–56.

"Ritual is Alive and Well in the U.S.A.! The Bad News Is . . ." *Pastoral Music* 16 (August–September 1992): 13–6.

"The Artist, the Senses and Worship," *Environment and Art* 5 (August 1992): 42–5.

"The Amen Corner: The Beauty of Holiness," *Worship* 66:4 (July 1992): 352–60.

"Ritual: A Forgotten Way of Doing Things?" *Praxis* (NPM/DDMD) 3:4 (1992): 3–5.

"The Amen Corner: Americans at Prayer," *Worship* 66:2 (March 1992): 177–84.

1991

"The Amen Corner: Sunday Morning," *Worship* 65:6 (November 1991): 540–7.

"The Amen Corner: Liturgy and Culture," *Worship* 65:4 (July 1991): 363–8.

"Full, Conscious and Active Participation Revisited," *Pastoral Music* 16 (October–November 1991): 34–41.

Book review: "*Reconciliation and Justification: The Sacrament and Its Theology* by Kenan Osborne," *Church* 7 (Spring 1991): 58.

"Second Thoughts: A Parish Full of Prodigals," *Church* 7 (Summer 1991): 48–50.

"Ordinary Time: Celebrating the Extraordinary," *GIA Quarterly* 2 (Spring 1991): 7–8.

"The Kingdom Journey of Justice," *Modern Liturgy* 18 (October 1991): 6–8.

"Bishop, Church, Eucharist: The Theology of Vatican II," *Assembly* 17 (September 1991): 534–40.

"A Generation Later," Assembly 17 (January 1991): 511–4.

1990

"The Evolution of the Novel," *Beyond Literacy: The Second Gutenburg Revolution,* ed. R. P. Howell, (Dallas: Saybrook, 1990), 34–9.

"Greeting of Peace: Deep Welcome," *Modern Liturgy* 17 (October 1990): 15–6.

"The Musician as Minister," *The Pastoral Musician: Pastoral Music in Practice,* ed. V. C. Funk (Washington: Pastoral Press, 1990).

"Leadership as Letting Go," *Assembly* 16:4 (June 1990): 488–90.

"Learning to Pray for Justice," *Liturgy* 8:4 (Summer 1990): 17–23.

1989

"Terms of Attachment: Conversion to Ministry," *Assembly* 16 (October 1989): 462–4.

1987

"Religious Communities: Christian Religious Orders," *The Encyclopedia of Religion,* vol. 12, ed. Mircea Eliade (New York: Macmillan, 1987), 308–12.

1985

Introductory material and notes in *Nobel Prize Conversations with Sir John Eccles, Roger Sperry, Ilya Prigogine, Brian Josephson,* with commentary by Norman Cousins (Dallas: Saybrook, 1985).

1983

Mission and Ministry: History and Theology in the Sacrament of Order (Wilmington: Michael Glazier / Collegeville: The Liturgical Press, 1983).

"Reform of Symbols: The Present Task," *Assembly* 9 (June 1983): 215–216.

1982

Cult and Controversy: The Worship of the Eucharist Outside Mass (Collegeville: The Liturgical Press, 1982).

Mission and Ministry: History and Theology in the Sacrament of Orders (Wilmington: Michael Glazier, 1982).

"The Spirituality of Christian Worship," *Spirituality Today* 34 (Spring 1982): 5–17.

"Papacy," *Encyclopedia Americana,* vol. 21 (Danbury CT: Grolier), 366–71.

1981

"The Sense of the Sacred," *Parish: A Place for Worship,* ed. Mark Searle (Collegeville: The Liturgical Press, 1981).

Book review: "*Disciples and Prophets,* by George Moloney," *Theological Studies* 42 (1981): 720–1.

"Teaching Worship in Seminaries: A Response," *Worship* 55:4 (July 1981): 319–32.

Book review: "*Ordinations inconstantes et Caractere inamissible,* by Cyrille Vogel," *Worship* 55:2 (March 1981): 171–3.

Book review: "*Die Aufbewahrung der Eucharistie,* by Otto Nußbaum," *Worship* 55:1 (January 1981): 78–80.

"The Liturgical Code in the Rule of Benedict," Appendix 3 in *RB 1980: The Rule of St. Benedict in Latin and English with Notes* (Collegeville: The Liturgical Press, 1981): 379–414.

"The Parable of Childhood," *Liturgy* 1 (1981): 3, 7–12.

1980

"Eucharistic Ordination in Benedictine Communities," *Benedictines* 35 (1980): 149–69.

"Education for Ecumenism: Shaping a New Perspective," *Mid–Stream: An Ecumenical Journal* 19 (1980): 21–31.

"The Rule of Benedict: Everyday Life is the Path," *Benedictines* 35 (1980): 14–24.

"Liturgical Education in Roman Catholic Seminaries: A Report and an Appraisal," *Worship* 54:2 (March 1980): 129–57.

Book review: "*Analecta Liturgica 1: Miscellanea Liturgica in honore di P. Burkhard Neunheuser,*" *Worship* 54:1 (January 1980): 79–81.

Book review: "*Centered on Christ: An Introduction to Monastic Profession,* by Augustine Roberts," *Theological Studies* 41 (1980): 243–4.

"Jesus' Vision of a New Community," *Liturgy* 1 (1980): 37–44.

"Liturgy and the Silent Minority," *Service,* Resources for Pastoral Ministry 4 (New York: Paulist Press, 1980), 85–9.

"The Musician as Minister," *Pastoral Music* 4 (1980): 27–31, 39–41.

1979

"Liturgy, 'Mystery,' Devotions," *Liturgy* 24:6 (1979): 39–40.

"Pain, Play and the Liturgy," *Liturgy* 24:4 (1979): 13–4.

"Social Origins of the Liturgical Movement," *Liturgy* 24:2 (1979): 9–10.

"Bread of Crisis, Bread of Justice," *Living Worship* 15 (March 1979): entire issue.

Book review: "*The Evolving Church and the Sacrament of Penance,* by Ladislas Orsy," *Theological Studies* 40 (1979): 786–7.

"All Those Lovely Liturgies—All Those Empty Pews," *Ministries* (premiere issue, October 1979): 17, 29–31.

"A God Who Hears," *Pastoral Music* 4 (1979): 29–35.

1978

The Rite of Penance: Commentaries, vol. III, editor and principal writer (Washington: The Liturgical Conference, 1978.)

Church, Eucharist and Liturgical Reform at Mercersberg: 1843–1857 (PhD diss., University of Notre Dame, 1978).

"Early Church Orders," *Liturgy* 23:4 (1978): 35–6.

"Blessing/Berakah," *Liturgy* 23:3 (1978): 44–5.

"Language in Liturgy," *Liturgy* 23:2 (1978): 37–9.

"Jewish Prayer in Jesus' Time," *Liturgy* 23:1 (1978): 29–30.

"Institution of Readers and Acolytes," *New Catholic Encyclopedia,* vol. 17 (Supplement, 1978), 293–4.

"Celibacy (Rite of Commitment)," *New Catholic Encyclopedia,* vol. 17 (Supplement, 1978), 98.

"Candidacy for Ordination," *New Catholic Encyclopedia,* vol. 17 (Supplement, 1978), 69.

"Putting the Pieces Together," *Pace* 9 (1978).

"Jesus at Walden Pond: Americans and the Meditation Movement," *Pace* 9 (1978).

"West Meets East: Christians Encounter Non-Christian Religions," *Pace* 9 (1978).

"Spirituality in the Space Age," *Pace* 9 (1978).

"Charismatic Spirituality: Christian Conversion and Christian Intimacy," *Pace* 9 (1978).

"Ethics and Earthiness: The Spirituality of Christian Worship," *Pace* 9 (1978).

"The Changing Role of the Pastoral Musician," *Pastoral Music* 2:5 (1978): 12–9.

"The Problem of Authority in Roman Catholicism," *Review and Expositor* 55 (1978): 195–209.

"Rediscovering the Spirituality of the New Testament," *Pace* 9 (1978).

"Changing Styles in Christian Spirituality," *Pace* 9 (1978).

"Six Minor Heresies in Today's Music," *Pastoral Music* 2:2 (1978): 8–10.

1977

"Jewish Prayer in Jesus'Time," *Liturgy* 22:7 (1977): 38–9.

"Liturgy and Life Cycles," *Liturgy* 22:6 (1977): 37–8.

"Music in Worship," *Liturgy* 22:5 (1977): 36–7.

"Ministry," *Liturgy* 22:4 (1977): 38–9.

"Eucharist: Drama or Meal?" *Liturgy* 22:2 (1977): 28–9.

"Useless Prayer," *Christians at Prayer*, ed. John Gallen (Notre Dame: University of Notre Dame Press, 1977), 1–25.

"The Adult Catechumenate in an Age of Pluralism," *Liturgy* 22:1 (1977): 11–7.

"Symbols Are Actions, Not Objects—New Directions for an Old Problem," *Living Worship* 31 (February 1977): entire issue.

"Old Hymnal Illustrates Roots of Catholic Music," *Pastoral Music* 1:6 (1977): 30–2.

"He Who Sings Prays a Lot? It Depends . . . " *Pastoral Music* 1:2 (1977): 16–9.

1976

"Learning From Liturgy's History," *Liturgy* 21 (1976): 316–7.

Book review: "*Sanctifying Life, Time and Space: An Introduction to Liturgical Study*, by Marion Hatchett," *Theological Studies* 37 (1976): 2–18.

"Monks and the Future of Worship," *Worship* 50:1 (January 1976): 2–18.

"Dissolution of the Rite of Christian Initiation," *Made Not Born*, ed. John Gallen (Notre Dame: University of Notre Dame Press, 1978), 50–82.

"Speaking about the Spirit," *Pace* 7 (1976).

"Thinking about the Holy Spirit—Some Guidelines," *Pace* 7 (1976).

1975

"The Once and Future Child: Toward a Theology of Childhood," *Living Light* (1975): 423–37.

Book review:"*A New Pentecost?*, by Leon Joseph Cardinal Suenens," *Theological Studies* 36 (1975): 569–70.

Book review:"*The Recovery of the Sacred*, by James Hitchcock," *Theological Studies* 36 (1975): 198–200.

"Social Sin and the Rite of Penance," *Liturgy* 20 (1975): 251–8.

1974

"Prayer:The Ecology of Worship," *Musart* 26:4 (1974): 9–14.

"Mystery (in Theology)," *New Catholic Encyclopedia*, vol. 16 (Supplement 1974): 309–10.

"Christian Initiation: Decline and Dismemberment," *Worship* 48:5 (September 1974): 458–79.

"Ministry Today: Problems and Prospects," *Worship* 48:4 (July 1974): 336–46.

"The Christian Eucharist: Sign of Community," *Pace* 5 (1974).

"What Does Christmas Really Celebrate?" *Pace* 5 (1974).

1973

"Christian Conversion and Initiation:Are They Still Happening?" *Pace* 4 (1973).

1972

The Grail of England and Nathan Mitchell, *Themes, Prayers and Intercessions* (Cincinnati:World Library Publications, 1972.)

1971

"Introduction: Eucharist Prayers and Eucharistic Piety," *Resonance* 6 (1971): 5–10.

Nathan D. Mitchell and Thomas J. Extejt, "The Second Eucharistic Prayer and the Anaphora of Hippolytus," *Resonance* 6 (1971): 21–32.

"Revolution:A Romance with the Wilderness," *American Benedictine Review* 22 (1971): 298–318.

1970

"Investigation into Analogia Entis," *Resonance* 5:2 (1970): 30–52.

1969

"Jewish Liturgy in the Talmudic Period," *Resonance* 4:1 (1969): 18–44.

"*Ordo Psallendi* in the *Rule:* Historical Perspectives," *American Benedictine Review* 20 (1969): 505–27.

Contributors

John F. Baldovin, SJ, is professor of historical and liturgical theology at Weston Jesuit School of Theology in Cambridge, Massachusetts. He has taught at Fordham University, the Jesuit School of Theology at Berkeley, the University of Notre Dame and St. John Vianney National Seminary in Pretoria, South Africa. A past president of both the North American Academy of Liturgy and the Societas Liturgica, he co-edited with Nathan Mitchell a volume in honor of Aidan Kavanagh, OSB, titled *Rule of Prayer, Rule of Faith* (1996).

Andrew D. Ciferni, OPraem, is a Norbertine priest of Daylesford Abbey in Paoli, Pennsylvania, where he is liturgy director and rector of the abbey church. He is the convener of the executive committee of the Catholic Academy of Liturgy. With Nathan Mitchell he graduated from the PhD program in liturgical studies at the University of Notre Dame in August of 1978.

Patrick W. Collins has been a priest of the diocese of Peoria since 1964. He holds a PhD in historical theology from Fordham University. He has published numerous articles and has written four books, including *Bodying Forth: Aesthetics and Liturgy* (1992) and *More Than Meets the Eye: Ritual and Parish Liturgy* (1983).

Michael S. Driscoll is an associate professor of liturgy and sacramental theology in the department of theology at the University of Notre Dame. He has published a monograph entitled *Alcuin et la pénitence à l'époque carolingienne,* LQF 81 (1999) and numerous articles in journals such as *Worship, Ecclesia Orans* and *Traditio.* He is a past president of the North American Academy of Liturgy and has served for many years as convener of the study group in medieval liturgy. He has also served as an advisor to the Bishops' Committee on the Liturgy, a standing committee of the United States Conference of Catholic Bishops.

Steve Erspamer, SM, whose art graces this book, is a Marianist brother who lives and works in St. Louis, Missouri. He studied at St. Mary University in San Antonio, Texas; the Art Institute of San Antonio; Creighton University in Omaha, Nebraska; and Boston University. He has traveled throughout Europe and India as a student of sacred art. He works in many media, including clay, stone, fresco, glass, silkscreen and cut paper. He has worked in many church building and renovation projects, and his art appears in many publications.

Edward Foley, CAPUCHIN, is professor of liturgy and music and the founding director of the ecumenical DMIN program at Catholic Theological Union in Chicago. Foley is a past president of the North American Academy of Liturgy, and a founder and originating member of the executive committee of the Catholic Academy of Liturgy. He has published thirteen books, including *Preaching Basics* (1998), *Mighty Stories, Dangerous Rituals* co-authored with Herbert Anderson (1997), *Ritual Music* (1995), *Developmental Disabilities and Sacramental Access* (1994), *From Age to Age* (1991), and *Worship Music: A Concise Dictionary* (2000), for which he served as general editor.

Clare V. Johnson is a doctoral candidate in liturgical studies at the University of Notre Dame, and is writing her dissertation under the direction of Nathan Mitchell. She has published articles in *Worship, Pastoral Music* and *The Summit*.

Maxwell E. Johnson, an ordained minister in the Evangelical Lutheran Church in America, is professor of liturgical studies at the University of Notre Dame. A frequent contributor to scholarly journals, he has most recently published the books *Images of Baptism* (2001) and *The Apostolic Tradition: A Commentary* co-authored with Paul Bradshaw and L. Edward Phillips (2002).

John Allyn Melloh, SM, is a professional specialist and director of the John S. Marten Program in Homiletics and Liturgics in the department of theology at the University of Notre Dame.

Gilbert Ostdiek, OFM, is professor of liturgy at Catholic Theological Union in Chicago. He is the author of numerous essays, articles and the book *Catechesis for Liturgy: A Program for Parish Involvement* (1986). He served as a member of the International Commission for English in the Liturgy for many years and is the founder and director of the Institute for Liturgical Consultants at CTU.

R. Kevin Seasoltz, OSB, a Benedictine from Saint John's Abbey in Collegeville, Minnesota, teaches in the school of theology at Saint John's University and is the editor of the liturgical journal *Worship*.

Raymond Studzinski, OSB, a monk of St. Meinrad Archabbey in Indiana, is an associate professor and chair of the department of religion and religious education at The Catholic University of America in Washington.

Robert F. Taft, SJ, is professor emeritus of Oriental liturgy at the Pontifical Oriental Institute, Rome. He is director of publications for the Institute and serves as the editor-in-chief of the series *Orientalia Christiana Analecta* and *Anaphorae Orientales*. A prolific writer, he has written fourteen books and edited seven in collaboration with other writers. He serves as Consultor for Liturgy for the Vatican Congregation for the Oriental Churches and is a member of several other Vatican commissions.